Innovation Drivers and Regional Innovation Strategies

In the global economy, regional development and innovation are increasingly an imperative to increase the competitive edge of EU economies. While European regions are different in many ways, the innovation capacity of regions, clusters, and firms is what makes them capable of building up new and diversified pathways for sustainable growth.

For this reason, *Innovation Drivers and Regional Innovation Strategies* looks to analyze different knowledge drivers (e.g., entrepreneurial or policy orientation, scientific and practice-based knowledge modes, institutional innovation support) that influence the innovative and competitive capacity of regions, clusters, and firms in Europe. The aim of this volume is to develop an in-depth understanding of these drivers and their implications for the way in which regional and cluster growth may be upgraded.

Innovation Drivers and Regional Innovation Strategies examines the construction of new innovation pathways for regions and clusters in different geographical contexts. The main themes are cluster evolution, regional innovation systems, and business innovation modes and capabilities. The objectives are centered on exploring the logic and mechanisms that can be activated as a means to promote innovation and competitiveness within regions and, within these, across and within firms.

Aimed at researchers and academics in the field, this is a thoughtful and innovative new volume that helps define the academic debate.

Mario Davide Parrilli is Associate Professor of Regional Economic Development, Faculty of Management, University of Bournemouth, United Kingdom.

Rune Dahl Fitjar is Professor of Innovation Studies at the UiS Business School, University of Stavanger, Norway.

Andrés Rodríguez-Pose is Professor of Economic Geography at the London School of Economics, United Kingdom.

Routledge Studies in Innovation, Organizations and Technology

For a full list of titles in this series, please visit www.routledge.com

13 **User-Innovation**
Barriers to Democratization and
IP Licensing
Victor R. G. Braun and Cornelius Herstatt

14 **Working on Innovation**
Edited by Christophe Midler, Guy Minguet and Monique Vervaeke

15 **Organization in Open Source Communities: At the Crossroads of the Gift and Market Economies**
Evangelia Berdou

16 **Theory and Practice of Triple Helix Model in Developing Countries**
Issues and Challenges
Edited by Mohammed Saad and Girma Zawdie

17 **Global Innovation in Emerging Economies**
Prasada Reddy

18 **Creativity and Innovation in Business and Beyond**
Social Science Perspectives and Policy Implications
Edited by Leon Mann and Janet Chan

19 **Managing Networks of Creativity**
Edited by Fiorenza Belussi and Udo Staber

20 **Managing Environmentally Sustainable Innovation**
Insights from the Construction Industry
Bart Bossink

21 **Management and Information Technology**
Challenges for the Modern Organization
Edited by Peter Dahlin and Peter Ekman

22 **Managing Organizational Ecologies**
Space, Management, and Organizations
Edited by Keith Alexander and Ilfryn Price

23 **Digital Virtual Consumption**
Edited by Mike Molesworth and Janice Denegri-Knott

24 **The Video Game Industry**
Formation, Present State, and Future
Edited by Peter Zackariasson and Timothy Wilson

25 **Marketing Technologies**
Corporate Cultures and Technological Change
Elena Simakova

26 **Public Sector Transformation through E-Government**
Experiences from Europe and North America
Edited by Vishanth Weerakkody and Christopher G. Reddick

27 **Innovation Policy Challenges for the 21st Century**
Edited by Deborah Cox and John Rigby

28 **Eco-Innovation and Sustainability Management**
Bart Bossink

29 **Creativity and Leadership in Science, Technology, and Innovation**
Edited by Sven Hemlin, Carl Martin Allwood, Ben R. Martin, and Michael D. Mumford

30 **Framing Innovation in Public Service Sectors**
Edited by Lars Fuglsang, Rolf Rønning, and Bo Enquist

31 **Management of Broadband Technology Innovation**
Policy, Deployment, and Use
Edited by Jyoti Choudrie and Catherine Middleton

32 **The Management Idea Factory**
Innovation and Commodification in Management Consulting
Stefan Heusinkveld

33 **The Cultural Side of Innovation**
Adding Values
Dany Jacobs

34 **Creativity Research: An Inter-Disciplinary and Multi-Disciplinary Research Handbook**
Eric Shiu

35 **Business Modeling for Life Science and Biotech Companies**
Creating Value and Competitive Advantage with the Milestone Bridge
Alberto Onetti and Antonella Zucchella

36 **Low-Cost, Low-Tech Innovation**
New Product Development in the Food Industry
Vijay Vyas

37 **The Entrepreneurial University**
Context and institutional change
Edited by Lene Foss and David V. Gibson

38 **Dynamics of Knowledge-Intensive Entrepreneurship**
Business strategy and public policy
Edited by Franco Malerba, Yannis Caloghirou, Maureen McKelvey and Slavo Radosevic

39 **Collaborative Innovation: Developing Health Support Ecosystems**
Edited by Mitsuru Kodama

40 **Innovation Drivers and Regional Innovation Strategies**
Edited by Mario Davide Parrilli, Rune Dahl Fitjar, and Andrés Rodríguez-Pose

Innovation Drivers and Regional Innovation Strategies

**Edited by Mario Davide Parrilli,
Rune Dahl Fitjar, and
Andrés Rodríguez-Pose**

NEW YORK AND LONDON

First published 2016
by Routledge
711 Third Avenue, New York, NY 10017

and by Routledge
2 Park Square, Milton Park, Abingdon, Oxon OX14 4RN

First issued in paperback 2018

*Routledge is an imprint of the Taylor & Francis Group,
an informa business*

Library of Congress Cataloging-in-Publication Data
Names: Parrilli, Mario Davide, editor. | Dahl-Fitjar, Rune, editor. |
    Rodrâiguez-Pose, Andrâes, editor.
Title: Innovation drivers and regional innovation strategies / edited by
    Mario Davide Parrilli, Rune Dahl-Fitjar, and Andrâes Rodrâiguez-Pose.
Description: New York : Routledge, 2016. | Series: Routledge studies in
    innovation, organizations and technology ; 40 | Includes bibliographical
    references and index.
Identifiers: LCCN 2015034339 | ISBN 9781138945326 (cloth : alk. paper) |
    ISBN 9781315671475 (ebook)
Subjects: LCSH: Regional planning—European Union countries. |
    Technological innovations—Economic aspects—European Union
    countries. | Economic development—European Union countries.
Classification: LCC HT395.E85 I56 2016 | DDC 338.94—dc23
LC record available at http://lccn.loc.gov/2015034339

ISBN 13: 978-1-138-61720-9 (pbk)
ISBN 13: 978-1-138-94532-6 (hbk)

Typeset in Sabon
by Apex CoVantage, LLC

Contents

List of Tables   ix
List of Figures   x
Foreword   xi
Note on Contributors   xiii

1 Innovation Drivers and Regional Innovation Strategies:
   Territorial and Business Insights   1
   MARIO DAVIDE PARRILLI, RUNE DAHL FITJAR,
   AND ANDRÉS RODRÍGUEZ-POSE

PART I
Regional Innovation

2 Identification of Regions With Less-Developed Research
   and Innovation Systems   23
   MICHAELA TRIPPL, BJÖRN ASHEIM, AND JOHAN MIÖRNER

3 Innovation Gaps: A Typology for Spain   45
   XABIER ALBERDI-PONS, JUAN JOSÉ GIBAJA MARTÍNS,
   AND MARIO DAVIDE PARRILLI

4 Path Development in Different Regional Innovation Systems:
   A Conceptual Analysis   66
   ARNE ISAKSEN AND MICHAELA TRIPPL

5 Mechanisms of Innovation-Based Cluster Transformation   85
   ZSUZSANNA VINCZE AND JUKKA TERÄS

 6 What About Disruptions in Clusters? Retaking
    a Missing Debate   105
    JOSÉ LUIS HERVÁS-OLIVER

PART II
Business Innovation

 7 Building High-Tech Clusters? The Case of the
    Competitiveness Cluster "Secure Communicating
    Solutions" in the French Provence-Alpes-Côte
    d'Azur Region   123
    CHRISTIAN LONGHI

 8 The Role of Open Innovation-Oriented Strategies in the
    Innovation Performance of Mechanical Engineering
    Start-Up Firms in Northern Italy   142
    SILVIA RITA SEDITA AND ROBERTA APA

 9 Firm Collaboration and Modes of Innovation in Norway   160
    RUNE DAHL FITJAR AND ANDRÉS RODRÍGUEZ-POSE

10 University Collaboration for Sustainable Competitive
    Advantage: A Resource-Based Perspective   179
    MARTIN GJELSVIK AND RUNE DAHL FITJAR

11 Business Innovation Modes: A Review From a
    Country Perspective   197
    MARIO DAVIDE PARRILLI, RUNE DAHL FITJAR,
    AND ANDRÉS RODRÍGUEZ-POSE

    Index   219

Tables

2.1 RIS Failures   25

2.2 Organizational and Institutional Thickness/Thinness of RIS   27

2.3 Differentiated Knowledge-Base Approach   28

2.4 Knowledge Bases and RIS Configurations   30

2.5 RIS Types and Regional Industrial Path Development Patterns and Challenges   33

3.1 Variables in the Study   52

5.1 Categories of Situational and Action-Formation Mechanisms   90

5.2 Transformational Mechanisms in Cluster Transformation   92

7.1 Centrality Measures   134

7.2 Short Heads of the Edges Weight Distribution   137

8.1 Descriptive Statistics   154

8.2 Determinants of Firms' Innovation Performance   155

9.1 Number and Share of Firms Collaborating With Different Types of Partners   167

9.2 Logit Regression Estimation of the Empirical Model   169

9.3 Share of Firms Collaborating With Partners Within and Outside the Region   172

9.4 Logit Regression Estimation of the Empirical Model   173

11.1 Comparative Methodology Parameters Across STI-DUI Studies   203

11.2 Development Indicators by Country   211

11.3 Associations Between Innovation Mode and Output in Different Studies   211

11.4 Critical Factors and Focus of Innovation Activities   214

Figures

1.1 The Interdependence Between Firms' and Systems'
    Innovation Capabilities   10
2.1 Regional Performance Groups in the Regional
    Innovation Scoreboard 2014   37
3.1 Correlation Circle   54
3.2 Global Display of Groups   55
3.3 Cluster Dendrogram   57
3.4 Spanish RISs' Integration Levels Map   58
5.1 Typology of Social Mechanisms   87
7.1 SCS Collective Learning Networks   131
7.2 Centrality Measures   133
8.1 Collaboration Networks of the Firms Interviewed   151
8.2 Spatial Distribution of Firms' Collaboration Networks   151
9.1 Percentage Share of Firms That Have Cooperated
    With Partner Type   171

Foreword

Faced with global competition, every policy-maker, businessman, and academic recognizes that innovation is a key driver for growth and welfare in their firms and territories. The new challenges imposed by the globalization of social, political, and economic relations require changes, transformations, and evolution of firms and systems (e.g., countries and regions, regional innovation systems, global value chains, industrial districts, and clusters) to retain competitiveness and growth potential. In short, innovation is crucial for the sustainability of the development model of economically advanced societies, being necessary for the development and growth of territories and agents that might otherwise find themselves caught in vicious circles and development traps (e.g., the case of Southern European countries with their budget burden and necessary cuts, traditional industries with their limited incremental innovation models, among others).

Consequently, the capacity to develop new knowledge and to manage innovation outputs has become part of new strategies oriented to achieving sustainable competitive advantage, i.e., a continuous competitive edge over global rivals. This idea is now acknowledged across European countries and regions. It has been part of the policy agenda pursued by the European Union since the early 2000s up until now and including the current Horizon 2020 agenda. It is also recognized in other developed countries, as exemplified by the US (Obama's) "Strategy for American Innovation: Securing Our Economic Growth and Prosperity," published in 2011, or the Japanese government's Basic Plan for Science and Technology 2011–2016.

In the social sciences, the role of research is to interpret and systematize what is happening in the world of business and institutional practice. Businessmen, managers, workers take the lead in developing innovation and new economic and social practices. This leads academics to work on data on country, regional, or business experiences so as to understand what is going on in the economy, the new trends, changes, and potentials that can be identified, measured, systematized, and prospected through adequate strategies or policy tools. In this respect, they support the primary work developed by the aforementioned social, institutional, and economic agents.

This is what we aimed to achieve in the 2013 "Regional Innovation Policy" conference in San Sebastian, where academics, policy-makers, and other stakeholders met and discussed relevant topics oriented to informing public policies for business strategy and for regional development. The present volume derives from the collaboration of a research group that convened at the conference and that forms a broad research network focused on the innovation dynamics of businesses, institutions, and regions. As part of the conference, Andrés Rodríguez-Pose, Rune Dahl Fitjar, and Mario Davide Parrilli developed a track on the heterogeneity of business innovation and regional innovation pathways, inviting a number of recognized colleagues to share the outcomes of their current research on these topics. This formed the basis for a valuable debate on innovation dynamics, which has led to the development of this volume.

The experts who have participated in this collective initiative work on innovation from two main disciplinary perspectives. The first is the perspective of the economics of innovation that takes into account the aggregate form in which economies grow, i.e., countries, regions, industries/sectors, and local production systems. The second is the management of innovation, which examines how individual businesses structure their activities so as to develop innovation. This combination of macro- and micro level perspectives provides a fertile ground for the generation of new inter- and multi-disciplinary opportunities for learning and new knowledge generation in the context of the economics of innovation and the management of innovation. Consequently, the present volume integrates both perspectives as complementary contributions to the debate on economic development and welfare in country and regional economies, as well as on the innovation and competitiveness achieved by individual businesses. The macro level is oriented to introducing the larger landscape and the mutual interactions, exchanges, and spillovers that the territory generates for the local business units, whereas the micro level is focused on introducing "creative disruptions" or fractures across aggregate behaviors and trends, which may open new phases of the economy toward newer and higher standards.

This volume is a synthesis of the efforts of these experts, who we would like to thank together with the other participants in the track who enriched the discussion with their insightful inputs. The organization of the Orkestra Institute of Competitiveness and the Deusto Business School of the University of Deusto in San Sebastian and Bilbao is also appreciated as it gave us the opportunity to develop the present initiative that we believe may deliver significant academic and policy inputs to our readers and academic colleagues.

Mario Davide Parrilli, Rune Dahl Fitjar, and Andrés Rodríguez-Pose
San Sebastian, Stavanger and London, July 2015

Note on Contributors

Andrés Rodríguez-Pose is a Professor of Economic Geography at the London School of Economics. He is the current holder of a European Research Council (ERC) Advanced Grant and President of the Regional Science Association International. He is a regular advisor to numerous international organizations on research and innovation-related issues, including membership of the European Commission's High Level Group Expert Group on Innovation (RISE) and the World Economic Forum's Global Agenda Council on the Economics of Innovation.

Arne Isaksen is Professor at the Department of Working Life and Innovation at the University of Agder, Norway, and Senior Researcher at Agderforskning. He has a PhD in economic geography from the University of Oslo. His research interest is theoretical and empirical studies of regional industrial development, focusing on regional clusters, innovation systems, companies' innovation modes, and policy tools and policy lessons.

Björn Terje Asheim is Professor in Economic Geography and Innovation Studies at University of Stavanger Business School/Centre for innovation research, Stavanger, Norway; CIRCLE (Centre for Innovation, Research and Competence in the Learning Economy), Lund University, Sweden; and Department of Innovation and Economic Organization, BI-Norwegian Business School, Oslo, Norway. His area of research is regional innovation studies.

Christian Longhi is a Senior Researcher in Economics in CNRS at the University of Nice Sophia-Antipolis, GREDEG. He specializes in the areas of industrial economics, ICT, and innovation with a special focus on regional and local development and high-tech centers.

Johan Miörner is a PhD student in Economic Geography at CIRCLE (Centre for Innovation, Research and Competence in the Learning Economy) and the Department of Human Geography, Lund University, Sweden. His main research interests include regional industrial change and regional innovation policy.

José Luis Hervás-Oliver is Full Professor at Polytechnic University of Valencia (Spain). His main research interest lies at the intersection of strategy, innovation, and economic geography, especially studying cluster firms and industrial districts.

Juan José Gibaja Martíns is Associate Professor in the Quantitative Methods department at DBS (University of Deusto). He holds a PhD degree in Business Administration and an MSc degree in Mathematics. His main research areas include the relationship between marketing and society and regional economic development.

Jukka Teräs *D.Sc. (Tech.)* is Senior Research Fellow at Nordregio, a Nordic research institute in the field of regional development and urban planning in Stockholm, Sweden. His main research areas include economic geography and innovation studies with a special focus on regional clusters and innovation environments.

Mario Davide Parrilli is Associate Professor of Regional Economic Development at the University of Bournemouth. He specializes in SME clusters, innovation systems, value chains, and social capital. He has been advisor for the EU, UNIDO, IADB, among others, and is a member of the research committee of the Regional Studies Association (RSA) and the Jorg Meyer-Stamer Foundation. For Routledge, he edited the volume *The Competitiveness of Clusters in Globalized Markets* in 2014.

Martin Gjelsvik is Research Manager at International Research Institute of Stavanger (IRIS) and holds a Prof II position at the Centre of Innovation Research, a joint venture between the University of Stavanger and IRIS. Gjelsvik earned his Dr. oecon at the Norwegian School of Economics (NHH) in 1998, specializing in strategy and management. His research is focused on innovation both at the regional and organizational level.

Michaela Trippl is Associate Professor in innovation studies at CIRCLE (Centre for Innovation, Research and Competence in the Learning Economy), Lund University, Sweden. Her main research areas include economic geography and innovation studies with a special focus on regional innovation policies, industrial path development, and the transformation of regional innovation systems.

Roberta Apa is Research Associate at the Department of Economics and Management, University of Padova, Italy. Her main research fields are innovation processes of start-ups and small and medium enterprises, business incubators, and entrepreneurial development.

Rune Dahl Fitjar is Professor of Innovation Studies at the UiS Business School, University of Stavanger. He received his PhD in Government from the London School of Economics in 2007. In 2013, he became the youngest professor at the University of Stavanger, and his work has been awarded the university's prizes for communication of research in 2012 and for research excellence in 2014. He has published numerous articles on regional development, innovation, politics, identities and culture, spanning political science, economic geography, and business studies.

Silvia Rita Sedita is Associate Professor of Management at the Department of Economics and Management, University of Padova, Italy. Her main research interest is the management of innovation in inter-organizational networks, industrial districts, and clusters.

Xabier Alberdi-Pons finalized his PhD at the University of Deusto in 2014 with a work on the role of intermediaries as catalysts of integration in regional innovation systems. He won a prize from the Jorg Meyer-Stamer Foundation for his PhD research project and spent a period as a visiting PhD student in Circle-University of Lund.

Zsuzsanna Vincze is Associate Professor at the Umeå School of Business and Economics at Umeå University in Sweden and Lecturer of international business at the University of Turku in Finland. Her main research areas include internationalization processes, cluster transformation, and innovation in low- and medium-technology firms.

1 Innovation Drivers and Regional Innovation Strategies

Territorial and Business Insights

Mario Davide Parrilli, Rune Dahl Fitjar, and Andrés Rodríguez-Pose

1. INTRODUCTION

As a consequence of the rapidly globalizing world economy, regions and countries of Europe are facing increasing competition and development challenges. In order to sustain high wages and standards of living, European territories need to maintain or improve their levels of productivity relative to competing and emerging regions. This can only be achieved through continuous innovation that consistently improves regional productivity levels. Yet the recipe for success for European regions is unclear. The European territory encompasses a variety of regional traditions, industrial structures, institutional strengths and weaknesses, all of which make for highly different requirements for regional development across different parts of the continent. Together with significant regional differences in terms of resource endowments, production specializations, institutions, social capital, and support programs, the innovation capacity of regions (including their clusters and firms) also varies strongly within Europe. Strengthening the innovation capacity therefore requires building up new and diversified pathways for sustainable growth across the heterogeneity of contexts that make up the European geography (Foray and Van Ark, 2007; Asheim, Boschma and Cooke, 2011; McCann and Ortega-Argilés, 2013). For this reason, the present volume is devoted to analyzing different knowledge drivers that influence this innovation capacity. These drivers are analyzed in the context of local and regional production systems and across firms, which are the critical agents of local and regional development.

The book is original on two counts. On the one hand, it includes a nested analysis of innovation processes, which combines a meso-level perspective on regions and innovation systems with a microlevel perspective on firms, to examine the dynamics of regional innovation and competitiveness both from the perspective of firms and of territories. This multilevel theoretical debate permits a more thorough understanding and discussion of the heterogeneity that exists in any territory in terms of agents, linkages, and potentials that orient (and constrain) the pathways available to improve the innovation and competitive capacity of regions. On the other hand, it also recognizes the mutual interdependence between the wider geographical frameworks of regions and the individual business units. The wider geographical framework provides the social, institutional, and economic context, as well as the shared traditions and competences/specializations that orient business approaches and outcomes. Meanwhile, the business units on their part are the crucial actors that can determine the innovation and development prospects of an entire production and innovation system.

In this introduction, we discuss the recent literature on regions and their knowledge drivers. We then produce a similar analysis on business knowledge capabilities and innovation modes in a way that shows how heterogeneous firms (can) contribute effectively to their own innovation processes and those of their territories. A synthetic section is later presented in which we develop the idea of mutual dependence or interdependence between the regional context and firm innovation processes in determining the potential for economic development within a territory. A short description of the different chapters follows with a similarly synthetic presentation of the research gaps they target.

2. INNOVATION IN A REGIONAL CONTEXT

2.1 Regional Evolution

The concept of innovation systems emerged along with related concepts such as clusters and industrial districts in the 1980s and 1990s to highlight the systemic interplay between firms and other economic agents in promoting or deterring innovation. A common theme in all these theories is that firms in regions are mutually interdependent in both their production and innovation processes. Consequently, a large body of research investigating the linkages and networks between firms and with other organizations has been developed, and this has been a central theme in a great number of studies of local and regional industries across many countries over the past 30 years (Piore and Sabel, 1984; Porter, 1998; Nadvi and Schmitz, 1999; Lastres and Cassiolato, 2005; Bellandi and Di Tommaso, 2005; Pietrobelli and Rabellotti, 2007; Becattini et al., 2009; Boix and Galletto, 2009). However, a growing number of contributions over the last 15 years has also emphasized the potential limitations of interaction within regions or clusters, noting that firms and regions must also develop trans-local networks of firms and organizations in order to escape lock-in situations (Henderson et al., 2002; Bathelt et al., 2004; Boschma, 2005; Glückler, 2007; Visser and Atzema, 2008; Rodríguez-Pose and Comptour, 2012). Nonetheless, recent years have seen a renewed interest in clusters revived in academia, as well as in policy-making circles (Menzel and Fornhal, 2010; Parrilli and Sacchetti, 2008; Boschma and Frenken, 2011; Martin and Sunley, 2011; Lorenzen and Mudambi, 2012; Delgado, Porter and Stern, 2014). This reflects the existence of more or less thick business agglomerations that rely on joint actions and external economies (Schmitz, 1995), the related coordinated division and specialization of labor (Piore and Sabel, 1984; Parrilli and Sacchetti, 2008), as well as a continued belief in the ability of clusters to promote the exchange of tacit knowledge. While earlier versions of cluster theory held that this type of knowledge exchange would take place almost automatically through the sheer physical proximity between the actors, recent versions have added alternative dimensions, such as cognitive, social, cultural, and institutional proximity, as potential mechanisms, theorizing that physical proximity would promote the development of proximity in these other dimensions (Audretsch, 1998; Malmberg and Maskell, 2002; Guerrieri and Pietrobelli, 2004; Giuliani, 2005; Belussi and Sedita, 2012; Parrilli, 2012). However, the empirical evidence of a link between non-geographical and physical proximity dimensions remains somewhat mixed, and the question of to what extent permanent physical proximity is actually necessary for successful knowledge exchange therefore also remains unresolved.

A large number of studies are currently developed on this topic, in particular in the European context, where the historic reliance of EU economies on this type of business and territorial configuration make this a pressing topic. This is motivated by the heavy dependence of these economies on small and medium-sized enterprises—SMEs—which may be more dependent on developing external economies to remain competitive. This has been acknowledged in the new approach of the European Commission to the so-called "regional innovation strategies for smart specialization—RIS3" (Foray and van Ark, 2007; European Commission, 2010; McCann and Ortega-Argilés, 2013), which is a coordinated development strategy set up to promote smart and diversified specialization across EU regions and countries.

Within the topic of regional development, the current academic debate focuses on the identification of different patterns of regional evolution across time. This novel topic replaces former approaches to regional development that were mostly centered on the identification of "models" that specific local production systems were supposed to target directly (see Humphrey, 1995). For this reason, a novel round of studies commenced in order to identify critical factors of regional evolution (Knorringa, 2002; Pietrobelli and Rabellotti, 2007; Parrilli, 2009), some of which were and are specifically focused on knowledge drivers (Guerrieri and Pietrobelli, 2004; Menzel and Fornahl, 2007; Ter Wal and Boschma, 2011; Boschma and Fornahl, 2011; Li and Bathelt, 2011; Martin and Sunley, 2011; Crespo, Suire, and Vicente, 2014).

Within this relatively novel approach, a debate is stirred about the strategies that are supposed to generate new competencies and innovation capacity at the local and regional level. The "related variety" approach postulates the importance of moving from current industrial/production specializations to proximate ones as a means to build up new competencies and capacities based upon the current absorptive capacity (Cooke, 2006; Asheim et al., 2011; Boschma and Frenken, 2011; Asheim et al. in this volume). Other scholars prioritize a process of "entrepreneurial discovery" in which entre-preneurs and other regional stakeholders actively explore potential new areas in which the region can build unique competitive advantage (Foray and van Ark, 2007; Foray and Goenaga, 2014). The two approaches may or may not complement each other, depending on whether the entrepreneurial discovery is based on the existing local/regional specializations or on exog-enously based capacities (e.g., FDI).

The general debate on the evolution of local and regional production systems as well as the more specific discussion on the most appropriate ter-ritorial knowledge management strategy raise the interest of local agents (e.g., firms, technology organizations, cluster associations, chambers of commerce, among others) and regional and local policy-makers. They are interested in this dynamic view of local development as it helps to identify the critical aspects that can activate vibrant processes of territorial growth (EC, 2010). Moreover, the evolutionary approach to regional development may help policy-makers to differentiate stages and instruments that help them plan appropriate, local-specific innovation, and development policies and programs (Tödtling and Trippl, 2005, 2011; EC, 2010; Komninos et al., 2012; Valdaliso et al., 2013).

2.2 Knowledge as a Driver for the Evolution of Regions and Innovation Systems

The importance of knowledge for regional evolution is emphasized in differ-ent phases of the cluster life cycle literature (Menzel and Fornahl, 2007; Ter Wal and Boschma, 2011), with particular reference to a large set of mecha-nisms that help to transcend existing stages (Boschma and Frenken, 2011; Li and Bathelt, 2011; Sisti et al., 2014) and path dependencies (Martin, 2011). This literature is based on a wider economics literature on innovation that highlights a number of partially overlapping concepts and drivers. This includes the role of Research and Development (R&D) expenditure; skilled workforce; absorptive capacity; cognitive, social, and institutional proxim-ity/distance; technological capabilities; industrial/sector competences; and related variety knowledge platforms, among others. All these concepts have been related to the development of local production systems more in general (Audretsch, 1998; Boschma, 2005; Menzel and Fornahl, 2007; Asheim et al., 2011). Among the different knowledge drivers, we focus on a few crit-ical aspects that are currently discussed in the literature and which can have crucial implications for policy-making. First of all, we introduce the concept of the knowledge relatedness of the industries involved in the innovation pro-cess (Asheim et al., 2011; Boschma and Frenken, 2011). Knowledge relat-edness concerns the absorptive capacity of firms and territories as well as the "cognitive proximity/distance" that is required to be able to absorb the type of knowledge that spurs novel and/or radical innovations (Nooteboom, 2000; Boschma and Frenken, 2011; Iammarino, 2011). This relatively new field of research is currently analyzed under a number of lenses/mechanisms (i.e., institutional, entrepreneurial, labor market, social capital, among others). However, there is an unresolved debate about the degree of openness that regions should pursue within a "related variety" approach. Is it better to favor a higher or a lower "related variety" within the territorial economy, thus a relative specialization? This has implications for the capacity of the local and regional economy to transform its production capacity and to react to exogenous shocks. In fact, once some exogenous shock hits specific industries, regions, and countries, a higher degree of "unrelated variety" may be a better solution, as it helps to reduce the negative impact on other regional and national industries. On the other hand, related variety means cognitive proximity and a higher capacity to extend the local knowledge on the basis of extant knowledge bases, thus making growth easier in periods of relative calm and growth of the economy (Parrilli and Zabala, 2014).

Such an approach has important implications for the investments and strategies that policy-makers set up to promote local and regional development. The question is whether the creation of new industries from scratch or, alternatively, the development of industrial branches that are closely related to (and possibly spin out from) their existing knowledge bases should be promoted. The debate might also stir deeper discussions on the adoption of policy approaches that are more in line with an "entrepreneurial discovery" market-driven type of approach (Foray and van Ark, 2007), vis-à-vis others, which may be connected with a more top-down, policy-inducement approach (Asheim et al. in this volume; Cooke, 2006).

Taking a different lens, the debate is also reflected in the discussion of the path dependence of innovation systems, which is in part mediated by the knowledge bases (analytic vs. synthetic or symbolic; see Asheim and Coenen, 2005) and the technological capabilities managed in the production and innovation system (Martin, 2011) and in part by other institutional and cultural aspects that may contribute in different ways to defining the options for knowledge exploration and market exploitation in regions and clusters (Amin and Thrift, 1994; Parrilli, 2009; Tödtling and Trippl, 2011; Rodríguez-Pose, 2013). Certain regions count with a thicker institutional framework based upon regional (e.g., the Basque Country, Emilia-Romagna) or national public and public/private organizations (e.g., German and French regions) that focus their activities on a reduced number of locally based industries, while other regions may benefit from a more dynamic and variable environment that responds quickly to market signals and/or new revolutionary scientific outputs (Cambridgeshire, south and southeast of England, Sophia-Antipolis in the south-east of France). Starting from these different institutional and social capital bases, processes of path dependence lead regions to develop more or less "related variety," affecting their ability to respond to the continuously new market challenges. Thus a range of diverse development options—pathways—(e.g., branching out of new sectors or creation of brand-new industries) are available, which may provide different results in different types of innovation systems (e.g., thick vs. thin RISs; Trippl and Isaksen in this volume; see also Martin, 2011).

The discussion on the pathways available to innovation systems needs to be complemented with a debate about the efficiency and effectiveness of such systems. This requires undertaking an in-depth analysis of the micro-components of the innovation systems that also affect the way production systems work. Particularly in the European context, there are a wide variety of agents that participate in the innovation dynamics of regions and production systems, including universities, technology centers, private research centers, business incubators, science and technology parks, venture capitalists, high-tech industries, and knowledge-intensive business services (KIBS), among others. Such variety may help to generate an innovation system, but it may also lead to overlaps and system failures that need to be addressed. This set of organizations may have a major (or minor) impact on the innovation and competitive capacity of regions, industries, and, within these, firms, particularly when these are small and medium-sized enterprises (Cooke, 2001; Parrilli et al., 2010). In particular, the understanding of how innovation systems work becomes crucial. Innovation systems may be disassembled in a number of parts and agents, some of which may be efficient, while others not (Hollanders et al., 2009; Nauwelaers and Wintjes, 2008; Alberdi et al., 2014; Trippl and Isaksen, and Asheim et al. in this volume). Disassembling innovation systems may help identify the actual gaps that exist in each regional innovation system to promote a more effective institutional (and policy) support, as well as a more direct business involvement.

The analysis of regions is crucial in the identification of development/evolutionary pathways that can be targeted and implemented through the dynamism of the private sector and the support of public agents. Notwithstanding this, the actual agents of development and innovation are the firms, thus a well-grounded analysis of the potential prospects for growth of regional economies needs to "zoom" in on these specific "actors" as a means of understanding their key features and overall heterogeneity. The firms are grounded in specific territories, industries, and institutions but also act upon their environments and transform them. Hence, this volume devotes a special section to the presentation and understanding of businesses and their strengths, features, and impacts on innovation and economic development.

3. BUSINESS DEVELOPMENT

3.1 The Firms and Their Innovation Context

Alongside the studies of factors and mechanisms related to the evolution of regions and their industries, the current volume integrates a closely related discussion on business knowledge capabilities and innovation modes. This theme complements the territorial research strand, as the development/evolution of both production and innovation systems rely on the competitiveness and innovation capacity and capabilities of firms. In any region, firms are the crucial actors behind innovation. The innovation capacity of any region or cluster is a function of its changing composition of firms and of the development of these firms. In order to understand the conditions under which regions can promote innovation and growth, we need to examine and understand how firms in different regions conduct their innovation processes and which factors determine their success or failure.

Importantly, these factors are not the same for firms across different industries or territories. Different industries have different requirements in terms of how innovation processes are organized (e.g., exploration, examination, exploitation), which are the most important knowledge inputs (e.g., R&D, learning-by-doing), how knowledge is transferred (e.g., codified and tacit knowledge), and the pace or extent of innovation (e.g., incremental or radical). The composition of industries in any given region is a function of its factor endowments, historical evolution, market conditions, and pure coincidence, and it therefore varies widely across regions. In addition, geographical and cultural idiosyncrasies may imply the generalized adoption of certain practices of innovation in a given region. The application is that regions also innovate in very different ways and have different requirements for promoting innovation.

In the innovation systems approach, these features, capabilities, and businesses innovation modes represent the "idiosyncratic foundations" of the competitiveness of clusters, innovation systems, and regions (Jensen et al, 2007; Lundvall, 2007). The innovation systems approach puts the spotlight on institutions, which shape the interaction between actors within a national or regional economy and create the conditions for systemic patterns of interaction. When this interaction—in particular between knowledge generators and knowledge appliers—works well, it creates fertile conditions for innovation and growth in the region. However, successful interaction requires an institutional setup that give actors the incentives, confidence, and opportunities to interact, whether in the form of formal institutions (e.g., laws, organizations) or informal institutions (e.g., trust, reputation).

Firms are conceptualized as part of the knowledge application subsystem within the regional innovation systems approach. According to this theory, firms apply knowledge generated by universities and R&D centers to develop new products and processes that provide additional value. From the perspective of firms, interaction within the system means communicating their needs to the centers of knowledge generation and identifying and applying the knowledge produced by these centers, which is relevant to their activities.

However, whether and to what extent firms actually apply knowledge generated within these regional innovation systems in their innovation activities is a question that still requires to be answered. Two topics currently dominate the debate: 1) how important is knowledge sourcing within the regional system relative to sourcing knowledge from outside the local area in firm innovation processes and 2) how important is knowledge derived from the knowledge-generating subsystem following a science and technology-driven linear model of innovation relative to experience-based learning-by-doing and using? Both topics represent research domains that may help to contextualize firm innovation processes within their specific regions and innovation systems. This is important in identifying which policy actions could be set up to make public investments more effective and efficient, thus promoting the development of production and innovation systems.

3.2 Knowledge Sourcing Within and Outside Regional Systems

Another question that has been high on the agenda of economic geographers in the current era of globalization is how firms balance sourcing knowledge from within their local areas and from elsewhere in the world. Globalization has been accompanied by increasing urbanization, which creates a paradox: while information technology has reduced the costs of communication across distances, firms increasingly tend to cluster in large cities and specialized production systems (Sonn and Storper, 2008). Why do firms want to locate in close proximity to other firms and economic agents? One possible answer to this paradox is that the modern economy is also more knowledge based, making access to novel information and flows of tacit knowledge increasingly important to firms (Leamer and Storper, 2001). Tacit knowledge travels badly, making it necessary to locate close to the sources of such knowledge, be they other firms, customers, or research centers.

However, firms relying exclusively on knowledge from within regional clusters run the risk that the absence of new information flowing into the clusters may limit their innovative potential (Rodríguez-Pose and Fitjar, 2013). In smaller regions in particular, the same set of agents might interact frequently, reducing the capacity for learning as the cognitive distance between them gradually disappears (Boschma, 2005). Unless new knowledge is continuously being fed into the system from outside, the region may become locked-in to a less innovative trajectory. Thus firms need to combine intra-regional sources of knowledge with links to knowledge hubs outside the region. These pipelines are often purpose-built connections to knowledge producers in faraway locations, which require an investment to discover the right partners and establish a relationship with them that allows for knowledge transfer (Bathelt et al., 2004).

An issue that has hitherto not been given a lot of attention in the literature is that the choice between intra-regional and extra-regional sources of knowledge may depend on characteristics of the region in which the firm is located (see Parrilli, Fitjar, and Rodríguez-Pose in this volume). Fitjar and Rodríguez-Pose (2015a) show that these choices are closely related to the R&D investment levels and educational attainment of the region. In regions with high investments in R&D, more knowledge is generated internally, and firms may rely more on intra-regional knowledge. Regions with a highly educated workforce have more capacity to identify and use knowledge from outside—more absorptive capacity (Cohen and Levinthal, 1990)—and may therefore make better use of extra-regional sources of knowledge.

3.3 Business Innovation Modes

The diversity of modes of innovation has also attracted attention of the knowledge sourcing literature (Jensen et al., 2007; Lundvall, 1992) distinguish between a scientific-technological approach to innovation in which innovation processes are mainly built around investments in in-house R&D and relations to universities and other research centers (the Science and Technology-based Innovation, or STI mode) and an experiential and practice-oriented innovation mode based on learning-by-doing and learning-by-interacting (the doing, using, and interacting, or DUI mode). Innovation policy and empirical measures of innovation have so far been based mainly on an STI logic, which emphasizes formal R&D leading to new patents, while a great deal of innovation within the DUI approach is more difficult to observe and to measure.

The importance of these innovation modes varies across different production systems and industries. While firms in some industries, e.g., biotechnology or computing, rely heavily on scientific knowledge as an input to innovation, experience- and practice-based learning is more important, for example, in many service-producing industries. Hence the balance between sourcing knowledge from universities and from suppliers or customers is different across sectors, leading to different ways of organizing the innovation process. For policy-makers, this carries the implication that it is important to understand the nature and logic of the innovation processes of the main regional industries in order to craft appropriate policy interventions. Hence policy choices of typical STI-oriented countries such as the United States, Japan, or Sweden may not be the most appropriate ones in environments dominated by more DUI-oriented industries.

However, this is not to say that the ideal way forward is to cultivate existing strengths in experience-based or science-based learning. In their study of Denmark, Jensen et al (2007) find that the best results are obtained by firms that combine the STI and DUI approaches to innovation and that are therefore able to build upon both scientific and practice-based knowledge in their innovation processes. Similarly, Fitjar and Rodríguez-Pose (2015b) find in the case of Norway that firms in some DUI-dominated industries, such as construction, benefit the most from interacting with scientific partners, as these may provide access to knowledge that is rare and novel within their industry.

4. THE ORIGINALITY OF THIS VOLUME

In addition to presenting specific valuable contributions on regional innovation pathways and taxonomies (e.g., Asheim et al.; Trippl and Isaksen; Hervás-Oliver; Longhi; Vincze and Teräs; Alberdi et al.) and on firm innovation capabilities and business innovation modes (Longhi; Sedita and Apa; Fitjar and Rodríguez-Pose; Gjelsvik and Fitjar; Parrilli et al.), an important contribution of this volume is its combination of the two spheres of analysis that refer to two different academic disciplines, i.e., economics of innovation and management of innovation. These two large strands of the literature on innovation contribute, to a different extent, to regional development dynamics due to their specificities and interdependencies for which they are likely to strengthen each other in a sort of circular process.

This nested analysis of innovation processes combines a meso-level focus on regional innovation systems and local production systems with a micro-level focus on individual business units. The advantage of the approach is that it allows the examination of dynamics of regional development from the perspective of both the firms (i.e., individual organizations) and the territories (i.e., aggregate and collective systems). A multilevel theoretical debate thus permits a more thorough understanding and discussion of the heterogeneity that exists in any territory in terms of agents, linkages, and growth potentials that orient (and constrain) the pathways available to improve the innovation and competitive capacity of regions. For instance, a rising group of radical innovators in a region that has always pursued incremental innovations may generate new horizons for other businesses, setting the bases for radical transformations also in other industries (e.g., the case of East Asian economies joining high-tech industries). Simultaneously, this work recognizes the mutual interdependence between the wider geographical frameworks of regions and the individual business units. The wider geographical framework provides the social and institutional context, traditions, and routines as well as specific competences and economic specializations that orient business approaches and outcomes (e.g., the regional

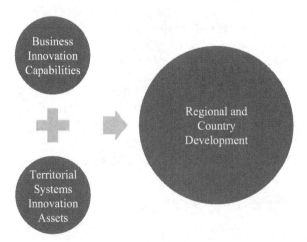

Figure 1.1   The Interdependence Between Firms' and Systems' Innovation Capabilities

propensity to institutionalize cooperation activities in Baden-Wurttenberg or in Emilia-Romagna). Meanwhile, the business units are the crucial actors that practically determine (maintain and/or transform) the innovation and development prospects of a region.

Interdependence is at the heart of this volume. Territories have their own social capital and institutional features that orient the activity of the firm (Granovetter, 1985; Amin and Thrift, 1995; Asheim and Gertler, 2005; Rodríguez-Pose, 2013). Hence the likelihood of starting up a business is intimately related to the conditions of the territory. The advantages of specialization in favorable institutional contexts in the Italian industrial districts have been a continuous source for the creation of new and dynamic firms. Production cooperatives have proven a rich basis for start-ups in areas characterized by strong ties, such as the Basque Country). The emergence of new businesses purely out of individual ambition, talent, and hard work in more market-oriented contexts (e.g., Anglo-Saxon countries and regions) is, however, not to be discarded as a fundamental source of start-ups (i.e., different kinds of social and institutional environments).

The "individual spirit" and the "entrepreneurial discovery" process are also continuously in motion (Foray and Van Ark, 2007). Many individuals and businesses rely on them in order to break the path dependence of their territorial industrial routines. They are also the source of "radical" innovations and new market opportunities. When businesses develop radical innovations, they can benefit and dynamize an entire local supply chain or cluster, such as in the case of Genentech and Amgen companies for the biotech industry clusters in California, the case of Nokia in the mobile phone market and local supply chain in Finland, the case of the Luxottica and the related glasses cluster in Treviso, Veneto, in Italy, or Zara in Galicia and its local supply chain. These, and many others, are cases of individual entrepreneurs and businesses that have been able to change paths and break the routine so as to develop new industries and new opportunities for several thousands of other people, entrepreneurs, and workers.

The aforementioned discussion shows that, in spite of existing path dependencies, there is not just one predefined path in regional innovative trajectories, but that the overall relation between firms and territories is bi- or multipolar and that these different poles may act and influence each other in a reciprocal form (Martin and Sunley, 2011). For this reason, we have decided to analyze the two types of actors simultaneously and to show their dynamics as well as their capacity to influence each other mutually.

5. A SYNTHETIC VIEW OF THIS VOLUME

This volume discusses the construction of new innovation pathways for regions and firms in the context of the multiform European geography. The objectives are centered on exploring the logic and mechanisms that can be activated as a means to promote innovation and competitiveness within regions and, within these, across and within firms. As a consequence, the book aims at developing an in-depth understanding of these drivers and the way in which they may activate growth in regions and firms. Additionally, the approach adopted in the book may offer useful insights and knowledge to the new approach developed by the European Commission, called "regional innovation strategies for smart specialization—RIS3" (European Commission, 2010), which is the coordinated development EC strategy set up to promote smart and diversified specializations across countries and regions. In this volume, we call attention to this topic by focusing on some key features of territorial evolution. In particular, we focus on core geographies of an appropriate RIS3 strategy, as well as on the options that different business capabilities and innovation modes offer for achieving higher regional development prospects.

The volume is divided into two main parts, a territorial (macro) development section that discusses the growth prospects of regions. The second part is about business innovation (micro), i.e., the way individual firms develop their organizations and their interfirm practices so as to be able to develop a significant output of innovation that makes them more competitive in current globalized markets.

Michaela Trippl and Johan Miörner (Circle-Lund University) and Björn Asheim (University of Stavanger and Circle-Lund University) developed the first chapter in the first part of this volume. They focus on regions with less-developed research and innovation systems. Moving from the analysis of different types of system failures (i.e., organizational thinness, lock-in, fragmentation), the authors stress the different development trajectories or paths available to regional innovation systems. Path extension, path renewal, and new path creation are the routes that distinct RISs can pursue on the basis of the knowledge bases managed in the territory, and the organizational and institutional thickness/thinness that can be found there. This chapter is complemented by a significant review of the current policy and academic efforts made to characterize these regional innovation systems and to measure their strengths and weaknesses. In the concluding section, the authors argue for a more thorough conceptual and empirical review to take into account the system failures, the organizational and institutional thickness and thinness, and the knowledge bases, as well as the impact of global innovation networks on the capacity of the regional innovation system to reorient their development process toward some of the most appealing trajectories.

The second chapter in part one of this volume is connected to the first in the attempt to study and assess the working of regional innovation systems. Its authors, Alberdi-Pons, Gibaja-Martíns, (Deusto Business School) and Parrilli (Bournemouth University), focus on the integration/fragmentation of regional innovation systems—with an empirical analysis based on the seventeen Spanish Autonomous Communities—and their related efficiency and effectiveness. In particular, the chapter aims to identify relevant gaps in the system (consistently with the work of Trippl et al. in the first chapter) and to try to measure their impact on the innovation capacity of the regional system. A typology of regions is thus proposed on the basis of their characteristics and their capacities to face the different gaps that may affect the innovation capacity of the system. Practical implications for policy-making are derived, which target the differentiated ability of the regions to perform in the selected fields of innovation.

Arne Isaksen (University of Agder) and Michaela Trippl (Circle-Lund University) developed the third chapter in part one. The authors take a more "prospective" approach to the identification of trajectories of development of a set of regional innovation systems. They focus on path dependence and path renewal within different types of regional innovation systems and identify specific policies that might respond to the weaknesses of these specific systems and support their increasing competitiveness. In particular, the authors identify and discuss the features and opportunities that organizationally "thick" and "thin" regional innovation systems have to deviate from the built-in path dependence and to promote dynamic regional development pathways. Particularly, this matters when it is considered together with the industry base of specialized versus diversified production, as this base paves the way for distinct types of path dependencies (e.g., technology lock-ins in the first case and lack of production depth/specialization in the second), which need to be surpassed as a means to open new waves of development across these systems. Once again, the importance of a specific-purpose public policy is discussed, as it needs to be adapted to the specific social capital, institutional, and industrial conditions of the production and innovation system located in the region.

Zsuzsanna Vincze (Umeå University) and Jukka Teräs (Nordregio) proposed the fourth chapter in part one in which they focus on cluster evolution from an institutional perspective. The novelty of this contribution refers to the identification of different types of mechanisms, part of which are directly derived from different sets of drivers, among which social mechanisms (individual and cultural values, beliefs, designs), operational (exchange and learning processes), and transformational mechanisms (business models, knowledge and identity structure). In particular, the latter are explored in depth in two different cases selected for analysis: Oulu in Finland and Örnsköldsvik in Sweden.

The fifth chapter, elaborated by José Luis Hervás-Oliver (Polytechnic University of Valencia), wraps up the first section of the book on territorial innovation and development. The analysis presented connects the discussion on regional development with the topic of business innovation and growth. Hervás-Oliver points out the relevance of radical innovation (capacity) as a basis for the reconfiguration of the cluster evolution and development prospects. Distance technologies, competence destruction, weak ties, and spin-offs are identified as crucial mechanisms for the promotion of such radical innovation capacity in the context of dynamic clusters that are able to continuously renew themselves as a means to respond to the changing global markets. The world-known case of the tile industry in Castellón is discussed in this chapter. The final output of this research delivers significant outcome in terms of the most fertile ground for radical innovation vis-à-vis the most likely obstacles to overcoming it: on the one hand, the connection to technology-distant industries, knowledge bases, and agents, including their weak-ties-based networks and on the other, the role of incumbent technology gatekeepers that tend to rely a lot on accumulated knowledge and strong local ties, which promote incremental innovations but are rather rigid in the adoption of breaking-ground kinds of knowledge insights and technological novelties.

Overall, these five chapters tackle the issue of regional development from a number of different perspectives, namely the regional innovation system approach and cluster perspectives. Such contributions aim at closing a few key research and policy gaps, such as understanding more in depth the options of different trajectories and policy targets of different types of production and innovation systems (Asheim et al. chapter, Trippl and Isaksen chapter, and Alberdi et al. chapter), the importance of breaking former competences and routines (Hervás-Oliver), and the relevance of identifying specific mechanisms and forms in which the context, particularly social capital, catalyzes changes and evolutions within local production systems (Vincze and Teräs).

Connecting the regional-level analyses with the chapters focusing more on the firm level is the contribution of Christian Longhi (University of Nice) on learning processes in interfirm collaborations. The author develops a network analysis that is embedded in the pole "Secure Communicating Solutions" created through a proactive cluster policy in the French Côte d'Azur Region near Marseille (Rousset-Gémenos) and Nice (Sophia-Antipolis). The two areas are well-known, high-technology clusters in France; the first one specialized in microelectronics and the latter in telecommunication, software, and multimedia. The focus of the chapter are the distinct endogenous innovation dynamics that have grown in these clusters. Local and international business networks emerge as the crucial means for developing positive knowledge spillovers across firms. Longhi's contribution connects the regional perspective with the business strategy perspective as specific territories are proved to benefit not just from generic geographical proximity but also from active business networking strategies, which often exceed the local boundaries of the cluster.

Longhi's chapter is very much in line with the next chapter realized by Silvia Rita Sedita and Roberta Apa (University of Padua). They investigate the role of open innovation strategies in explaining firm innovation performance. They explore how differences in search strategies among firms influence their ability to achieve different levels of novelty in their innovative output. In this respect, relationships with clients, suppliers, industrial partners, consultants, universities, and public research organizations are analyzed through the two key dimensions of breadth and depth, at the global and the international, national, and regional levels. This study examines the innovation performance (in 2012) among a sample of 188 start-up firms operating in the mechanical engineering sector in the north of Italy that were born in the period 2004–2007. The findings establish that, in this context, depth does not matter much, whereas breadth does. A wider inclusiveness or openness of innovation collaborations helps new start-ups to be more innovative and competitive. In geographical terms, the international scope of these collaborations guarantees the strongest innovation output generated by firms.

Rune Dahl Fitjar (University of Stavanger) and Andrés Rodríguez-Pose (London School of Economics) elaborated a complementary chapter. Their work integrates the debate on science, technology, and innovation mode (STI) vis-à-vis the experience and interaction-based innovation mode (DUI) and analyses the approach taken by firms in the context of Norway. In particular, the analysis is centered around the geographical reach of these innovation modes with a view to analyzing whether businesses tend to adopt the archetypical STI or DUI mode at the regional or non-regional level and which one reaches the most significant and highest impact on innovation output (i.e., product and process innovation). The results show the criticality of non-local relations of collaboration vis-à-vis local relations. Between the two specified modes—STI and DUI—it is DUI-type collaborations at the non-local scale that matter most for innovation output, although—to a lower extent—STIs at both the non-local and local levels are also significantly correlated with innovation output. The overall outcome of the study is the emphasis delivered on non-local sources of collaboration for innovation vis-à-vis the local, and the importance assumed by the DUI mode (collaborations with supply-chain agents) vis-à-vis the STI approach when critical collaborations are developed.

Martin Gjelsvik (International Research Institute of Stavanger) and Rune Dahl Fitjar (University of Stavanger) proposed a further critical contribution on business innovation. The chapter focuses on the relationship between businesses and universities in the promotion of innovation, stressing that this relationship is far from linear as firm-university relationships of collaboration, in the form of collaborative research, consulting, teaching, and informal networking, can lead to the mutual enhancement of their absorptive capacity, thus leading to a range of significant outcomes. In particular, in this contribution, Gjelsvik and Fitjar identify and emphasize the type of mechanisms (i.e., good governance and knowledge-sharing routines) that help make this university-business relationship more effective. Fine-tuning their activation in specific joint initiatives leads to spilling over mutual positive effects, such as, for example, the formation of human capital by universities and the activation of a more sophisticated business demand that leads to continuous innovation upgrades.

Moving back to the topic of STI and DUI innovation modes, Mario Davide Parrilli, Rune Dahl Fitjar, and Andrés Rodríguez-Pose offer a meta-study review of the several studies realized on business innovation modes, which represent the innovation strategies undertaken by firms (i.e., based on scientific and technology drivers vs. those based on learning-by-doing and by-interacting). Echoing the seminal contribution of Jensen et al. (2007), a relevant number of studies have been performed in several country contexts (Denmark, Norway, Sweden, Austria, Spain, Portugal, China, Colombia, Belarus). The results seem to show divergent trends, i.e., specific drivers (e.g., scientific human capital vs. general education, R&D investments vs. investments in machinery and equipment) operate actively in different types of countries. As a result, the relevance of country specificities is to be reckoned both in research and policy practice as a means to correctly interpret and strategically address specific country needs and potentials.

The chapters of the second part of the book focus on how businesses are affected by, but also shape and even transform their industries and territories. This represents the second message of this collective research endeavor. Business strategies, capabilities, and innovation modes are conditions to increase the innovation capacity and the competitiveness of firms and their territories in the current competitive global markets. This is a level of analysis that is critical also for regional (and country) development, because the latter relies upon the aggregated trend of such business strategic behaviors and drivers. In addition, this level offers a detailed view of the heterogeneity of businesses when innovation capabilities and strategies are taken into account.

This whole discussion matters for policy-making, as the territorial specificities—that exist—cannot be taken for granted. Even in the context of territories that count on a significant social and institutional capital in addition to a traditional industrial-based competitiveness, the aforementioned heterogeneity of firms implies a higher or lower capacity to adapt the territorial competitiveness basis to the exogenous changes that derive from new situations, shocks, and transformation that occur in global markets. Policy-makers are thus required to recognize the business heterogeneity and their effective capacities in order to set up differentiated plans, programs, and instruments/mechanisms that offer such businesses a response to their specificities, assets, and limitations.

REFERENCES

Alberdi, X., Gibaja, J. J. and Parrilli, M. D. (2014). Evaluación de la fragmentación en los sistemas regionales de innovación: una tipología para España. *Investigaciones Regionales*, 28, 7–35.

Amin, A. and Thrift, N. J. (1994). *Globalisation, institutions and regional development in Europe*. Oxford: Oxford University Press.

Asheim, B. T. and Coenen, L. (2005). Knowledge bases and regional innovation systems: Comparing nordic clusters. *Research Policy*, 34(8), 1173–1190.

Asheim, B., Boschma, R. and Cooke, P. (2011). Constructing regional advantage: Platform policies based on related variety and differentiated knowledge bases. *Regional Studies*, 45(7), 893–904.

Asheim, B. and Gertler, M. (2005). The geography of innovation: Regional innovation systems. In J. Fagerberg, D. Mowery and R. Nelson (eds.), *The Oxford handbook of innovation* (291–316). New York: Oxford University Press.

Audretsch, D. B. (1998). Agglomeration and the location of innovative activity. *Oxford Review of Economic Policy*, 14(2), 18–29.

Bathelt, H., Malmberg, A. and Maskell, P. (2004). Clusters and knowledge: Local buzz, global pipelines and the process of knowledge creation. *Progress in Human Geography*, 28(1), 31–56.

Becattini, G., Bellandi, M. and De Propris, L. (2009). *Handbook of industrial districts*. Cheltenham: Elgar.

Bellandi, M. and Di Tommaso, M. (2005). The case of specialized towns in Guangdon, China. *European Planning Studies*, 13(5), 707–729.

Belussi, F. and Sedita, S. R. (2012). Industrial districts as open learning systems. *Regional Studies*, 46(2), 165–184.

Boix, R. and Galletto, V. (2009). Innovation and industrial districts. *Regional Studies*, 43(9), 1117–1133.

Boschma, R. A. (2005). Proximity and innovation: A critical assessment. *Regional Studies*, 39(1), 61–74.

Boschma, R. A. and Frenken, K. (2011). Technological relatedness, related variety and economic geography. In P. Cooke et al. (eds.), *Handbook of regional innovation and growth* (187–197). Cheltenham: Edward Elgar.

Cohen, W. and Levinthal, D. (1990). Absorptive capacity: A new perspective on learning and innovation. *Administrative Science Quarterly*, 35, 128–152.

Cooke, P. (2001). Regional innovation systems, clusters and the knowledge economy. *Industrial and Corporate Change*, 10(4), 945–971.

Cooke, P. (2006). Reflections on the research and conclusions for policy. In P. Cooke, C. De Laurentis, F. Tödtling and M. Trippl (eds.), *Regional knowledge economies* (296–329). Cheltenham: Elgar.

Crespo, J., Suire, R. and Vicente, J. (2013). Lock-in or lock-out? How structural properties of knowledge networks affect regional resilience. *Journal of Economic Geography*, 14(1), 199–219.

Delgado, M., Porter, M. and Stern, S. (2014). Clusters, convergence and economic performance. *Research Policy*, 43(10), 1785–1799.

European Commission. (2010). *Regional policy contributing to smart growth in Europe 2020*. SEC (2010) 1983, Brussels.

Fitjar, R. D. and Rodríguez-Pose, A. (2015a). Networking, context and firm-level innovation: Cooperation through the regional filter in Norway. *Geoforum*, 63(1), 25–35.

Fitjar, R. D. and Rodríguez-Pose, A. (2015b). Interaction and innovation across different sectors: Findings from Norwegian city-regions. *Regional Studies*, 49(5), 818–833.

Foray, D. and Goenaga, X. (2014). *The goals of smart specialization*, S3 Policy Brief 01/2013. Brussels: European Commission.

Foray, D. and Van Ark, B. (2007). Smart specialization, policy brief no.1, expert group knowledge for growth, European Commission, Brussels, http://ec.europa.eu/invest-in-research/pdf/download_en/policy_brief1.pdf.

Giuliani, E. (2005). Cluster absorptive capacity: Why do some clusters forge ahead and others lag behind. *European Urban and Regional Studies*, 12(3), 269–288.

Glückler, J. (2007). Geography of reputation: The city as the locus of business opportunity. *Regional Studies*, 41(7), 949–962.

Granovetter, M. (1985). Economic action and social structure: the problem of embeddedness. *American Journal of Sociology*, 91, 481–510.

Guerrieri, P. and Pietrobelli, C. (2004). Industrial districts' evolution and technological regimes: Italy and Taiwan. *Technovation*, Elsevier, 17(11), 899–914.

Henderson, J., Dicken, P., Hess, M. and Yeung, H. W. (2002). Global production networks and the analysis of economic development. *Review of International Political Economy*, 9(3), 436–464.

Hollanders, H., Tarantola, S. and Loschky, A. (2009). *Regional innovation scoreboards*. Brussels: Pro Inno Europe.

Humphrey, J. (1995). Industrial organization in developing countries: from models to trajectories. *World Development*, 23(1), 149–162.

Iammarino, S. (2011). Regional innovation and diversity. In P. Cooke et al. (eds.), *Handbook of regional innovation and growth* (143–153). Cheltenham: Edward Elgar.

Jensen, M., Johnson, B., Lorenz, E. and Lundvall, B. A. (2007). Forms of knowledge and modes of innovation. *Research Policy*, 36, 680–693.

Knorringa, P. (2002). Cluster trajectories in developing countries. In M. P. Van Dijk and H. Sandee (eds.), *Innovation and small firms in the Third World* (48–65). Cheltenham: Elgar.

Komninos, N., Pallot, M. and Schaefer, H. (2012). Special issue on smart cities and the future of Internet in Europe. *Journal of Knowledge Economy*, doi: 10.1007/s13132–012–0083-x.

Lastres, A. and Cassiolato, J. (2005). Innovation systems and local productive arrangements. *Innovation, Management, Policy and Practice*, 7(2), 172–187.

Leamer, E. and Storper, M. (2001). The economic geography of the Internet age. *NBER Working Papers* no. 8450.

Li, P. F., & Bathelt, H. (2011). A relational-evolutionary perspective of cluster dynamics. *Spatial Aspects Concerning Economic Structures—SPACES online*, 9(2), 1–18.

Lorenzen, M. and Mudambi, R. (2012). Clusters, connectivity and catch-up: Bollywood and Bangalore in the global economy. *Journal of Economic Geography*, doi: 10.1093/jeg/lbs017.

Lundvall, B. A. (1992). *National systems of innovation*. London: Pinter.

Lundvall, B. A. (2007). National innovation systems. *Industry and Innovation*, 14(1), 95–119.

Malmberg, A. and Maskell, P. (2002). The elusive concept of localization economies: Towards a knowledge-based theory of spatial clustering. *Environment and Planning*, 34, 429–449.

Martin, R. (2011). Regional economies as path dependent systems: Some issues and implications. In P. Cooke et al. (eds.), *Handbook of regional innovation and growth* (198–210). Cheltenham: Edward Elgar.

Martin, R. and Sunley, M. (2011). Conceptualizing cluster evolution: Beyond the lifecycle model. *Regional Studies*, 45(10), 1299–1318.

Maskell, P. and Malmberg, A. (2002). Localised learning and industrial competitiveness. *Cambridge Journal of Economics*, 23, 167–185.

McCann, P. and Ortega-Argiles, R. (2013). Modern regional innovation policy. *Cambridge Journal of Regions, Economy and Society*, 6(2), 187–216.

Menzel, M. P. and Fornhal, D. (2010). Cluster lifecycle: Dimensions and rationales of cluster evolution. *Industrial and Corporate Change*, 19(1), 205–238.

Nadvi, K. and Schmitz, H. (1999). Clustering and industrialization: Introduction. *World Development*, 27(9), 1503–1514.

Nauwelaers, C. and Wintjes, R. (2008). *Innovation policy in Europe—measurement and strategy*. Cheltenham: Edward Elgar.

Nooteboom, B. (2000). Institutions and forms of coordination in innovation systems. *Organization Studies*, 21(5), 915–939.

Parrilli, M. D. and Sacchetti, S. (2008). Linking learning with governance in networks and clusters. *Entrepreneurship and Regional Development*, 20(4), 387–408.

Parrilli, M. D. (2009). Collective efficiency, policy-inducement and social embeddedness: Drivers of district development. *Entrepreneurship and Regional Development*, 21(1): 1–24.

Parrilli, M. D. (2012). Heterogeneous social capital: A window of opportunities for local economies. In P. Cooke, M. D. Parrilli and J. L. Curbelo (eds.), *Innovation, global change and territorial resilience* (230–245). Cheltenham: Edward Elgar.

Parrilli, M. D., Aranguren, M. J. and Larrea, M. (2010). Interactive learning to close the innovation gap in SME-based economies. *European Planning Studies*, 18(1), 351–370.

Parrilli, M. D. and Zabala, J. M. (2014). Interrelated diversification and internationalization: Critical drives of global industries. *Revue d'Economie Industrielle*, 145, 63–93.

Pietrobelli, C. and Rabellotti, R. (eds.). (2007). *Upgrading to compete*. Cambridge, Mass.: Harvard University Press.

Piore, M. and Sabel, C. (1984). *The second industrial divide*. New York: Basic Books.

Porter, M. (1998a). Clusters and the new economics of competition. *Harvard Business Review*, November–December, 77–90.

Porter, M. (1998b). *On competition*. Cambridge, Mass.: Harvard Business School.

Rodríguez-Pose, A. (2013). Do institutions matter for regional development? *Regional Studies*, 47(7), 1034–1047.

Rodríguez-Pose, A. and Comptour, F. (2012). Are clusters the solution? In P. Cooke, M. D. Parrilli and J. L. Curbelo (eds.), *Innovation, global change and territorial resilience* (274–293). Cheltenham: Edward Elgar.

Rodríguez-Pose, A. and Fitjar, R. D. (2013). Buzz, archipelago economies and the future of intermediate and peripheral areas in a spiky world. *European Planning Studies*, 21(3), 355–372.

Schmitz, H. (1995). Collective efficiency: Growth path for small-scale industry. *Journal of Development Studies*, 31, 529–566.

Sisti, E., Parrilli, M. D. and Zubiaurre, A. (2014). The role of social capital in resilient territories: Mechanism for growth. In H. Pinto (ed.), *Resilient territories: Innovation and creativity for new modes of regional development* (30–61). Cambridge: Cambridge Scholars Publishers.

Sonn, J. W. and Storper, M. (2008). The increasing importance of geographical proximity in knowledge production: An analysis of US patent citations. *Environment and Planning A*, 40, 1020–1039.

Ter Wal, A. and Boschma, R. (2011). Co-evolution of firms, industries and networks in space. *Regional Studies*, 45(7), 919–933.

Tödtling, F. and Trippl, M. (2005). One size fits all?: Towards a differential regional innovation policy approach. *Research Policy*, 34(8), 1203–1219.

Tödtling, F. and Trippl, M. (2011). Regional innovation systems. In P. Cooke et al. (eds.), *Handbook of regional innovation and growth* (455–466). Cheltenham: Elgar.

Valdaliso, J., Navarro, M., Aranguren, M. J. and Magro, E. (2013). A holistic approach to regional strategies. *Science and Public Policy*, doi: 10.1093/scipol/sct080.

Visser, E. and Atzema, O. (2008). With or without clusters: Facilitating innovation through a differentiated and combined network approach. *European Planning Studies*, 16(9), 1169–1188.

Part I

Regional Innovation

2 Identification of Regions With Less-Developed Research and Innovation Systems

Michaela Trippl, Björn Asheim, and Johan Miörner

1. INTRODUCTION[1]

Smart specialization has become the new innovation policy paradigm in the European Union. This policy concept

> is about placing greater emphasis on innovation and having an innovation-driven development strategy in place that focuses on each region's strength and competitive advantage. It is about specialising in a smart way, i.e. based on evidence and strategic intelligence about a region's assets and the capability to learn what specialisations can be developed in relation to those of other regions.
>
> (European Union, 2011, p. 7)

Smart specialization shares a number of commonalities with and has been inspired by other modern and influential policy concepts, such as the Constructing Regional Advantage (CRA) approach (European Commission, 2006; Asheim et al., 2011a; Asheim, 2014; Boschma, 2014a). It considers knowledge and innovation as key determinants of regional development and emphasizes the need to avoid imitation of successful policies pursued in other regions and "one-size-fits-all" strategies (Tödtling and Trippl, 2005). Smart specialization strategies are place-based policy strategies that aim to promote economic diversification of regions (McCann and Ortega-Argiles, 2013; Boschma, 2014a) taking into account their unique characteristics and assets. Specialized diversification or diversified specialization (Asheim 2014) should thus rank high on policy agendas. The identification and selection of prioritized areas for policy intervention are suggested to be the outcome of an "entrepreneurial discovery process," a notion that has been heavily debated in the recent past (Foray and Goenaga, 2013; Foray and Rainoldi, 2013; Asheim, 2014; Boschma, 2014a). There seems to be an agreement, however, that an inclusive approach to the identification of policy priorities (that is, inclusive governance structures that allow for the involvement of regional stakeholders in selecting promising areas for innovation policy) is important for the success of smart specialization.

A key question is if smart specialization strategies are applicable to any type of regions. It has been argued that regions with less-favored research and innovation systems have a low potential to diversify into new industrial areas due to unfavorable economic structures and a weak endowment of knowledge organizations (Boschma, 2014b, Isaksen and Trippl, see chapter 4 in this volume). In addition, some less-developed regional research and innovation systems suffer from weak policy and governance capacities, which could curtail the effective use of Cohesion policy funds (Charron et al., 2014) and may form major barriers to the successful formulation and implementation of smart specialization strategies (Rodríguez-Pose et al., 2014).

The aim of this chapter is to contribute to the debate on how to identify regions with less-developed research and innovation systems. It would be beyond the scope of this chapter to engage in a discussion of how the specific elements of these systems influence the opportunities for smart specialization or how the challenges faced by these regions might be overcome to enhance the impact of smart specialization strategies. However, this chapter paves the way for such analyses by discussing several conceptual and empirical contributions to identify regions with less-developed research and innovation systems, focusing in particular on key barriers and missing elements that may be found in these systems. For the sake of clarity, it is important to note that in the following parts of this chapter, only the notion "regional innovation system" (RIS) will be used, because we consider the regional research system as a subsystem of RIS.

The remainder of this chapter is organized as follows. Section 2 reviews the conceptual debate on RIS, system failures, organizational and institutional thinness, knowledge bases, and regional industrial path development and demonstrates how these concepts can contribute to identifying various types of regions with less-developed RIS. In section 3, we provide a critical discussion of empirical approaches to categorize less-developed RIS based on measurements of their innovation performance. Finally, section 4 concludes and outlines some key issues that should receive due attention in future research.

2. CONCEPTUAL APPROACHES

Research on RIS has grown significantly since the notion's first articulation and development in the early 1990s (for an overview on the theoretical antecedents and origins of the RIS approach, its development over the past two decades, and recently made advances see Asheim et al., 2011b). RISs come in many shapes and various typologies have been suggested to capture this variety (see, for instance, Asheim and Isaksen, 2002; Cooke, 2004; Asheim and Gertler, 2005; Asheim and Coenen, 2006). In this section, we focus on those conceptual ideas (and the typologies that emanate from them) that are most relevant for identifying less-developed RIS. We review contributions on system failures, organizational and institutional thinness, knowledge bases, and new regional industrial path development to shed light on potential factors and dimensions in RIS that can restrain regional innovation and change.

2.1 System-Failure Approaches

A well-known conceptual approach for identifying less-developed innovation systems draws attention to various types of system deficiencies or system failures that result in low levels of innovation activities. Several typologies of system failures exist (see, for instance, Lundvall and Borras, 1999), enabling us to spot various dimensions of innovation systems that may be less developed or not working adequately. Klein Woolthuis et al. (2005), for example, distinguish between infrastructural failures, institutional failures (hard and soft institutional problems), interaction failures (strong and weak network failures), and capability failure. Recent work on transformational system failures (Weber and Rohracher, 2012) has further advanced the debate, pointing to a set of factors that limit a system's capacity to undergo processes of transformative change toward sustainability. A distinction between four types of transformational failures can be drawn: i) directionality failure, ii) demand articulation failure, iii) policy coordination failure, and iv) reflexivity failure (Weber and Rohracher, 2012). In the context of this debate, innovation systems might be referred to as "less developed" if they exhibit a weak capacity to foster transformative change. These insights are highly relevant for smart specialization, as the promotion of sustainability and social innovation are often seen as key aims of such strategies.

Tödtling and Trippl (2005) have applied the system-failure approach to the regional level to analyze various deficiencies of RIS. The authors propose a typology that distinguishes between three forms of system deficiencies, namely, organizational thinness, negative lock-in, and fragmentation (Table 2.1).

Table 2.1   RIS Failures

System failure / deficiencies	Type of region
Organizational thinness: crucial elements of a RIS are missing: low levels of clustering and weak endowment with key organizations	Peripheral regions
Negative lock-in: overembeddedness and overspecialization	Old industrial areas
Fragmentation: lack of interaction between RIS elements	Metropolitan regions

Source: Tödtling and Trippl (2005)

This provides the foundation for discerning three main types of less-developed RIS (Tödtling and Trippl, 2005; Martin and Trippl, 2014):

- *Organizationally thin RISs* are systems in which essential elements are only weakly developed or even missing. Examples include the lack of a critical mass of innovative firms, a weak endowment of other key organizations and institutions and low levels of clustering. Organizationally thin RISs are often present in peripheral areas. These regions are characterized by insufficient levels of R&D and innovation due to the dominance of SMEs in traditional sectors, the lack of assets to nurture new industries, a weak capacity to absorb knowledge from outside the region, and a thin structure of supporting organizations (Doloreux and Dionne, 2008; Karlsen et al., 2011).
- *Locked-in RISs* are characterized by an overembeddedness and over-specialization in mature sectors and out-dated technologies. Locked-in RISs often prevail in old industrialized areas. The capacity of firms in these areas to generate radical innovation is limited and the supporting organizations tend to be too strongly oriented on traditional industries and technologies. Various forms of negative lock-in (functional, cognitive, and political ones) keep these regions in ancestral development paths (Grabher, 1993; Trippl and Otto, 2009; Hassink, 2010).
- *Fragmented RISs* suffer from a lack of connectivity due to a suboptimal level of networking and knowledge exchange between actors in the system, leading to insufficient levels of collective learning and systemic innovation activities. Fragmented RISs can frequently be found in metropolitan areas (Blazek and Zizalova, 2010; OECD, 2010). In this type of region, fragmentation is often the outcome of too much diversity and a lack of related variety, resulting in levels of regional knowledge exchange and innovation below what could be expected given the often rich endowments of knowledge exploration as well as exploitation organizations found in metropolitan regions.

The application of the system-failure approach to the regional level has provided important insights into potential misconfigurations of RIS, pointing to a variety of elements that might be less developed or functioning inadequately. However, the key notion of "thickness" is defined in a rather simple way (number of organizations) and remains poorly conceptualized. In particular, the role of institutions for regional development and innovation (Gertler, 2010; Rodríguez-Pose, 2013; Charron et al., 2014), that is, the institutional dimension of thickness, is only insufficiently captured.

More recently, an attempt has been made to elaborate on the notions of thickness and thinness of RIS. Based on a comprehensive review and critical discussion of the respective literature, Zukauskaite et al. (2014) advocate a clear distinction between the organizational and institutional dimension of thinness. Organizational thickness (thinness) refers to the presence (absence) of a critical mass of firms, universities, research bodies, support organizations, unions, associations, and so on. Institutional thickness (thinness) is defined as the presence (absence) of both formal institutions (laws, rules, regulations) and informal institutions (such as an innovation and cooperation culture, norms, and values) that promote collective learning and knowledge exchange.

Departing from this clear-cut distinction, we advance the argument that RIS may suffer from institutional thinness, organizational thinness or a combination of both dimensions of thinness. This leads us to distinguish between three types of less-developed RIS (see Table 2.2):

- Institutionally thick *but* organizationally thin RIS: Good examples for this type of RIS are industrial districts in the Third Italy and regions in the North of Europe. Italian districts are well known for a pronounced culture of cooperation (institutional thickness), but they lack specific RIS elements, such strong research organizations or science-based firms (organizational thinness) that are essential for the generation of more radical forms of innovation. Nordic peripheral regions benefit from a high quality of government institutions (institutional thickness) but are only poorly endowed with innovation-relevant organizations (organizational thinness).
- Organizationally thick *but* institutionally thin RIS: This type of RIS can often be found in larger cities in Southern and Eastern Europe but also some old industrial areas in Western Europe may fall under this category. These places are characterized by the existence of a critical mass of firms as well as research, educational, and other supporting organizations (organizational thickness). However, innovation activities are seriously curtailed by the absence of an innovation and cooperation culture as well as a low quality of government institutions (institutional thinness).
- Institutionally thin *and* organizationally thin RIS: Such constellations tend to prevail in peripheral regions located in the South and East of Europe. More often than not, these areas are poorly endowed with innovation-relevant organizations (organizational thinness) and suffer from an institutional setup that is not conducive to innovation (institutional thinness).

Table 2.2   Organizational and Institutional Thickness/Thinness of RIS[2]

	Organizational thickness	Organizational thinness
Institutional thickness	Metropolitan/city-regions in Northern and Western Europe	Industrial districts in the Third Italy, Nordic peripheral regions
Institutional thinness	Larger cities in Southern and Eastern Europe, OIA in Western Europe	Southern and Eastern peripheral regions

Source: Authors' compilation

2.2 Knowledge-Base Approach

The literature on differentiated knowledge bases (Asheim and Gertler, 2005; Asheim et al., 2011a) has sharpened our view that all industries, and not only high-tech ones, can be innovative, and it has provided the analytical tools for explaining intersectoral variations of innovation patterns. Three types of knowledge bases can be distinguished: analytical, synthetic, and symbolic (see Table 2.3). Scholarly work on knowledge bases clearly challenges old approaches that equate innovation with R&D and high-tech activities. Innovation systems that are characterized by lower levels of R&D and a dominance of mature industries (that often are knowledge intensive but not high tech) cannot automatically be categorized as less-developed ones.

Table 2.3   Differentiated Knowledge-Base Approach

	Analytical (science based): genetics, biotech, IT, nanotech	Synthetic (engineering based): industrial machinery, shipbuilding	Symbolic (arts based): film, TV, design, fashion
Rationale for knowledge creation	Developing new knowledge about natural systems by applying scientific laws	Applying or combining existing knowledge in new ways	Creating meaning, desire, aesthetic qualities, affect, symbols, images
Development and use of knowledge	Scientific knowledge, models	Problem solving, custom production	Creative process
Actors involved	Collaboration within and between research units	Interactive learning with customers and suppliers	Experimentations in studios, project teams
Knowledge types	Strong codified knowledge content, highly abstract, universal	Partially codified knowledge, strong tacit component, more context specific	Creativity, cultural knowledge, sign values; strong context specificity
Importance of spatial proximity	Meaning relatively constant between places	Meaning varies substantially between places	Meaning highly variable between place, class and gender

Source: Asheim et al. (2011a, p. 898; author's modification)

An analytical knowledge base prevails in research-intensive industries, such as biotechnology or nanotechnology, where innovation is driven by scientific progress. Radically new products and processes are developed in a systematic manner involving mainly basic but also applied research. Firms usually invest heavily in intramural R&D but rely also on knowledge generated at universities and other research organizations. Linkages between firms and public research organizations are thus pivotal and occur more frequently than in other industries. The "science, technology, and innovation" (STI) mode clearly dominates in analytical industries, while synthetic and symbolic sectors rely more on the "doing, using, and interacting" (DUI) mode of innovation (for a detailed discussion of the STI and DUI modes of innovation, see Lorenz and Lundvall, 2006; Jensen et al., 2007; Asheim, 2012).

A synthetic knowledge base is dominant in mature industries operating in fields, such as industrial machinery or food processing. Innovation is often more incremental in nature, based on the use and new combination of existing knowledge and learning-by-doing, using, and interacting (mainly along the value chain, that is, with customers and suppliers). Linkages between university and industry are relevant but occur more in applied research and education, and less in basic research.

The symbolic knowledge base is present in creative and cultural industries (advertisement, fashion, new media, and design). Innovation is devoted to the creation of intangible dimensions, such as aesthetic value and images. Symbolic knowledge is highly context specific; the meaning and the value associated with it can vary considerably across places. More often than not, innovation occurs through experimentations in studios and the formation of temporary project teams.

A key question that follows from the discussion about knowledge bases concerns the relation between RIS configurations and different knowledge types. Arguably, different types of knowledge bases require different types of RISs. Asheim and Gertler's (2005) distinction between narrowly defined and broadly defined RISs is eminently important in this regard (Table 2.4). A *narrowly defined RIS* is constituted by two subsystems and the systemic interaction between them to support the STI mode of innovation: the knowledge exploration and diffusion subsystem (universities, technical colleges, R&D organizations, technology transfer agencies, business associations, and finance organizations) and the knowledge exploitation subsystem (firms in regional clusters and their support industries). A *broadly defined RIS*, in contrast, also benefits the DUI mode of innovation. It includes the wider setting of organizations and institutions (such as a specialized labor market that provides experienced workers, applied research centers, non-R&D-based business services, local technical culture, and so on) that support knowledge creation, learning, and innovation and their interactions with firms located in the region.

A narrowly defined RIS forms an adequate setting for analytical industries and the STI mode of innovation. Although synthetic and symbolic

Table 2.4   Knowledge Bases and RIS Configurations

Knowledge bases	RIS
Analytical knowledge base (basic research), synthetic and symbolic knowledge bases (applied research)	Narrowly defined RIS (linkages between universities, R&D institutes, TTOs, and firms in the region)
Synthetic and symbolic knowledge bases	Broadly defined RIS (systemic interactions between wider system of organizations supporting learning and innovation and firms)

Source: Asheim and Gertler (2005)

sectors may also benefit from some elements of a narrowly defined RIS (in particular applied research), they need a broader defined RIS (a wider set of organizations and institutions) that supports the DUI mode of innovation to prosper and innovate. If a RIS is weakly developed (and what specific RIS elements are missing) can thus only be determined in relation to knowledge bases and modes of innovation. An innovation system can be considered as "less developed", if one or more of the aforementioned elements are absent or if the existing ones are not "fine-tuned" to the knowledge bases that dominate in the region. The theoretical advancement made by the differentiated knowledge-base approach and insights offered on modes of innovation clearly challenge too "one-dimensional" definitions of RIS and narrow policy approaches that put too much emphasis on R&D only and ignore other important sources of regional innovativeness and competitiveness.

The approaches discussed earlier have shed light on various elements and dimensions of RIS that may be weak or even missing. They have also allowed for the development of different typologies of less-developed RIS, and they have led to valuable policy suggestions (see Tödtling and Trippl (2005) for policy implications following from RIS failures and Asheim et al. (2011a) as well as Martin and Trippl (2014) for policy conclusions drawn from the knowledge-base approach).

The RIS concept, however, has also been criticized for providing a rather static perspective. Uyarra (2010, p. 129), for instance, notes that many analyses of RIS are "inventory-like descriptions of regional systems, with a tendency to focus on a static landscape of actors and institutions". Recent scholarly work, however, has essentially contributed to the development of a more dynamic view. Advances in evolutionary economic geography and the literature on related variety (Frenken et al., 2007, Boschma and Frenken 2011) and combinations of knowledge bases (Asheim et al., 2011a, 2013; Strambach and Klement, 2012) have enhanced our understanding of key sources of regional industrial change. Isaksen and Trippl (see Chapter 4 in this volume) integrate RIS in the analysis of such change processes and explore conceptually the link between different types of RIS and various forms of regional path development (see the following section). This is highly relevant for the purpose of this chapter. Regional economies and innovations systems increasingly face the challenge to renew their industrial structures and embark on new growth paths. Promotion of such processes is one of the core aims of smart specialization strategies.

2.3 Regional Innovation Systems and New Path Development

Recent work on regional industrial path development provides important insights into the ways regions change over time. This work moves beyond traditional approaches of path dependence, which are primarily concerned with illuminating the continuation and persistence of regional industrial structures and restrictive lock-ins, and seeks to explain economic renewal and new path development in regions. A distinction between three main forms of regional industrial path development is drawn (Asheim et al., 2013; Tödtling and Trippl, 2013; Isaksen, 2014; Isaksen and Trippl, see chapter 4 in this volume).

- *Path extension* occurs through mainly incremental innovations in existing firms and industries. However, such *intra-path changes* may, in the long run, lead to stagnation and decline due to a lack of renewal (Hassink 2010). Regional industries are then locked into innovation activities that take place along existing technological paths limiting their opportunities for experimentation and space to maneuver into radical innovation. Ultimately, this erodes regional competitiveness and can lead to *path exhaustion.*
- *Path renewal* takes place when existing firms and industries located in the region switch to different but possibly related activities and sectors. This is in line with the notions of regional branching and related diversification (Boschma and Frenken, 2011; Boschma, 2014b) as well as combinatorial knowledge bases and the integration of STI and DUI modes of innovation (Jensen et al., 2007; Asheim et al., 2011a, 2013; Manniche, 2012, Strambach and Klement, 2012; Grillitsch and Trippl, 2014).
- *New path creation* corresponds to unrelated diversification (Boschma, 2014b) as it refers to the establishment of firms in entirely new sectors or to the introduction of products new to the market (i.e., radical innovations) (Martin and Sunley, 2006; Tödtling and Trippl, 2013). New path creation is often research driven and requires active policy interventions (Asheim et al., 2013) and the creation of supportive organizational and institutional structures.

Several scholars have argued that macro-institutional structures have a major influence on directions of regional change. Storper (2011) claimed that path renewal is typical for Europe while the United States has a stronger tendency for radical innovations and new path creation. Boschma and Capone (2014) provided empirical evidence that national institutions in liberal market economies promote unrelated diversification (new path creation), while coordinated market economies encourage related diversification (path renewal), as their less flexible institutions do not allow them to move in more unrelated fields of activities. However, such tendencies found in coordinated market economies can be compensated by strong proactive policy interventions as is seen, for example, in Sweden by VINNOVA's (Swedish Governmental Agency for Innovation Systems) center of expertise policy of building regional innovation systems or strong regional research and innovation milieus. This perspective has important implications for the potential of a smart specialization strategy as well as how to design and implement such a strategy.

Recent conceptual work that points to varying capacities of regional economies (Boschma, 2014b) and RIS (Isaksen and Trippl, see chapter 4 in this volume) to renew their economic structures is highly relevant given the purpose of this chapter. Boschma (2014b) argues that regions characterized by industrial diversity, weak ties, and a loosely coherent institutional structure have better chances to develop new growth paths. Isaksen and Trippl (see chapter 4 in this volume) explore the relation between RIS configurations and various forms of regional industrial path development. They distinguish between three different types of RIS: organizationally thick and diversified systems, organizationally thick and specialized systems, and organizationally thin systems. Through a conceptual analysis, it is demonstrated that these three RIS types differ enormously in their capacity to promote new path development (Table 2.5).

Thick and diversified RIS offer excellent conditions for path renewal and new path creation due to the presence of related variety, combinatorial knowledge dynamics, academic entrepreneurship, and a favorable setup of knowledge-generating organizations. Organizational thick and specialized RIS, in contrast, tend to support path extension but face the risk of path exhaustion if positive lock-in turns into negative lock-in. However, some RIS belonging to this group benefit from a sufficiently large generic competence in their field of specialization, which may form the basis for path renewal processes. Investment into the region's research infrastructure to strengthen and widen the exploration capacity of the RIS can essentially enhance such processes (Asheim and Grillitsch, 2014). Path renewal may also be triggered by the inflow of nonlocal knowledge and its combination with the highly specialized assets available within the region. Organizationally thin RISs have a limited capacity of promoting path extension and thus they have to deal with the danger of path exhaustion (although for different reasons than organizationally thick ones).

Both organizationally thick and specialized regions and especially organizationally thin regions have thus weakly developed RIS structures for supporting new regional industrial path development. The main development

Table 2.5 RIS Types and Regional Industrial Path Development Patterns and Challenges

	Characteristics	Typical development patterns	Weak RIS structures for . . .
Organizationally thick and diversified RIS	Wide range of heterogeneous (but related) industries and knowledge bases → high potentials for cross-sectoral knowledge flows and recombinations of knowledge, strong research organizations → high potentials for commercializing research, bridging (and bonding) social capital	Path renewal and new path creation	. . . path extension (too little exploitation) → lack of industrial focus, emerging paths may not achieve critical mass, instability in institutional arrangements (fragmentation)
Organizationally thick and specialized RIS	Narrow industrial base, specialized knowledge, and support structure; bonding (and bridging) social capital	Path renewal Path extension (positive lock-in) Path exhaustion (negative lock-in)	. . . switching to new growth paths (lack of industrial and organizational variety, too little exploration)
Organizationally thin RIS	Weakly developed clusters, poor endowment with knowledge and support organizations, bonding social capital	Path exhaustion	. . . new path development (lack of critical mass of actors, little variety)

Source: Authors' compilation based on Isaksen and Trippl (see chapter 4 in this volume)

challenge for these RIS types is to avoid being caught in the "path exhaustion trap." Organizationally thick and diversified regions, in contrast, may suffer from weak structures for path extension mainly due to a reduced industrial production (exploitation) capacity. A too strong focus on and use of assets and resources for knowledge exploration and new path development can lead to a too rapid decrease in knowledge exploitation capacity, causing fragmentation problems.

2.4 Summary

To summarize, the system-failure approach, the notions of organizational and institutional thinness, the knowledge-base concept as well as recent work on the relation between RIS types and new path development offer many insights into what exactly might be less developed in RIS. A RIS can be seen as less developed if it is ill equipped to generate innovations along existing industrial and technological paths (static view). However, it might also be less developed in the sense that it lacks the capacity to support the renewal of the regional economy over time (dynamic view). Given the fact that smart specialization strategies aim at initiating regional transformation, it is the latter aspect that should deserve more attention in future research. Key issues that remain poorly understood include, among others, the role of exogenous sources (external connectedness of regions) of regional change (Isaksen and Trippl, 2014) and how multiscalar institutional frameworks shape path renewal and new path creation (Gertler, 2010).

3. EMPIRICAL APPROACHES

This section takes a closer look at two empirical approaches to measure innovation activities in regions and to identify less-developed RISs. The approaches selected for a critical examination include the Regional Innovation Scoreboard (European Commission, 2014) and the typology of regions suggested by the OECD (2011). The section is concluded by a short discussion of the empirical approach suggested by Alberdi-Pons et al. (see chapter 3 in this volume).

3.1 Regional Innovation Scoreboard

The Regional Innovation Scoreboard provides a comparative assessment of 190 regions within the European Union, Norway, and Switzerland and is complementary to the Innovation Union Scoreboard, which benchmarks innovation performance at the national level. The latest Regional Innovation Scoreboard was completed in 2014, using the same methodology as the Innovation Union Scoreboard. Due to problems of data availability, however, it is based on fewer indicators. Three main groups of variables with regard to innovation are considered: enablers, firm activities, and outputs (European Commission, 2014).

In the Innovation Union Scoreboard three types of *enablers* are covered: human resources, research systems, and finance and support. Due to a lack of regional data, they are only considered to a limited extent in the Regional Innovation Scoreboard. Only two indicators are included, namely "percentage of population aged 25–64 having completed tertiary education" as a measure for human resources, and "R&D expenditure in the public sector as % of GDP" as an indicator for finance and support. No indicators for measuring the openness and attractiveness of research systems are available. Indicators for *firm activities* are grouped into firm investments, linkages and entrepreneurship, and intellectual assets. Firm investments are measured by "R&D expenditures in the business sector as % of GDP" and by "non-R&D innovation expenditures as % of turnover" in SMEs. The latter indicator is based on CIS data and is supposed to indicate the diffusion of new production technology and ideas by measuring, for example, investments in equipment and machinery or the acquisition of patents and licenses. Data from CIS is also used for the two indicators on linkages and entrepreneurship to measure the share of SMEs that have innovated in-house and are involved in innovation cooperation with others. Intellectual assets are covered by the number of European Patent Office (EPO) patent applications in relation to regional GDP.

The indicators of innovation *outputs* aim to measure the innovative outputs of firms (the innovators) and the regional effects. Based on CIS data, two indicators are used for measuring the performance of innovators: the share of SMEs introducing product or process innovations, and the share of SMEs introducing marketing or organizational innovations. As regards economic effects, the Regional Innovation Scoreboard considers the share of employment in knowledge-intensive activities and the sales of new-to-market and new-to-firm innovations in relation to turnover.

In addition to the lack of regional data for a number of indicators, almost 30% of data for the indicators included in the Regional Innovation Scoreboard is missing. For some of the indicators, such as "sales of new-to-market and new-to-firm innovations" and "non-R&D innovation expenditure," data availability is only around 50%. Furthermore, data availability differs between countries. In Bulgaria, the Czech Republic, and Slovakia, the availability is 100%, while in Denmark, Croatia, and Switzerland it is below 30%. To increase data availability, a technique for regionalization has been adopted from CIS, followed by a number of imputation practices for the remaining missing CIS data and for the indicators using other data (primarily Eurostat) (European Commission, 2014).

Using the Regional Innovation Scoreboard, regions in Europe can be categorized in four categories based on their relative performance, with thresholds at the same levels as in Innovation Union Scoreboard. *Innovation leaders* are those regions performing 20% or more above the EU average. In the

Regional Innovation Scoreboard 2014, these regions have the highest performance in all indicators except the share of SMEs involved in innovation cooperation with other companies. Among the key strengths of innovation leaders are business activities and higher education. *Innovation followers* are regions at levels between 90% and 120% of the EU average. They are performing well on indicators measuring SMEs cooperation in innovation activities and share of SMEs innovating in-house but less well on indicators related to the performance of their business sector. *Moderate innovators* are performing between 50% and 90% of the EU average and *modest innovators* perform below 50% of the EU average, the latter with low scores on all indicators except being equipped with a relatively well-educated population (72% of the EU average).

Following the map laid out in Figure 2.1, we can observe that the regions belonging to the modest innovators are largely to be found in the post-socialist transition economies. Others are to be found in Croatia and the islands off the Mediterranean coast of Spain. Moderate innovators are more broadly distributed across Europe, with significant groupings in the southern member states (Spain, Portugal, Italy, and Greece) the Czech Republic, and parts of Slovakia, Hungary, and Poland. Furthermore, there are pockets of moderate innovators in countries that generally exhibit higher levels of performance, such as Northern France (surrounding Ile de France) and Norway.

The features that characterize these modest and moderate innovators vary across regions and national context, and we suggest that the patterns illustrated earlier provide the basis for identifying three key categories: first, regions and countries experiencing post-socialist transitions; second, regions and countries located in Southern Europe; and third, regions underperforming in comparison with their surrounding context.

In a comparison of the initial performance levels and the change in performance between 2004 and 2010 for all regions in the Regional Innovation Scoreboard, no "catching-up" processes can be observed. Less-performing regions are not growing faster than well-performing ones during this time period. However, most regions have improved their innovation performance during the observation period. In regions located in Southern Europe and regions underperforming in comparison with their surrounding context, a decrease in innovation performance is seen in some regions, such as the east coast of Spain, but the main pattern is that innovation performance is increasing. In regions experiencing post-socialist transitions, innovation performance growth is more divergent, most notably with groups of decreasing regions in Eastern Poland, Croatia, and Western Romania. Here we have a number of lesser-performing regions experiencing a relative decline of innovation performance over time.

The Regional Innovation Scoreboard suffers from several shortcomings. As already mentioned earlier, it is based on a rather low number of indicators and data is missing for many regions. For some indicators, survey data

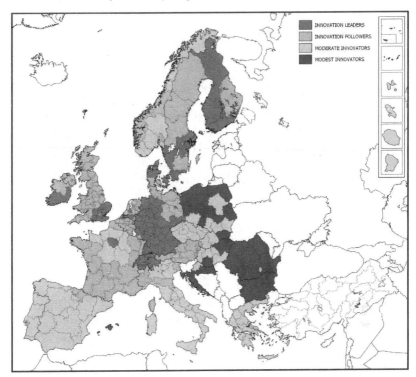

Figure 2.1   Regional Performance Groups in the Regional Innovation Scoreboard 2014

Source: European Commission, 2014, p. 16

is used, while others are based on register data. Another problem is that the Regional Innovation Scoreboard sometimes corresponds to NUTS1 and sometimes to NUTS2 regions. Among the indicators in the Regional Innovation Scoreboard, there is a bias toward measuring R&D-driven innovation activities, and even though non-R&D activities are targeted (for example, through non-R&D expenditure as % of turnover in SMEs), it remains obscure what is covered in this regard. While some indicators are broad and can include a wide variety of innovations, most are more narrow and targeted toward measuring analytical knowledge, the STI mode of innovation, and narrowly defined RIS. Neither does the Regional Innovation Scoreboard recognize some of the conceptually convincing characteristics suggested earlier in the section on RIS typologies. For example, it does not take into account the degree of regional specialization, neglecting, for instance, the possible dependence of regions on industrial mono-structure, fragmentation problems, or a lack of positive lock-ins. Thus it fails to identify what system failures or system deficiencies are prevailing in the region.

Moreover, it does not offer insights into problems of organizational and institutional thinness, nor does it capture the capacity of regions to support regional industrial change.

3.2 OECD Approach

By using data from the Organization for Economic Cooperation and Development (OECD) Regional Database, Ajmone Marsan and Maguire (2011) suggest a categorization of regions with the aim of capturing the regional socioeconomic and production structure as well as variables associated with innovation activities. This is the approach used to categorize regions in the report "Regions and Innovation Policy" (OECD 2011). Based on the availability of data in the OECD Regional Database, twelve variables are selected to reflect the regional socioeconomic structure, industrial structure, and some input and output indicators "commonly associated with an innovation-friendly environment" (Ajmone Marsan and Maguire, 2011, p. 11). When selecting variables, there was a trade-off between the breadth of variables and the number of countries with available data in an effort to maximize the number of regions for the analysis.[3] Three broad categories are identified and a majority of regions (60%) are categorized as *industrial production zones*, characterized by an industrial structure that faces specific challenges for restructuring and transformation. The highest wealth levels and best performance on science- and technology-based, innovation-related indicators are found in the *knowledge hubs*, constituting 15% of all regions. Finally, 24% of all regions are *non-S&T-driven regions*, sharing a peripheral location and are lacking knowledge absorption and generation capacity to keep up with other OECD regions.

The non-S&T-driven regions are divided into "structural inertia or deindustrializing regions" and "primary-sector-intensive regions" and account for only 8% of the sample GDP (compared to 14% of the population). These are regions that face processes of deindustrialization or experience structural inertia and regions with a significant share of their economies in primary sector activities or low-technology manufacturing, located across primarily Eastern and Southern Europe. The primary-sector-intensive regions are lagging behind all other groups in terms of GDP per capita and innovation-related indicators. These regions largely correspond to regions experiencing post-socialist transitions and regions in Southern Europe and are considered by Ajmone Marsan and Maguire (2011) to capture the peripheral economies in Europe. However, with the exception of two regions in Southern France, no regions underperforming compared to their surrounding context are found. This probably relates to the methodology used, measuring the industrial structure by the share of employment in broad sectoral terms (primary, public, manufacturing, and service sectors), leading to a spatial clustering of regions within the same category.

The indicators proposed by Ajmone Marsan and Maguire (2011) are useful for identifying regions with weak economic structures, as well as weak innovation capabilities. They do not, however, take into consideration the characteristics of different types of RISs. Measurement of innovation is restricted to variables such as R&D and patenting intensity that may capture activities in analytical sectors and the STI mode of innovation but are inadequate to assess the performance of other knowledge bases, innovation modes, and broadly defined RIS (see the following section). Furthermore, these indicators are mainly targeting the current economic state of the region and, as the authors themselves acknowledge, are lacking a dynamic dimension. The OECD typology does not consider what factors are determining the transformative capacity of a RIS or what factors are resulting in a lack of such capacity. Moreover, as already stated earlier, the indicators used in the OECD typology approach to proxy the innovation environment are mainly measuring analytical knowledge and narrowly defined RIS. Neither do they cover the degree of specialization in the regional industrial structure. In addition, even though non-S&T-driven regions are identified as lesser-performing regions, the OECD approach does not take into consideration the heterogeneity existing within this group. This issue is also seen in the case with regions categorized as industrial production zones, where this approach acknowledges that these regions are facing challenges for restructuring and transformation but treats these challenges as specificities to each region, failing to provide insights into more general innovation and transformation problems that might curtail development in these regions.

3.3 Innovation Gaps

An empirical approach that could be used to identify less-developed RISs is suggested by Alberdi-Pons et al. (see chapter 3 in this volume). It is argued that a well-functioning RIS is characterized by a high degree of connectivity and interactions (referred to as "interactivity" by Alberdi-Pons et al.), and by evaluating the presence or absence of "innovation gaps" the level of integration in a RIS could be examined. Furthermore, it is brought forward that the level of integration is largely correlated with other aspects, such as innovative capabilities and efficiency in a broader sense. In their study of Spanish regions, variables relating to four different gaps (managerial gaps, openness and learning gaps, technological gaps, and financial gaps) are quantitatively assessed, leading to the identification of four different types of regions: 1) dense and industry-oriented, integrated RISs, 2) dense and service-oriented, integrated RISs, 3) moderately integrated RISs, and 4) thin (or inexistent) RISs.

This approach is promising, as it takes into account some recent conceptual advancements in the effort of constructing more sophisticated indicators for RIS analysis. The approach broadly recognizes the importance of interaction between RIS elements. For example, organizational and institutional thickness/thinness and fragmentation problems are recognized by measuring variables related to cross-organizational learning among firms and gaps in technological capabilities of firms that prevent effective interactions. However, as the authors acknowledge, too dense networks might lead to lock-in effects and the approach does not measure variables indicating the degree of specialization in industries or technologies. Yet overall, this approach provides an interesting basis for further empirical work both in terms of examining a wider selection of regions and in terms of engaging in partial analyses of specific gaps in different types of regions.

4. CONCLUSIONS AND OUTLOOK

The critical review and discussion of conceptual and empirical approaches to identify less-developed RISs has shed light on a large number and variety of barriers and weaknesses that may curtail innovation and regional industrial change. The RIS concept offers many insights in this regard and allows for the development of useful typologies of less-developed RISs that are highly relevant for the current debate on the design and implementation of smart specialization strategies.

There are several challenges for future research. First, future conceptual research should further advance our understanding of opportunities and challenges for regional industrial change in different types of RIS. Recent work on the relation between RIS configurations and new path development has made an important contribution in this regard. The focus has thus far been on how the degree of organizational thickness and the degree of specialization of industrial structures shape the direction of regional industrial change. The institutional dimension of RIS has received less attention in this work. A key issue of future research is thus to explore how institutions at various spatial scales and institutional change affect new path development in different RIS types. Another core question that deserves due attention in future work concerns the role of exogenous sources of regional industrial change. New path development has thus far been conceptualized as a process that builds on endogenous assets. The role of global innovation networks and other forms of exogenous development impulses (and their interplay with locally available knowledge) have been underplayed in the literature and remain poorly understood. There is thus a need for systematic analyses of how extra-regional knowledge flows and external connectedness affect the extension, renewal, and creation of regional industrial paths. Furthermore, little is known about the nexus between RIS transformation and regional industrial change. Future research should thus address the question of how various RIS types transform themselves as a result of path renewal and new path creation.

Second, existing empirical approaches fall short of taking account of conceptual insights into system failures, organizational and institutional thinness, misconfigurations of RIS in relation to knowledge bases, and weak RIS structures for different forms of path development. In other words, advances that have been made in conceptual debates on specificities of less-developed regions are only partly reflected in existing empirical approaches. There is still a tendency to measure narrowly defined RIS, analytical (R&D-based) knowledge, and the STI mode of innovation and build typologies based on the findings of these exercises. There is a need to consider in particular recent findings on the role of different types of knowledge bases and innovation modes (as well as their combination) and broadly defined RIS in empirical research that aims at revealing misconfigurations of RIS. In addition, the transformative potential of RIS—that is, their capacity to support new path development, is hardly captured. There is a need for developing new measures and indicators to be used in quantitative research as well as new designs for qualitative case studies that take into consideration the issues raised earlier. Building on the analytical insights provided in this chapter, current research in the context of Smart Specialisation could make a valuable contribution to enhance understanding of how diversified specialization or specialized diversification can be achieved among the heterogeneity of European regions.

NOTES

1 This chapter is based on work within Work Package 3 of the project "Smart Specialisation for Regional Innovation" (funded by the European Commission in the context of the seventh framework program, grant agreement no. 320131). We are grateful to our colleagues Markus Grillitsch and Teis Hansen at CIRCLE, Lund University for inputs to an earlier version of this chapter.

2 This matrix is based on an idea by Björn Asheim, outlined in a project application for the Marianne and Markus Wallenberg Foundation.

3 All OECD countries except Australia, Chile, Estonia, Iceland, Israel, Japan, Mexico, New Zeeland, Turkey, Slovenia, and Switzerland are included in the analysis.

REFERENCES

Ajmone Marsan, G. and Maguire, K. (2011). *Categorisation of OECD regions using innovation-related variables.* OECD regional development working papers, 2011/03. OECD: Paris.

Alberdi Pons, X., Gibaja Martíns, J. J. and Davide Parrilli, M. (2016). Innovation gaps: A typology for Spain. In M. Davide Parrilli, R. Dahl Fitjar and A. Rodríguez-Pose (eds.), *Innovation drivers and regional innovation strategies.* London: Routledge, this volume.

Asheim, B. (2012). The changing role of learning regions in the globalizing knowledge economy: A theoretical re-examination. *Regional Studies*, 46(8), 993–1004.

Asheim, B. (2014). *North Denmark Region RIS3. An expert assessment on behalf of DG regional and urban policy.*

Asheim, B., Boschma, R. and Cooke, P. (2011a). Constructing regional advantage: Platform policies based on related variety and differentiated knowledge bases. *Regional Studies*, 45, 893–904.

Asheim, B., Bugge, M., Coenen, L. and Herstad, S. (2013). *What does evolutionary economic geography bring to the table? Reconceptualising regional innovation systems*. CIRCLE Working Paper no. 2013/05, Circle: Lund University.

Asheim, B. and Coenen, L. (2006). Contextualising regional innovation systems in a globalising learning economy: On knowledge bases and institutional frameworks. *Journal of Technology Transfer*, 31, 163–173.

Asheim, B. and Gertler, M. (2005). The geography of innovation: Regional innovation systems. In J. Fagerberg, D. Mowery and R. Nelson (eds.), *The oxford handbook of innovation* (291–317). New York: Oxford University Press.

Asheim, B. and Grillitsch, M. (2014). *Regional Report on More og Romsdal*. Circle: Lund University.

Asheim, B. and Isaksen, A. (2002). Regional innovation systems: The integration of local 'sticky' and global 'ubiquitous' knowledge. *Journal of Technology Transfer*, 27(1), 77–86.

Asheim, B., Lawton Smith, H. and Oughton, C. (2011b). Regional innovation systems: Theory, empirics and policy. *Regional Studies*, 45, 875–891.

Blazek, J. and Zizalova, P. (2010). The biotechnology industry in the Prague Metropolitan Region: A cluster within a fragmented innovation system? *Environment and Planning C: Government and Policy*, 28(5), 887–904.

Boschma, R. and Capone, C. (2014). *Institutions and diversification: Related versus unrelated diversification in a varieties of capitalism framework*. Papers in Evolutionary Economic Geography, No. 2014/21. Utrecht University.

Boschma, R. and Frenken, K. (2011). Technological relatedness and regional branching. In H. Bathelt, M. P. Feldman and D. F. Kogler (eds.), *Beyond territory: Dynamic geographies of knowledge creation, diffusion, and innovation* (64–81). London and New York: Routledge.

Boschma, R. (2014a). Constructing regional advantage and smart specialisation: Comparison of two European policy concepts. *Scienze Regionali*, 13(1), 51–68.

Boschma, R. (2014b). Towards an evolutionary perspective on regional resilience. *Regional Studies*, doi:10.1080/00343404.2014.959481.

Charron, N., Dijkstra, L. and Lapuente, V. (2014). Regional governance matters: Quality of government within European Union member states. *Regional Studies*, 48(1), 68–90.

Cooke, P. (2004). Regional innovation systems—an evolutionary approach. In P. Cooke, M. Heidenreich and H. J. Braczyk (eds.), *Regional innovation systems: The role of governance in a globalized world* (2–24). New York: Routledge.

Doloreux, D. and Dionne, S. (2008). Is regional innovation system development possible in peripheral regions? Some evidence from the Case La Pocatière, Canada. *Entrepreneurship and Regional Development*, 20(3), 259–283.

European Commission. (2006). *Constructing regional advantage: Principles—perspectives—policies*. Final report from DG Research Expert Group on 'Constructing Regional Advantage.' Brussels: DG Research, European Commission.

European Comission. (2014). *Regional innovation scoreboard 2014*. Brussels: European Commission.

European Union. (2011). *Regional policy for smart growth in Europe 2020*. Brussels: EU Publications Office.

Foray, D. and Goenaga, X. (2013). *The goals of smart specialisation. S3 Policy Brief, 01/2013*. Seville: Institute for Prospective Technological Studies.

Foray, D. and Rainoldi, A. (2013). *Smart specialisation programmes and implementation. S3 Policy Brief, 02/2013*. Seville: Institute for Prospective Technological Studies.

Frenken, K., Van Oort, F. and Verburg, T. (2007). Related variety, unrelated variety and regional economic growth. *Regional Studies*, 41(5), 685–697.

Gertler, M. (2010). Rules of the game: The place of institutions in regional economic change. *Regional Studies*, 44, 1–15.

Grabher, G. (1993). The weakness of strong ties: The lock-in of regional development in the Ruhr Area. In G. Grabher (ed.), *The embedded firm: On the socio-economics of industrial networks* (255–277). London: Routledge.

Grillitsch, M. and Trippl, M. (2014). Combining knowledge from different sources, channels and geographical scales. *European Planning Studies*, 22(1), 2305–2325.

Hassink, R. (2010). Locked in decline? On the role of regional lock-ins in old industrial areas. In R. Boschma and R. Martin (eds.), *The handbook of evolutionary economic geography* (450–468). Cheltenham: Edward Elgar.

Isaksen, A. (2014). Industrial development in thin regions: Trapped in path extension. *Journal of Economic Geography*, doi:10.1093/jeg/lbu026, 1–16.

Isaksen, A. and Trippl, M. (2014). *New path development in the periphery*. Papers in Innovation Studies, No 2014/31. CIRCLE: Lund University.

Isaksen A. and Trippl, M. (2016), *Path development in different regional innovation systems: a conceptual analysis*, in M.D. Parrilli, R. Dahl Fitjar and A. Rodriguez-Pose (eds.), *Innovation drivers and regional innovation strategies*, Routledge, New York, this volume.

Jensen, M. B., Johnson, B., Lorenz, E. and Lundvall, B.-A. (2007). Forms of knowledge and modes of innovation. *Research Policy*, 36, 680–693.

Karlsen, J., Isaksen, A. and Spilling, O. (2011). The challenge of constructing regional advantages in peripheral areas: The case of Marine Biotechnology in Tromsø, Norway. *Entrepreneurship and Regional Development*, 23(3–4), 235–257.

Klein Woolthuis, R., Lankhuizen, M. and Gilsing, V. A. (2005). A system failure framework for innovation policy design. *Technovation*, 25(6), 609–619.

Lorenz, E. and Lundvall, B.-A. (eds.). (2006). *How Europe's economies learn: Coordinating competing models*. Oxford: Oxford University Press.

Lundvall, B. A. and Borras, S. (1999). *The globalising learning economy: Implications for innovation policy*. Brussels: European Commission, DG XII.

Manniche, J. (2012). Combinatorial knowledge dynamics: On the usefulness of the differentiated knowledge bases model. *European Planning Studies*, 20, 1823–1841.

Martin, R. and Sunley, P. (2006). Path dependence and regional economic evolution. *Journal of Economic Geography*, 64(4), 395–437.

Martin, R. and Trippl, M. (2014). System failures, knowledge bases and regional innovation policies. *The Planning Review*, 50(1), 24–32.

McCann, P. and Ortega-Argilés, R. (2013). Modern regional innovation policy. *Cambridge Journal of Regions, Economy and Society*, 6(2), 187–216.

OECD. (2010). *Higher education in regional and city development: Berlin, Germany 2010*. OECD: Paris.

OECD. (2011). *Regions and innovation policy. OECD reviews of regional innovation*. OECD: Paris.

Rodríguez-Pose, A. (2013). Do institutions matter for regional development? *Regional Studies*, 47(7), 1034–1047.

Rodríguez-Pose, A., di Cataldo, M. and Rainoldi, A. (2014). *The role of government institutions for smart specialisation and regional development*. S3 Policy Brief, 04/2014. Seville: Institute for Prospective Technological Studies.

Storper, M. (2011). Why do regions develop and change? The challenge for geography and economics. *Journal of Economic Geography*, 11, 333–346.

Strambach, S. and Klement, B. (2012). Cumulative and combinatorial micro-dynamics of knowledge: The role of space and place in knowledge integration. *European Planning Studies*, 20, 1843–1866.

Tödtling, F. and Trippl, M. (2005). One size fits all? Towards a differentiated regional innovation policy approach. *Research Policy*, 34, 1203–1219.

Tödtling, F. and Trippl, M. (2013). Transformation of regional innovation systems: From old legacies to new development paths. In P. Cooke (ed.), *Reframing regional development* (297–317). London: Routledge.

Trippl, M. and Otto, A. (2009). How to turn the fate of old industrial areas: A comparison of cluster-based renewal processes in Styria and the Saarland. *Environment and Planning A*, 41(5), 1217–1233.

Uyarra, E. (2010). What is evolutionary about regional systems of innovation? Implications for regional policy. *Journal of Evolutionary Economics*, 20(1), 115–137.

Weber, K. M. and Rohracher, H. (2012). Legitimizing research, technology and innovation policies for transformative change. Combining insights from innovation systems and multi- level perspectives in a comprehensive 'failures' framework. *Research Policy*, 41(6), 1037–1047.

Zukauskaite, E., Plechero, M. and Trippl, M. (2014). *Institutional thickness: Redefining the concept*. CIRCLE: Lund University.

3 Innovation Gaps

A Typology for Spain

Xabier Alberdi-Pons, Juan José Gibaja Martíns, and Mario Davide Parrilli

1. INTRODUCTION

A regional innovation system (RIS) is understood as a system of innovation networks and institutions located within a certain geographic area, with strong, regular, internal interaction (Kostiainen, 2002). However, interaction does not necessarily come about in an automatic fashion, meaning systems might not always be dense or well integrated. The article tackles this issue and presents an estimation of the level of integration of Spanish RISs based on the evaluation of several innovation gaps that have mainly been described in a theoretical fashion, although not yet systematic (Isaksen, 1999; Nauwelaers and Wintjes, 1999; Woolthuis et al., 2005; Trippl, Asheim, and Mjorner in this volume). Though key agents might be present (i.e., universities, technology centers, regional innovation agencies, intermediaries, etc.), the lack of innovation collaboration may block beneficial mixes of dissimilar tacit and explicit knowledge bases (Nonaka and Takeuchi, 1995) which may lead to the emergence of certain gaps that hinder systemic upgrading. Therefore, the existence of innovation gaps may exhibit inadequate attitudinal behaviors stemming from certain agents according to their own associative practices, whose supervision and correction should be at the purview of both political and economic parties involved.

Interactivity is, broadly speaking, overlooked as a crucial property of well functioning—dense—RISs (Ibid.), albeit its impact on the creation, development and diffusion of knowledge had already been recognized (Lundvall, 1992; Isaksen, 1999; Nauwelaers and Wintjes, 1999). The linear distinction between *"factor-driven," "efficiency-driven,"* and *"innovation driven"* economies (Porter, 1990) sets the mind of most academics, politicians, and consultants on the last step, all agreeing on the claim that innovation[1] is the key factor promoting competitiveness. Choosing the high-road strategy was thought to be identical to the promotion of high-tech, R&D intensive industries (Asheim and Parrilli, 2012, p.2). Analogously, the evaluation of the implemented strategies along with the pervasive behavior of RISs has been steered toward the analysis of the capabilities that systems show when turning (mainly knowledge-based) inputs into (mainly technological) outputs. Instead, our approach will be slightly different and will focus on the evaluation of the gaps across the regions. Accordingly, the chapter will complement a—first—literature tradition that builds on the use of econometric techniques to evaluate RISs. This tradition gathers typologies that seize the diversity and the variety of innovation and efficiency patterns (Susiluoto, 2003; Zabala-Iturriagagoitia et al., 2007; Hollanders et al., 2009; Navarro and Gibaja, 2012). Our approach will also add to a second tradition that focuses on the description and exemplification of innovation gaps that coexist at different layers of a given RISs. The latter tradition revolves around a number of "managerial," "openness and learning," "technological" and "financial" gaps that produce disintegrated RISs. Our evaluation of the gaps will build on these traditions to produce a systematic and empirical examination that will blend most significant approaches together.

The chapter is organized into five sections. The second presents system components, presents the gaps of the study, and sets an illustration that facilitates analyses. The following section operationalizes quantitative variables to evaluate these gaps. It also presents the data and the methodology employed. The fourth section develops the empirical results of the study. The analysis shows that the behavior of the gaps is asymmetric not only across a given RIS but also when comparing them with its pairs in other regions, setting grounds for further developments that could produce innovation policy recommendations. The final section presents conclusions and acknowledges a number of limitations.

2. INTERPRETATIVE FRAMEWORK OF THE STUDY

Innovation systems consist of two kinds of constituents. First, systems are disaggregated into their main "components." Second, the interactions among these components are emphasized[2] (Ingelstam, 2002; Edquist, 2005; Parrilli, 2013). These components—or subsystems—compose a coherent framework that facilitates the study of manifold attributes. First, the "knowledge exploitation" subsystem would consist mainly of firms, especially where these firms display clustering tendencies[3] (Autio, 1998; Cooke and Morgan, 1998; Isaksen, 1999; Asheim and Gertler, 2005; Gielsing and Nooteboom, 2006). Second, the "knowledge exploration" subsystem would include colleges, technology transfer agencies, vocational training organizations, etc. (Ibid.). Third, the "regional policy" subsystem would be composed of government organizations and regional development agencies (Tödtling and Trippl, 2005; Trippl and Tödtling, 2007; Martin and Trippl, 2013).

As stated, in order to have a sharp view of the performance of RISs, one has to open the boxes of its subsystems, identify their elements, and specify those interactions between and within the subsystems that have importance (Fischer, 2001). Interaction leads to collective learning and innovation and thus it is considered to be a central feature of highly innovative regions (Trippl and Tödtling, 2007). Consequently, a well-functioning and dense system should stand out for its high level of integration, both between and within its components, which could also be explained by the absence of innovation gaps. Therefore, systemic density constitutes an outstanding property that should be observed to evaluate integration levels.

Accordingly, the main driving force of our analysis is to come up with a detailed or "microscopic" description of the specific "densities" of Spanish RISs. To this end, the study of the gaps will bring back illustrative and intuition-guided "photographs" of existing differences among RISs. This approach will round up both literature strands introduced. While the econometric strand evaluates performance, it does not pursue an exhaustive report on the interaction of their components and innovation-relevant organizations; the second one, more theoretical, describes problems but lacks empirical grounding to support analyses on a spatial basis.[4] To begin with, there is an implicit need for disentangling and listing gaps in a systematic way, so they can be evaluated coherently. We onward list and describe a number of innovation gaps:

Gap 1: "Managerial gaps" originate as an aftereffect of the lack of or poorly developed management capabilities of private firms, especially present in smaller and less experienced ones, when setting innovation processes (Bessant and Rush, 1995; Nauwelaers and Wintjes, 1999). These processes would not be successful or long lasting if firms do not show proper inner competences (i.e., marketing, organizational, strategy, distribution, commercial, and so on). Building on these recommendations, our evaluation will observe to what extent these capabilities are present in Spanish "exploitation subsystems."

Gap 2: "Openness and learning gaps[5]" occur when firms lack new "antennas" or networks. This means that firms that benefit from a favored network position are likely to perform better because of their superior access to novel information and knowledge (Burt, 1992; Hargadon and Sutton, 1997; Nauwelaers and Wintjes, 1999). Consequently, our study focuses on the evaluation of the linkages or "antennas" Spanish firms have, as a means to interpret the density of the Spanish "exploitation subsystems."

Gap 3: The "technological gap" could be described as the lack of technological capabilities of private firms (Nauwelaers and Wintjes, 1999; Dalziel, 2010; Parrilli et al., 2010). Though there are grounds for believing that linkages between technological and business worlds will start to multiply (Yusuf, 2008), we still witness disparity in goals and performance measures that prevent organizations from effective interactions that would provoke valuable learning and innovation outcomes (Dalziel, 2010; Parrilli et al., 2010). As in previous cases, we will evaluate these capabilities over the Spanish "exploitation subsystems."

Gap 4: Lastly, there is a "financial gap" when the "regional policy" component has not developed tools to help firms overcome the lack of available finance supporting their activity (Nauwelaers and Wintjes, 1999). While the existence of resources supporting innovation might be a desirable feature of well-functioning financial markets (i.e., banks), these markets often choose more secure investments. Thus policy intervention is often considered an alternative solution to bridge this gap. Our evaluations focus on understanding whether the regional policies have intervened in financial markets and settled the means necessary for the creation of alternative tools (i.e., venture capitalists).

Onward we connect the innovation gaps together with the corresponding system components. This theoretical evolution produces a new interpretative framework that will enrich evaluation in a number of ways. First, this framework adds a new spatial dimension that complements previous approaches (Nauwelaers and Wintjes, 1999; Woolthuis et al., 2005). It presents the gaps that will be evaluated in the current study, while it also permits the identification and empirical evaluation of other gaps that are currently out of scope (i.e., managerial gaps within other components). Second, our structure will also facilitate the development and interpretation of empirical analyses. This implies that innovation gaps will be assessed according to the quantity of interactions that occur both between but also within these components being presented. All in all, it will permit completing the scope of previous econometric investigations whose end product often came to be a rank of region´s performance showing their capability to achieve certain (mainly technological) outputs (e.g., patents). These studies often lacked theoretical grounds to suggest further innovation policy measures and actions that could relate to specific problems that remained unobserved.

3. VARIABLES, DATA, AND METHODOLOGY OF THE STUDY

3.1 Presentation of the Variables

Our explanation of the level of integration of Spanish RISs will build on the evaluation of the presence or absence of innovation gaps. In order to do so, we will produce a quantitative evaluation that will leverage on the use of a number of variables. These variables will be employed to form sets that will explain each of the gaps of the study. The choice of the variables builds on previous approaches that deal with the evaluation of innovation and efficiency-related aspects within RISs. Particularly, we leverage on the work of authors who employ indicators to evaluate and present typologies both of

Spanish and international RISs (Buesa et al., 2002, 2007; Martínez-Pellitero, 2002; Susiluoto, 2003; Iammarino, 2005; Zabala-Iturriagagoitia et al., 2007; Hollanders et al., 2009; Navarro and Gibaja, 2009, 2010, 2012; Chaminade et al., 2012). Additionally, we introduce three supplementary variables (AGR, IND, and SERV) that attest the analysis performed on the gaps. These variables provide an intuitive reference with regard to the quality of the results fed back, albeit they have no influence whatsoever over the core empirical findings.

A first and necessary step to estimate integration is to introduce a theoretical framework where innovation gaps could be settled together with affected components. Second, we need to operationalize a number of quantitative variables that would permit the assessment of the problems: "Gap 1," "Gap 2," "Gap 3" and "Gap 4" over the Spanish RIS. Table 3.1 summarizes the sources of information we have scrutinized in search of adequate variables, and their time periods. We have selected a number of indicators that proxy the information we would like to gather to estimate the integration level of Spanish RISs.

A fundamental problem is the excessive—path dependent—foci of both international (Ecotec, 2005; OECD, 1997/2006; UNU-MERIT, 2009) and national (Spanish) (INE) statistics on both "firms" and their "technological capabilities." The latter coupling constitutes the main stress of questionnaires in most surveys focused on development and innovation dynamic. This implies that most indicators are based on a firm-based *input-output* dichotomous perspective, which limits the scope of evaluation. As a matter of fact, innovation scholars will lack the observation of certain organizations and system components (e.g., regional agencies, universities, public organizations, entrepreneurs, among others) that have an increasing role in regional innovation performance. Consequently, these scholars will not be able to carry out accurate systemic diagnoses (Lundvall, 1992; Tödtling and Trippl, 2005; Woolthuis et al., 2005; Edquist, 2011; Asheim and Parrilli, 2012; Chaminade et al., 2012; Martin and Trippl, 2013). As a consequence of the former, policy designs will always be limited to available data, blind to the performance of the organizations and components exemplified. Therefore, policy-makers will often continue in the position of making crucial decisions at their expense (Edquist, 2011; Chaminade et al., 2012), leveraging on a very narrow and biased approximation on the real dynamics of a given RIS.

Though we find these important limitations, a number of variables may constitute a beta step to evaluate the introduced gaps, as presented in Table 3.1. Gap 1 evaluates to what extent firms make use of "qualified resources in management." A number of indicators (G11 to G14) approximate certain characteristics of private companies that might be explained by sophisticated managing practices. We claim that "higher educational levels" (G11), and the "ability to employ foreign languages" (G12), are descriptive of managers and businessmen who are better qualified to coordinate the internal, external, and the international activity of the organization. On the other hand, a "higher number of doctors performing research activity" (G13) and a higher number of "staff with a computer and internet access" (G14) are descriptive of managers and businessmen who are sensitive to the importance of learning and the firm's "absorptive capacity"[6] (Cohen and Levinthal, 1990). Put together, these indicators are intended to proxy sophisticated managerial practices but fail in the evaluation of other important characteristics that remain veiled.[7]

Gap 2 evaluates to what extent firms "learn from others and develop antennas in exploitation subsystems" of RISs. In order to do that, we add two new indicators (G21 to G22) that proxy an evaluation of the "density" and the "quality" of beneficial interactions occurring among private companies of the "exploitation component." We claim that "private companies joined or associated to a corporate group" (G21), and "private companies that consider the Spanish market (businesses) an important source of innovation" (G22) would have a better chance to update their knowledge by getting in touch with the "local buzz," as a consequence of the existence of crucial "knowledge spillovers" in these networks that firms benefit from (Zucker, Darby, and Armstrong, 1998; Bathelt et al., 2004). Thus if more firms engage in networks, the "exploitation subsystem" would turn a denser and more interactive spatial dimension. Of course, very dense networks can bring about other key undesired externalities such as "lock-in"[8] problems (Isaksen, 1999; Nauwelaers and Wintjes; 1999; Tödtling and Trippl, 2005; Martin and Trippl, 2013). Thus future approximations would aim to grasp the "related variety" of the networks firms belong to[9] (Asheim et al., 2011).

Gap 3 is represented by a set of indicators (G31 to G35) that aim at explaining to what extent firms "screen for technological options and adapt state-of-the-art to their own situation." As stated, the "technological outlook" of the sources of innovation employed (INE) permits a closer approximation to the evaluation of this gap. The "purchase of R&D" (G31 and G32), the "number of external consultants performing R&D" (G33), the "percentage of private companies that consider the exploration subsystem an important source of innovation" (G34), and the "number of researchers developing R&D activity in private companies" (G35) are good proxies to evaluate the density of interactions between exploration and exploitation components that facilitate the evaluation of firms' technological adoption.[10]

Gap 4 evaluates to what extent "a regional policy component has developed tools to help firms overcome financial difficulties" (when markets prefer secure investments with short-term return. We employ two complementary indicators to measure this (G41 and G42). A higher "venture capital portfolio" (G41) would imply a higher commitment of the "regional-policy component" to foster the creation of new firms and projects. A higher number of "new technology-based firms born" (G42) is an output indicator that actually shows the effectiveness of the system, which contributes to explaining a good functioning of the regional-policy component when it comes to nurturing the creation of new projects and firms. Of course we find important limitations. "Venture capital" is not only "public" capital. Consequently, new indicators could return a better approximation to the evaluation of this gap.[11]

To finish the section, we claim this is still a very preliminary estimation. First, our framework puts together system problems that mainly deal with the firm´s purview (Burt, 1992; Bessant and Rush, 1995; Hargadon and Sutton, 1997; Nauwelaers and Wintjes, 1999; Dalziel, 2010; Parrilli et al., 2010; Parrilli, 2013). This view could be completed with important interactions "between and within" other components that, to this point, have been overviewed both by the literature and by policy-makers[12] (Isaksen, 1999; Nauwelaers and Wintjes, 1999; Tödtling and Trippl, 2005; Woolthuis et al., 2005; Edquist, 2011; Chaminade et al., 2012; Martin and Trippl, 2013). Second, the evaluation of these problems is not intended to be finalistic, as the current state-of-art prevents the employment of important variables.

3.2 Data

The data we gathered for the empirical analysis are based on ad hoc exploitations sourced on various studies conducted by the Spanish Official Statistical Institute (INE). The special condition of an indicator employed in Gap 4 demanded new data sourced from the Spanish Venture Capital Association (ASCRI) (2006–2012).[13] Table 3.1 gathers all sources of information employed in the assessment of our unit of analysis (Spanish regions).

Our data is gathered in a matrix (Appendix 1) whose rows correspond to Spanish regions, while its columns stand for four separated sets of continuous variables that have been grouped under the names of "Gap1," "Gap2," "Gap3," "Gap4," and relate to the problems of interest.

3.3 Methodology

Due to the size of the dataset, our first aim is to review and reduce its dimensionality. Multiple Factor Analysis (MFA) (Escofier and Pagès, 1990, 1998; Pagès, 2004) allows integrating unlike groups of variables *(each gap under assessment)* describing the same observations *(Spanish regions[14])* (Abdi and Valentin, 2007). The procedure will return an integrated image of the observations and the relation among the groups of variables (Navarro and Gibaja, 2010). Second, we will complete our empirical study performing a cluster analysis[15] over the findings. This analysis will help us classify regions.

In terms of data analysis, the following outputs stem from the analysis carried out using R (R Development Core Team, 2011) and the FactoMineR package (Lê et al., 2008; Husson et al., 2011; R Development Core Team, 2011).

Table 3.1 Variables in the Study

Component of the model	Code	Indicator	UNIT	Source of information	PERIOD
GAP 1	G11	Percentage of businessmen, managing directors, and executives that have completed third-level education times the percentage of not businessmen who have also completed it.	Percentage	Survey on Adult Population Involvement in Learning Activities. Spanish Official Statistical Institute (INE)	2007
	G12	Percentage of businessmen, managing directors, and executives capable of using languages other than their "mother tongue" times the percentage of employees who are also capable of using them.			
	G13	Doctors performing research activity in private companies.	Per hundred thousand people	Innovation in companies´ survey. Spanish Official Statistical Institute (INE)	2008–2009
	G14	Private company´s staff with a computer and an Internet connection.	Percentage	Survey on ICT. Usage and e-commerce in companies. Spanish Official Statistical Institute (INE)	2011–2012
GAP 2	G21	Private companies joined or associated to a corporate group.		Innovation in companies´ survey.	2008–2009
	G22	Private companies that consider the Spanish market an important source of innovation.			
GAP 3	G31	Private companies that have purchased R&D services to joined, associated companies or other Spanish market sources.			

Code	Description	Units	Source	Period
G32	Private companies that have purchased R&D services to joined, associated companies or other foreign market sources.		Spanish Official Statistical Institute (INE)	2008–2010
G33	External consultants performing R&D activity within private companies.	Per hundred thousand people		
G34	Private companies that consider Spanish "exploration subsystems" an important source of innovation.	Percentage		
G35	Researchers that develop R&D activity in private companies.	Per hundred thousand people		
GAP 4 G41	Total venture capital portfolio.	€ per thousand people	Spanish Venture Capital Association (ASCRI) Statistics about R&D activities 2010	2005–2011
G42	New technology-based firms born.	Per hundred thousand people	Innovation in companies' survey. Spanish Official Statistical Institute (INE)	2008–2009
SUPPLEMENTARY VARIABLES (SUP) *AGR*	*Employed population by branch of activity, sex, and AC: Agriculture.*	*Thousands of employed population over thousands of working age population*	*Survey on Adult Population Involvement in Learning Activities. Spanish Official Statistical Institute (INE)*	2012
IND	*Employed population by branch of activity, sex, and AC: Industry.*			
SERV	*Employed population by branch of activity, sex, and AC: Services.*			

4. A TYPOLOGY FOR SPANISH RISs

4.1 Representation of the Gaps

1. We accomplish a MFA with the four groups of variables summarized in Table 3.1 and the Spanish regions. The correlation circle (Figure 3.1) displays the positions of these variables regarding the two latent factors. The first factor, measured along the horizontal axis explicates 42.45% of the variance. The second factor is represented along the vertical axis and explicates 17.47% of the variance
2. [16]The first axis is correlated to variables belonging to the four groups. It will oppose two clouds of regions.

Figure 3.2 presents the position of these regions regarding the factors. From right to left, we first find a cloud that could be decomposed into two groups. First, a subgroup composed by Navarre and the Basque Country; then, a second subgroup composed by Madrid, Catalonia and La Rioja. Then, the rest of Spanish regions are found in a second cloud that could also be further decomposed into two subgroups. On the one hand, we find Extremadura, Castile Leon, Asturias, Valencia, Cantabria, Galicia and Aragon; then, a second subgroup formed by Balear Islands, Canary Islands, Andalusia, Castile La Mancha and Murcia.

The first cloud shows high coordinates on the first axis, which is characterized by a positive association with variables related to systemic integration (i.e., limited technological gaps). Thus we can infer that Navarre and Basque Country show higher integration levels when compared with other communities evaluated. Symmetrically, the level of integration of

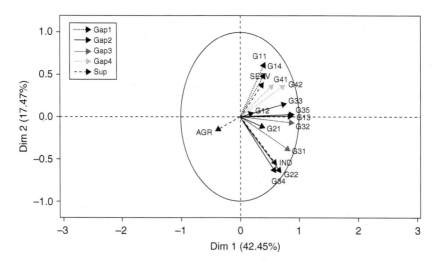

Figure 3.1   Correlation Circle

the rest of the communities fades away as they get closer to the left margin of the figure, which leads us to intuit that interactivity could be correlated to the economic development and to the overall innovative capabilities of the regions under assessment (Navarro and Gibaja, 2009, 2012).

The second axis (Figure 3.2) also provides distinct clouds of individuals. From the top to the bottom of the figure, we first find Madrid covering a lonely and outstanding position. Second, covering a central position, we find a group that congregates most of the regions. The group gathers all the remaining communities except La Rioja, which stands alone in the south of the picture. The smaller variance of the second axis makes it more complex to find a pattern for these observations. We could state that Madrid is set apart from the rest, being the region ranking highest measures along indicators, such as "sophisticated managerial practices" (G11 and G14) and for the "regional-policy commitment to help firms overcome financial difficulties" (G41 and G42). On the other hand, we find La Rioja in the south of the picture, which is set apart for its negative correlation measures along the second dimension. This community has a high "number of private companies that consider the Spanish market (businesses) an important source of innovation" (G22) and a high number of "private companies that have purchased R&D services to associated companies or other Spanish market sources" (G31). It also shows high rates regarding "private companies that deem Spanish exploration subsystems important sources of innovation."

All in all, Figure 3.2 shows that Navarre and Basque Country outstand for their "inner technological integration" (axis 1), which might imply that

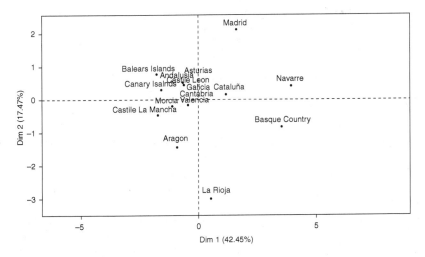

Figure 3.2 Global Display of Groups

policy intervention could have nurtured interaction between firms and technology infrastructures. On the other hand, the second axis demands for more attention. Communities in the north of the picture (as Madrid) would outstand for their "managerial and financial market integration" levels. On the other hand, communities placed in the south of the picture (as La Rioja) would outstand for their "market network integration" levels. Put together, we could sum up the second axis as the "interior-market general integration."

It is important to underline that Figure 3.1 also presents three supplementary variables named "AGR," "IND," and "SERV," which go hand in hand with the interpretations of the analysis. These variables are placed in the quadrant that one would intuitively find them, though the greater influence of the first axis (42.45%) provokes "IND" be placed in the first quadrant instead of the second, as expected. These variables help us explain that the second axis also distinguishes between "service-oriented integrated markets" (Madrid), and more "industry-oriented systems" (Basque Country, Navarre).

4.2 Cluster Analysis

The cluster analysis performed over the findings of the MFA helps us classify communities in homogeneous groups. The analysis outputs in the creation of four groups of regions that reveal dissimilar integration levels along their RISs (Figure 3.3).

The features of the four groups are summarized in the following titles:

- **Group 1: Dense and Industry-Oriented Integrated RISs:**
  Navarre and Basque Country.
- **Group 2: Dense and Service-Oriented Integrated RISs:**
  Madrid and Catalonia.
- **Group 3: Moderately Integrated RISs:**
  La Rioja and Aragon.
- **Group 4: Thin (or Inexistent) RISs:**
  Balear Islands, Canary Islands, Andalusia, Castille La Mancha, Murcia, Extremadura, Castille Leon, Asturias, Valencia, Cantabria and Galicia.[17]

Our typology can also be compared to other typologies based on the use of quantitative variables. We underline that our Spanish integration-level map (Figure 3.4) reveals a strong north (center and east)-south pattern that resembles these studies (Coronado and Acosta, 1999; Buesa et al., 2002; Martínez-Pellitero, 2002; Buesa and Heijs, 2007; Navarro and Gibaja, 2009, 2010, 2012). This is an outstanding aspect of our investigation, as it correlates the level of integration—or density—of RISs with other

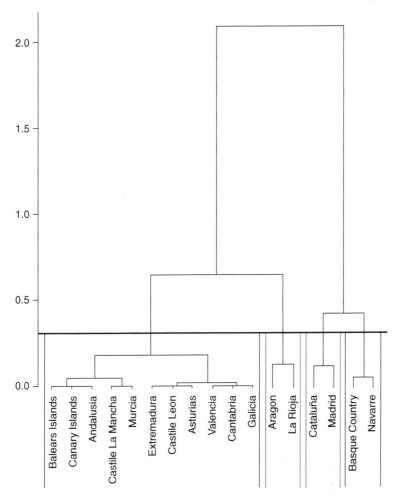

Figure 3.3   Cluster Dendrogram

aspects, as their efficiency or, more broadly, their overall innovative capabilities (Zabala-Iturriagagoitia, 2007; Navarro and Gibaja, 2012). Nevertheless, while this pattern is common to most typologies, there are aspects
that characterize the results. The fact that the final projections of these
analyses could apparently be similar, brings about quite different—and
complementary—information inputs. Space limitations prevent us from
interpreting the "partial analyses"[18] of the gaps and regions. The latter
could return important insights to design better, problem-based, and more
effective innovation policy recommendations.

Figure 3.4   Spanish RISs' Integration Levels Map

5 CONCLUDING REMARKS

This chapter permits a systemic observation of the level of integration of Spanish RISs thanks to the evaluation of a number of innovation gaps. In doing so, it makes a number of theoretical, methodological, and empirical contributions. First, our framework permits the identification of a significant number of innovation gaps, thus helping to move beyond a more general identification of system's inefficiencies. Second, it eases the operationalization of a few sets of quantitative variable sets that help produce practical assessments. All in all, it completes the scope of previous investigations whose end products often came to be a rank of a region´s performance resulting in myopic economic outlook descriptions.

Third, with regard to its methodological contribution, the article rounds up other studies and literature traditions (Nauwelaers and Wintjes, 1999; Susiluoto, 2003; Parrilli et al., 2010; Chaminade et al., 2012; Navarro and Gibaja, 2012; Trippl et al. in this volume). While econometric studies did not pursue an exhaustive description of RIS´s levels of integration, theoretical studies lacked important empirical foundations.

All in all, this chapter abounds in the construction of more sophisticated tools for regional analysis. Fourth, this chapter puts forward a number of empirical contributions. It presents a new typology that classifies Spanish regions according to their levels of integration and similarities. The results come to be asymmetric not only across a given RIS but also when comparing them with its pairs in other Spanish regions. Thus integration levels should not be considered a homogeneous characteristic of RIS, as it may vary depending on historic and cultural idiosyncrasies, institutional thickness, and private sectors proactive behavior, among others. However, while the work provides some general grounds for guidance, the development of "partial analyses" (i.e., analysis of specific gaps in specific regions) is reserved for future work. Together with other inputs, the authors believe these specifications could speed up the design of novel and more detailed innovation policy directions.

Last, certain limitations were identified here. First, we found strong difficulties to employ variables due to the fact that statistics often bypass the importance of critical regional organizations and institutions. Thus the chapter's novelties are far from definitive, as the current state of the art prevents the employment of broader indicators. Second, a longitudinal outlook would also contribute to assess the influence of time over integration. To finish with, we presume that social network analysis (Wasserman and Faust, 1994) could facilitate the comprehension of certain interactive practices that remain hidden, which would definitely enrich the "black box" of RIS's integration.

ACKNOWLEDGMENTS

This chapter was finished during the corresponding author's stay as a guest researcher at the Center for Innovation, Research and Competence in the Learning Economy (CIRCLE), Lund University, Sweden, between August and November 2013. Accordingly, the authors thank Michaela Trippl, Cristina Chaminade, Markus Grillitsch, and Roman Martin for their outstanding contributions and insightful comments during the stay. An earlier version of this chapter was awarded with the fourth edition of the JMS Scholarship for young development researchers and development practitioners, sponsored by the SEPT program at the University of Leipzig. This version was also presented at the EU-SPRI Early Career Researcher Conference, Lund, 2–3 October 2013, "Innovation in a Globalized Economy: On the Role of Knowledge Dynamics, Institutions and Innovation Policies."

Appendix 1: Data Standardized

Data (standardized)	GAP 1				GAP 2		GAP 3					GAP 4		SUP		
	G11	G12	G13	G14	G21	G22	G31	G32	G33	G34	G35	G41	C42	AGR	IND	SER
Andalusia	-0.03	-0.03	-0.62	-0.17	-0.21	-0.87	-1.05	-0.76	-0.44	-0.81	-0.62	-0.7	0.15	0.08	0.09	0.11
Aragon	-2.47	-0.09	-0.3	-0.17	-1.19	0.43	0.46	0.16	0.42	0.16	-0.14	-0.7	-1	0.06	0.18	0.10
Asturias	0.35	0.94	-0.06	0.05	-1.01	-0.24	-0.29	-0.59	-0.41	-0.13	-0.18	0.73	0.21	0.04	0.15	0.11
Balear Islands	0.3	0.39	-0.81	0.72	0.47	-1.3	-1.22	-0.76	-0.54	-1.74	-0.83	-0.85	-1.51	0.01	0.07	0.12
Canary Islands	-0.44	-0.09	-0.8	-0.66	1.16	-1.41	-1	-1.26	-0.59	-1.04	-0.82	-0.89	-0.2	0.03	0.05	0.11
Cantabria	0.72	2.14	-0.67	-0.74	-0.79	0.17	-0.22	-0.3	-0.51	0.26	-0.44	-0.21	0	0.03	0.16	0.11
Castille Leon	-0.07	-0.03	-0.19	-0.73	-1.93	-0.37	-0.12	0.12	-0.57	-0.2	-0.3	0.62	0.27	0.07	0.16	0.09
Castille La Mancha	-0.9	-2.98	-0.58	-1.22	-0.7	-0.61	-0.39	-0.72	-0.38	-0.37	-0.69	-0.36	-0.8	0.07	0.17	0.09
Catalonia	-0.77	-0.03	0.79	1.44	1.54	0.19	0.06	1.21	0.22	-0.55	0.35	0.22	0.62	0.02	0.19	0.13
Valencia	0.06	-0.21	-0.27	0.82	0.65	-0.19	-0.29	-0.21	-0.43	0.47	-0.26	-0.77	-0.68	0.04	0.17	0.11
Extremadura	-0.07	-0.39	-0.74	-0.56	0.42	-0.69	0.17	-0.3	-0.63	-1	-0.79	1.8	-0.82	0.11	0.11	0.07
Galicia	0.88	-0.45	-0.45	0.35	-0.15	0.09	-0.34	-0.51	-0.34	0.58	-0.39	-0.39	0.18	0.08	0.16	0.10
Madrid	2.25	0.21	1.04	2.58	-0.64	-0.26	0.13	0.79	1.23	-0.6	1.41	0.5	0.95	0,00	0.10	0.19
Murcia	-0.44	-0.33	-0.46	-1.1	-0.64	-0.22	-1.29	-1.22	-0.5	0.12	-0.53	-0.66	0.39	0.14	0.13	0.11
Navarre	0.84	0.51	1.4	-0.11	1.42	1.11	1.96	2.3	3.36	0.89	1.57	2.61	2.04	0.04	0.25	0.10
Basque Country	0.51	-0.33	2.94	0.53	0.76	1.73	2.04	1.67	0.43	1.97	2.78	-0.01	1.69	0.01	0.21	0.14
La Rioja	-0.73	0.75	-0.21	-1.02	0.85	2.43	1.4	0.37	-0.32	2	-0.12	-0.94	-1.51	0.05	0.24	0.10

NOTES

1 On the basis of the "Oslo Manual" endorsed by OECD (1997/2006).

2 Both these components and relations should form a coherent whole. Systems should also have a function, i.e., they should perform or achieve something. Lastly, it should be possible to discriminate between the system and the rest of the world; i.e., it must be possible to identify the boundaries of the system. The latter is a key aspect when it comes to making empirical studies of specific systems (Ingelstam, 2002).

3 These tendencies would constitute a desirable feature of well-functioning "knowledge exploitation subsystems" as agglomeration facilitates desirable external economies, such as knowledge spillovers, locally available skilled labor, or transaction costs reduction.

4 Our work adds to a promising path of studies that pay attention to systemic problems (Isaksen, 1999; Nauwelaers and Wintjes, 1999; Woolthuis et al., 2005; Edquist, 2011; Chaminade et al., 2012). The work conducted by Woolthuis and Edquist, facilitates the diagnostic analysis of innovation systems, due to the interpretive frameworks introduced. Chaminade et al., (2012) is probably one of the first empirical studies on systemic problems in innovation systems, which facilitates the investigation of mismatches between policies and problems.

5 Some authors name these gaps as "structural holes" (Burt, 1992; Hargadon and Sutton, 1997).

6 "Absorptive capacity" is described as a firm's ability to recognize the value of new information, assimilate it, and apply it to commercial ends.

7 Future approximations could complete the current view by adding variables that would describe crucial characteristics of sophisticated managerial practices, such as the "number of markets in which the firm operates," the "DUI or STI styles of firm innovation" (Jensen et al., 2007), the "organizational working environment," or "their investment in training."

8 Lock-in situations occur when the system is too closed and the networks are too rigid (Isaksen, 1999; Nauwelaers and Wintjes; 1999; Tödtling and Trippl, 2005).

9 New indicators could be added to evaluate the longitudinal interactivity among firms along the level of trust existing in these networks.

10 It is crucial to underline that some RISs will be more prone to show intensive collaboration between the exploration and exploitation subsystems than others. This would have to do with the predominating type of innovation that prevails (Jensen et al., 2007) and the existing—analytic, synthetic, symbolic—knowledge bases of the region itself (Martin and Trippl, 2013). Consequently, new variables could improve future approximations by adding new indicators that, as in the case of gap 1, regarded DUI or STI styles of firm innovation (Jensen et al., 2007).

11 First, the amount of private loans demanded by private firms (general debt ratio) could contribute to uncover a firm's financial difficulties and its access to loans, credit guarantees, and equity. Second, the "number of private firms that closed the business as a consequence of financial problems" could also be a good indicator to measure the existence of policy tools adequately adapted to a firm's financial difficulties.

12 This view could be completed with new gaps across subsystems and organizations. An example of the latter could be the evaluation of a fifth gap between the "policy component" and the "knowledge exploration subsystem." This would lead researchers to assess the involvement of regional policy-makers in fostering basic research and new knowledge production. Some indicators could

shed some light on the issue such as the public expenditure on universities or the number of academics in the region.

13 Though the employment of different sources could bias results, we decided to include it as it provides us with valuable and precious high quality information.

14 We mean to Spain´s seventeen Autonomous Communities (ACs). Nomenclature of Territorial Units for Statistics (NUTS-2) by regional level. We chose this level of disaggregation because subsidies that Europe provides to ACs are based in NUTS-2 classification. For this reason, both design and implementation of corrective measures destined to overcome functioning problems within RISs would need be implemented under the coordination and supervision of autonomous governments. In order to get more information with regard to this issue, "NUTS-2 is employed as a basis for distributing cohesion funds, using eligible population, regional and national prosperity, and unemployment as variables for calculating the financial amounts corresponding to each country" (Pavía and Larraz, 2012: 131).

15 We conduct an algorithm for hierarchical classification by calculating the incremental sum of squares (Ward´s method) and Euclidean distances among the observations of the study.

16 Put together, these two dimensions gather around 60% of the variance, meaning we lose 40% of the information as a consequence of reducing the complexity contained in the database. Thirteen dimensions are reduced into two latent variables, which are represented by the horizontal and vertical axes of the visual outputs of the study.

17 The position of Valencia and Cantabria in this group is unexpected. Typologies of Spanish communities set these communities according to their output level. This level usually sets them closer to better-performing RISs, such as La Rioja or Aragon.

18 Partial individuals represent each region viewed in terms of each of the gaps assessed and its barycenter (Pagès, 2004; Abdi and Valentin, 2007).

REFERENCES

Abdi, H. and Valentin, D. (2007). Multiple factor analysis. In N. Salkind (ed.), *Encyclopedia of measurement and statistics* (657–663). Thousand Oaks, CA: Sage.

ASCRI. (2006–2012). *Informe 2012. Capital Riesgo y Private Equity en España.* Madrid. 2012.

Asheim, B. T., Boschma, R. and Cooke, P. (2011). Constructing regional advantage: Platform policies based on related variety and differentiated knowledge bases. *Regional Studies*, 45(7), 893–904.

Asheim, B. T. and Gertler, M. S. (2005). The geography of innovation. Regional innovation systems. In J. Fagerberg, D. C. Mowery and Y. R. R. Nelson (eds.), *The oxford handbook of innovation* (291–317). Oxford: Oxford University Press.

Asheim, B. T. and Parrilli, M. D. (2012). Introduction: Learning and interaction—Drivers for innovation in current competitive markets. In B. T. Asheim and M. D. Parrilli (eds.), *Interactive learning for innovation: A key driver within clusters and innovation systems* (1–28). Basingstoke: Palgrave Macmillan.

Autio, E. (1998). Evaluation of RTD in regional systems of innovation. *European Planning Studies*, 6(2), 131–140.

Bathelt, H., Malmberg, A. and Maskell, P. (2004). Clusters and knowledge: Local buzz, global pipelines and the process of knowledge creation. *Progress in Human Geography*, 28(1), 31–56.

Bessant, J. and Rush, H. (1995). Building bridges for innovation: The role of consultants in technology transfer. *Research Policy*, 24, 97–114.

Buesa, M. and Heijs, J. (2007). *Sistemas regionales de innovación: nuevas formas de análisis y medición*. Madrid: Fundación de las Cajas de Ahorros.

Buesa, M., Heijs, J. and Martínez-Pellitero, M. (2002). Una tipología de los sistemas regionales de innovación en España. *Madrid monografías*, 5, 81–89.

Buesa, M., Heijs, J. and Martínez-Pellitero, M. (2007). Novel applications of existing econometric instruments to analyze regional innovation systems: The Spanish case. In J. Suriñach, R. Moreno and E. Vaya (eds.), *Knowledge externalities, innovation clusters and regional development* (145–165. Cheltenham: Edward Elgar.

Burt, R. (1992). *Structural holes*. Cambridge: Harvard University Press.

Chaminade, C., Intarakumnerd, P. and Sapprasert, K. (2012). Measuring systemic problems in National Innovation Systems: An application to Thailand. *Research Policy*, 41, 1476–1488.

Cohen, W. M. and Levinthal, D. A. (1990). Absorptive capacity: A new perspective on learning and innovation. *Administrative Science Quarterly*, 35, 128–152.

Cooke, P. and Morgan, K. (1998). *The associational economy: Firms, regions and innovation*. Oxford: Oxford University Press.

Coronado, D. and Acosta, M. (1999). Innovación tecnológica y desarrollo regional. *Información Comercial Española*, 781, 103–116.

Dalziel, M. (2010). *Why do innovation intermediaries exists?* Paper presented at Summer Conference 2010: "Opening Up Innovation: Strategy, Organizational and Technology" at Imperial College London Business School, June 16–18.

Ecotec. (2005). *The territorial impact of EU research and development policies*. ESPON 2.1.2.

Edquist, C. (2005). Systems of innovation. Perspectives and challenges. In J. Fagerberg, D. C. Mowery, Y. R. R. Nelson (eds.), *The oxford handbook of innovation* (514–552). Oxford: Oxford University Press.

Edquist, C. (2011). Design of innovation policy through diagnostic analysis: Identification of systemic problems (or failures). *Industrial and Corporate Change*, 20, 1725–1753.

Escofier, B. and Pagès, J. (1990). Multiple factor analysis. *Computational Statistics & Data Analysis*, 18, 121–140.

Fischer, M. (2001). Innovation, knowledge creation and systems of innovation. *Regional Science*, 35, 199–216.

Gielsing, V. and Nooteboom, B. (2006). Exploration and exploitation in innovation systems: The case of pharmaceutical biotechnology. *Research Policy*, 35, 1–23.

Hargadon, A. and Sutton, R. (1997). Technology brokering and innovation in product development firm. *Administrative Science Quarterly*, 42, 716–749.

Hollanders, H., Tarantola, S., and Loschky, A. (2009). *Regional innovation scoreboard* (RIS) 2009. Maastricht Economic and Social Research and Training Centre on Innovation and Technology, Joint Research Centre, Institute for the Protection and Security of the Citizen (IPSC), Maastricht.

Howells, J. and Edler, J. (2011). Structural innovations: Towards a unified perspective? *Science and Public Policy*, 38(2), 157–167.

Husson, F., Josse, J., Lê, S. and Mazet, J. (2011). *FactoMineR: Multivariate exploratory data analysis and data mining with R*. R package version 1.16. http://CRAN.R-project.org/package=FactoMineR

Iammarino, S. (2005). An evolutionary integrated view of regional systems of innovation: Concepts, measures and historical perspectives. *European Planning Studies*, 13(4), 495–517.

INE. (several years): *Survey on adult population involvement in learning activities*. Madrid.

INE. (several years): *Innovation in companies´ survey*. Madrid.

INE. (several years): *Survey on ICT. Usage and e-commerce in companies*. Madrid.

Ingelstam, L. (2002). System—att tänka över samhälle och teknik (Systems: To reflect over society and technology—in Swedish). *Energimyndighetens förlag*.

64   *Xabier Alberdi-Pons et al.*

Isaksen, A. (1999). National and regional contexts for innovation. In P. R. Christensen, A. Cornett and K. Philipsen (eds.), *Innovations and innovation support for SMEs-The triangle region of Denmark. Chapter 3, Centre for small business research.* South Denmark, Kolding: Southern Denmark University. SMEPOL report n°2.

Jensen, M. B., Johnson, B., Lorenz, E. and Lundvall, B. (2007). Forms of knowledge and modes of innovation. *Research Policy,* 36, 680–693.

Kostiainen, J. (2002). *Urban economic development policy in the network society.* Doctoral dissertation, Tekniikan Akateemisten Liitto, Helsinki.

Lê, S., Josse, J. and Husson, F. (2008). FactoMineR: An R package for multivariate analysis. *Journal of Statistical Software,* 25(1), 1–18.

Lundvall, B.-A. (ed). (1992). *National systems of innovation: Towards a theory of innovation and interactive learning.* London: Pinter Publishers.

Martin, R. and Trippl, M. (2013). *System failures, knowledge bases and regional innovation policies.* Center for Innovation, Research and Competence in the Learning Economy (CIRCLE): Lund University. Paper n° 2013/13.

Martínez-Pellitero, M. (2002). *Recursos y resultados de los sistemas de innovación: elaboración de una tipología de sistemas regionales de innovación en España.* IAIF working paper, 34.

Nauwelaers, C. and Wintjes, R. (1999). *SME policy and the regional dimension of innovation: The cases of Wallonia and Limburg*(1–20). SMEPOL report n°4. Maastricht, MERIT: Maastricht University.

Navarro, M. and Gibaja, J. J. (2009). Las tipologías en los sistemas regionales de innovación. El caso de España. *Ekonomiaz,* 70.

Navarro, M. and Gibaja, J. J. (2010). Tipologías de innovación basadas en análisis estadísticos para las regiones europeas y españolas. In M. D. Parrilli (ed.), *Innovación y aprendizaje: lecciones para el diseño de políticas* (158–205). Innobasque, Bilbao: Agencia Vasca de la Innovación.

Navarro, M. and Gibaja, J. J. (2012). Typologies of innovation based on statistical analysis for European and Spanish regions. In B. T. Asheim and M. D. Parrilli (eds.), *Interactive learning for innovation: A key driver within clusters and innovation systems* (134–173). Basingstoke: Palgrave Macmillan.

Nonaka, I. and Takeuchi, H. (1995). *The knowledge-creating company. How Japanese companies create the dynamics of innovation.* New York, Oxford: Oxford University Press.

OECD. (1997/2006). Oslo manual: Guidelines for collecting and interpretating innovation data. OECD-EUROSTAT, Paris, various editions.

Pagès, J. (2004). Multiple factor analysis: Main features and application to sensory data. *Revista Colombiana de Estadística,* 27, 1–26.

Parrilli, M. D. (2013). Unveiling the black-box of innovation: A methodological tool for the analysis of the efficiency of regional innovation systems. *Journal of Strategic Management Education,* 9(1), http://www.senatehall.com/strategic-management?article=461.

Parrilli, M. D., Aranguren, M. J. and Larrea, M. (2010). The role of interactive learning to close the innovation gap in SME-based local economies: A furniture cluster in the Basque Country and its key policy implications. *European Planning Studies,* 18, 351–370.

Pavía, J. M. and Larraz, B. (2012). Regional size, wealtz and EU regional policy. *Investigaciones Regionales,* 23, 127–141.

Porter, M. (1990). *The competitive advantage of nations.* London: The MacMillan Press.

R Development Core Team. (2011). *R: A language and environment for statistical computing. R Foundation for Statistical Computing.* Vienna, Austria. ISBN 3-900051-07-0, http://www.R-project.org/.

Susiluoto, I. (2003). Effects of ICT on regional economic efficiency. Helsinki City Urban Facts Office, *Web Publications*, ISSN 1458–5707, ISBN 952–473–146–0.

Tödtling, F. and Trippl, M. (2005). One size fits all? Towards a differentiated regional innovation policy approach. *Research Policy*, 34, 1203–1219.

Trippl, M., Asheim, B. and Mjorner, J. (2015). Identification of regions with less developed research and innovation systems. In M. D. Parrilli, R. Dahl Fitjar and A. Rodríguez-Pose (eds.), *Innovation drivers and regional innovation strategies.* New York: Routledge.

Trippl, M. and Tödtling, F. (2007). Developing biotechnology clusters in non-high technology regions: The case of Austria. *Industry and innovation*, 14, 47–67.

UNU-MERIT. (2009). *European innovation scoreboard 2008. Comparative analysis of innovation performance.* Pro Inno Europe INNO METRICS. http://ec.europa.eu/enterprise/policies/innovation/files/proinno/eis-2008_en.pdf.

Wasserman, S., and Faust, K. (1994). *Social network analysis: Methods and applications.* New York and Cambridge: Cambridge University Press.

Woolthuis, R. K., Lankhuizen, M. and V. Gilsing. (2005). A system failure framework for innovation policy design. *Technovation*, 25, 609–619.

Yusuf, S. (2008). Intermediating knowledge exchange between universities and businesses. *Research Policy*, 37, 1167–1174.

Zabala-Iturriagagoitia, J. M., Voigt, P., Gutiérrez-Gracia, A. and Jiménez-Sáez, F. (2007). Regional innovation systems: How to assess performance. *Regional Studies*, 41, 661–672.

Zucker, L., Darby, M. and Armstrong, J. (1998). Geographically localized knowledge: Spillovers or markets. *Economic Inquiry*, 36, 65–86.

4 Path Development in Different Regional Innovation Systems
A Conceptual Analysis

Arne Isaksen and Michaela Trippl

1. INTRODUCTION

Over the last years, models of path dependent regional industrial development have come to exercise increasing influence over academic work in economic geography, innovation studies, and related academic fields (see, for instance, Martin and Sunley 2006; Martin 2010; Boschma and Frenken 2011; Neffke et al., 2011). A key argument advanced in this literature is that preexisting industrial and institutional structures form the regional environment and context in which current economic and innovation activities take place and new ones emerge. This may result in the long-term persistence of regional industrial structures and institutional setups.

Conceptual approaches to path dependent regional industrial development have thus far been primarily concerned with explaining the continuation of existing pathways and less so with offering detailed insights into structural change processes (see, Martin 2010, 2012 for a critical appraisal of this literature). Recently, however, a growing body of conceptual and empirical work has enriched our understanding of new path creation and transformation processes in regional economies (Martin and Sunley 2006; Frenken et al. 2007; Boschma and Frenken 2011; Boschma 2014a). This chapter aims to contribute to the burgeoning debate on regional industrial renewal and the nature of path development activities across regions. We investigate conceptually to what extent and in what ways different types of regions can reconfigure their economic structures over time and embark on new growth paths.

Academic work on regional industrial path development tends to focus on firm-specific routines, norms, and tacit knowledge that are seen as crucially important "ingredients" to path extension; that is, intra-path changes based on mainly incremental innovations in existing regional industries and along well-established technological trajectories. This chapter suggests two major extensions of this framework. First, we intend to move beyond the notions of path dependence and path extension as these concepts provide explanations of continuity and stability but do not offer an adequate framework for analyzing change. We focus attention on alternative forms of regional industrial path development that relate to various routes of transformation of regional economies and innovation systems. A distinction between two main forms—that is, path renewal and new path creation—is drawn. Path renewal is defined here as the diversification of existing industries into new but related ones (Boschma and Frenken 2011), while path creation is referred to as the rise of entirely new industries in the region (Martin and Sunley 2006; Asheim et al. 2013).

Second, we go beyond microlevel, firm-based accounts of path development that are prevalent in evolutionary economic geography (see MacKinnon et al. 2009; Pike et al. 2009; Asheim et al. 2013; Hassink et al. 2014 for a critique of the microlevel approach). Drawing on insights provided by the regional innovation system (RIS) approach, we highlight that an institutional perspective can essentially enhance our understanding of how regions transform over time. By doing so, we overcome the strong focus on dynamic growth regions, whose experiences often create at least implicitly the basis for current conceptualizations and analyses of path dependent regional industrial development (Dawley, 2014, Isaksen, 2014). Focusing on two key dimensions of RISs—that is, density and degree of specialization of economic and institutional structures—enables us to identify different types of regions and to explore for each of them how RIS structures may influence directions and sources of regional change. We distinguish between organizationally thick and diversified RISs (often found in advanced core regions), organizationally thick and specialized RISs (commonly found in old industrial areas and industrial districts), and organizationally thin RISs (often found in peripheral areas).

Both the influence of policy actions at various spatial scales and the transformative potential of exogenous development impulses have been underplayed in models of path dependent regional industrial development. Only recently, scholarly work has begun to explore the role of exogenous sources of regional growth and change (see, for instance, Boschma and Iammarino, 2009; MacKinnon, 2012). Apart from a few notable exceptions (Asheim et al., 2011; Simmie, 2012; Asheim et al., 2013; Morgan, 2013, Boschma, 2014b; Dawley, 2014), the importance of policy interventions has received little attention so far in conceptual considerations and empirical analyses of regional path development. What is particularly missing is a systematic account of and more thorough reflections on how policy can promote new path creation and path renewal in a variety of regional settings.

This chapter seeks to address some of the aforementioned research gaps. We explore how different types of RISs vary in their transformation capacity, and we depict major development challenges that can be found in each RIS type. We also intend to contribute to the regional innovation policy debate by discussing adequate policy approaches for different types of regions. More precisely, the chapter deals with the following research questions:

- To what extent and in which ways do different types of regions vary in their capacity to renew their industrial structures over time? Which forms of regional industrial path development are promoted by different types of RISs and what is the role of intraregional and extra-regional development impulses in this regard?
- Which development challenges emanate from these regional development patterns? What is the scope of policy-supported or policy-led regional industrial path development? What are sound policy options to promote regional industrial renewal in different types of RISs?

We deal with these questions through a conceptual analysis. The remainder of this chapter is organized in three main parts. Section 2 provides definitions and a critical discussion of the key notions and concepts that establish the analytical framework used in this chapter. In section 3, we draw attention to different types of RISs, and we explore conceptually which forms of regional industrial path development are likely to take place in each of them. Furthermore, we identify key development and transformation challenges in various types of regions. This creates a basis to elaborate on adequate policy approaches and measures to promote new path development in different RIS types. Finally, section 4 summarizes the main findings of the chapter and draws some lessons.

2. DEFINITION OF KEY CONCEPTS: PATH DEVELOPMENT AND REGIONAL INNOVATION SYSTEMS

The analytical framework includes two main theoretical constructs, path dependent regional industrial development and regional innovation systems. Understanding of these notions is required before they are combined in analyses of, among other things, the type of path development that is particularly stimulated by specific types of regional innovation systems.

Path Development

The concept of path dependence is mainly used to explain the economic specialization of regions that includes lock-in effects that push a technology, an industry, or a regional economy along one path rather than another (Strambach, 2010). The approach assumes that the past economic development in a region "sets the possibilities, while the present controls what possibilities to be explored" (Martin and Sunley, 2006, p. 403). The preexisiting industrial and institutional structures constitute the regional environment in which current activities occur and new activities arise.

Path dependence means that regional industries may enter into *path extension* through mainly incremental product and process innovations in existing industries and technological paths. In situations of growth, this results in continuity or more of the same in a regional economy. In such situations, regional industries may, sooner or later, experience stagnation and gradual decline due to lack of renewal (Hassink, 2010). Regional industries thus face a risk of *path exhaustion*, which refers to situations wherein the innovation potential of local firms has been severely reduced or innovations take place only along a restricted technological path. Such situations may reflect high connectivity between regional actors but with few linkages to the outside world. External developments may be overlooked or recognized too late. Firms may become uncompetitive and decline, so the regional industry shrinks; although sometimes path revitalization is also possible (Martin, 2010).

Recent theoretical contributions supplement these notions of path dependent processes that focus on continuity and lock-in with alternative paths dealing with changes that may follow from different forms of reorientation of regional industries (Garud et al., 2010; Martin, 2010, 2012; Neffke et al., 2011; Boschma, 2014a). *Path renewal* takes place when existing local firms switch to different, but possibly related, activities and sectors (Boschma and Frenken, 2011). The possibilities for path renewal are strengthened when a region's industry includes related variety; that is, when the region has a wide range of industries that are technologically related (Frenken et al., 2007). The potential for inter-industry learning and new recombination of knowledge then exist. Regions may develop new growth paths "as new industries tend to branch out of and recombine resources from existing local industries to which they are technologically related" (Boschma, 2014a: 8). This means that knowledge and other resources that exist in regional firms will shape the type of renewal that occurs (Neffke et al., 2011). Path renewal is then often industry driven as regional industry mutates and widens the industrial structure (Boschma and Frenken, 2011), but such processes also make the border between path extension and path renewal fuzzy (Henning et al., 2013).

Path creation denotes the most wide-ranging changes in a regional economy. It includes the establishment of new firms in new sectors for the region or firms that have different variants of products, employ new techniques, or organize differently than what have hitherto dominated in the region (Martin and Sunley, 2006). Tödtling and Trippl (2013) distinguish two kinds of new industries in a region: first, the rise of established industries that are new for the region (regional path formation in established industries) and second, the rise of totally new industries (path creation in new industries). Path formation may be caused by inward investments and/or sectoral diversification of existing firms. The second case of new path creation is often research driven, focusing on commercialization of research results and grows up through the establishment of new firms and spin-offs. In this case, new sectors may not be "related to the existing regional industrial base" (Henning et al., 2013: 1353). Research driven, new path development is not considered in the regional branching and related variety approaches, and the importance of research for the development of new growth paths marks the main difference between path renewal and path creation. Path creation might demand the building of new knowledge organizations and institutional change (Tödling and Trippl, 2013). It is thus often policy initiated and demands proactive policy actions (Asheim et al., 2013).

Different paths may be combined in regions and other paths than the four types mentioned earlier are possible. Strambach (2010: 407) argues for opening up the path dependency thinking by focusing on path plasticity "which describes a broad range of possibilities for the creation of innovation within a dominant path of innovation systems." This leads to the argument that radical innovation activities can occur within existing institutional settings and within a path and do not necessarily lead to breaking out of a path and to the creation of a new path. From the perspective of technological path development in particular Sydow et al. (2012: 158), see path dependence and path creation as only two possible paths, "others are intentional path defence or extension, unintended path dissolution, or breaking a path without creating a new one". Still, the conceptual discussion in this chapter focuses on the three main forms of regional industrial path development, that is, path extension, renewal, and creation.

Regional Innovation System

The second building block in our conceptual analysis is the regional innovation system (RIS) approach. By using the RIS notion, an explicit institutional dimension is introduced to supplement the mainly evolutionary approach of the "path dependence school". Theorizing of path dependence focuses much on microlevel processes, which we here extend with an institutional approach that centers on elements in the wider regional environment that influence the innovation capability of firms.

A RIS is seen as a specific framework in which close interfirm interactions, knowledge and policy support infrastructures, and sociocultural and institutional environments may stimulate collective learning, continuous innovation, and entrepreneurial activity (Asheim and Isaksen, 2002, Tödtling and Trippl, 2005, Asheim et al., 2013). The RIS approach builds on the fact that innovative firms supplement their internal competence with external, specialist competence from a number of different actors (Lundvall, 2010). Formal and informal institutions stimulate cooperation among different actors in RISs and reduce uncertainty in innovation processes. Institutions contribute to path dependency as institutions may be slow in adapting to changes in the economic structure (Strambach, 2010). RISs thus "exhibit a high degree of inertia" (Tödtling and Trippl, 2013: 297).

Studies of RISs also rarely deal with how these systems transform over time. RIS studies are mostly snapshots focusing on the characteristics, and strengths and weaknesses, of particular systems, while the historical development of the systems is less reflected upon (Doloreux and Parto, 2005). Path creation may therefore presume "the breaking of institutional stability and the creation of new institutions for further innovation" (Strambach, 2010: 406). The RIS approach is still better equipped to study change, or path renewal and creation, than the related notion of regional clusters that consists of industries that "form specialised concentrations in particular locations" (Asheim et al., 2006). RISs may include several clusters and other types of firms that give possibilities to combine different types of knowledge across local industries and firms and to stimulate path renewal. A single cluster, on the other hand, includes few combinatory options at the local scale and therefore "few potential sources for renewal and diversification" (Boschma, 2014a: 7). Furthermore, knowledge organizations have an independent role in RISs, while these organizations in clusters mainly are seen to provide adapted knowledge to the dominating industry in the clusters. This means that knowledge organizations in the RIS approach can contribute to path creation.

Regional innovation systems, however, differ in many respects, which also affect the possibilities of RISs to contribute to path renewal and creation. The transformation of individual RISs, the extent and type of changes, and the mechanisms of change are therefore likely to differ much. Important differentiating elements in RISs are the number of firms and knowledge organizations, and the extent, width, and reach of knowledge exchange. The type of knowledge exchange depends much on the type of institutions that dominate in a regional industry. "By lowering uncertainty and information costs, institutions are believed to smooth the process of knowledge and innovation transfer within and across regions" (Rogriguez-Pose, 2013: 1038). Among informal institutions, trust and social capital have attracted the greatest attention (op. cit.: 1036), and we focus on social capital in the succeeding conceptual discussion of RISs. Social capital is defined as "social networks and relations held together by common norms and values (of which trust is one)" (Westlund and Kobayshi, 2013: 5). This definition relates to a distinction between two types of social capital: structural social capital seen in the social networks of actors and cognitive social capital, which refers to shared norms, values, attitudes, beliefs, and trust (Malecki, 2012: 1026). Another relevant distinction is between bonding and bridging social capital. Bonding refers to the internal network of a group or organization and the value and norms that keep the members together, while bridging social capital links to actors in other groups and organizations (Westlund and Kobayshi, 2013: 5–6).

Social capital is relevant in our context as it differs between regions (Eliasson et al., 2013: 115). "Social capital is part of a region's collective personality" (Malecki, 2012: 1033) of which one outcome is variation among regions "in the degree to which people—individually and within their organizations—trust and interact with one another" (op. cit.: 1023). Variation in social capital "explains why some regions shoot ahead through innovation while others are left behind in the development race" (Landa-baso, 2012: 375).

Tödtling and Trippl (2005) characterize some regions, often peripherally located ones, as having *organizationally thin* RISs. These systems have low levels of firm clustering and a weak endowment with knowledge generation and diffusion organizations. Due to few actors, little regional knowledge exchange takes place, and the exchange occurs mainly among local actors as (at least) rural regions usually have developed bonding social capital (Westlund and Kobayashi, 2013). Other RISs are *organizationally thick* but may differ in the configuration of their knowledge network with regard to the variety of involved actors and their location. Some regions, particularly old industrial areas, have rather specialized and relatively closed, regionally oriented inter-firm and interorganizational networks (Tödtling and Trippl, 2005); that is, they are also dominated by bonding social capital. Other regions, most often larger and more central regions, have diverse and geographically open knowl-edge networks. Social capital becomes more heterogeneous, i.e., it includes both bonding and bridging networks, in such regions (Malecki, 2012). Open knowledge networks coupled with firm and sector heterogeneity are favor-able settings for regional industries to branch out into new but related fields, building on existing competences (Boschma and Frenken, 2011), which is typical for path renewal. Based on this discussion, we distinguish in our sub-sequent analysis between organizationally thin RISs, organizationally thick and specialized RISs, and organizationally thick and diversified RISs.

3. TYPES OF RISs AND REGIONAL PATH DEVELOPMENT

This section explores the relation between different types of RISs and vari-ous forms of regional path development. As noted earlier, there are strong reasons to assume that regions vary enormously in their transformation capacity—that is, in their ability to set in motion endogenous processes of path renewal and new path creation. We substantiate this view by investigat-ing conceptually the forms of path development one can expect to observe in different types of RIS. We also analyze typical regional development chal-lenges that can be found in each RIS type. This provides the foundation for discussing policy approaches that are adequate for promoting regional transformation in different types of RIS.

3.1 Organizationally Thick and Diversified Regional Innovation Systems

3.1.1 *Typical Form of Regional Industrial Path Development*

Organizationally thick and diversified RISs host a relatively large number of different industries and a critical mass of knowledge and supporting organizations that promote innovation and development in a wide range of economic and technological fields. Such constellations are often found in large, well-performing core regions, such as metropolitan areas and advanced technology regions (Tödtling and Trippl, 2005). Some smaller "islands of innovation" that host several distinct clusters of "high technology" and knowledge-intensive business service activities (see, for instance, the case of Cambridge (UK), Martin and Sunley, 2006) may also fall into this category.

Organizationally thick and diversified areas offer favorable conditions for path renewal and new path creation. Unsurprisingly, current theorizing of regional industrial path development draws at least implicitly on experiences from these areas (Dawley, 2014; Isaksen, 2014). The strong capacity of these RISs to set in motion endogenous transformation processes is essentially nurtured by the existence of industrial and institutional variety. Industrial diversity and associated "Jabobsian externalities" are considered as eminently conducive to innovation and new path development activities. The wide range of heterogeneous (but related) industries located in this type of region leads to high potentials for cross-sectoral knowledge flows and new recombinations of knowledge (Boschma, 2014a). What is more, organizationally thick and diversified RIS often exhibit diverse and geographically open knowledge networks. Social capital in these areas is characterized by heterogeneity, that is, it includes both bonding and bridging networks (Malecki, 2012). Industrial heterogeneity along with open knowledge networks constitute favorable conditions for path renewal—that is, the evolution of existing regional industries into new but related ones through firms' diversification processes, labor mobility, spin-offs, and networking (Boschma and Frenken, 2011; Boschma, 2014a).

Regional transformation, however, might not only be based on firm-driven, path renewal processes. Organizationally thick and diversified RISs also offer excellent potentials for research-driven routes of regional change. These RISs are usually well endowed with strong universities and other research organizations, which can be an important source of regional transformation. They serve as seedbeds of academic spin-offs and promote other forms of commercialization of research results that might lead to the emergence of science-based industries and entirely new regional growth paths.

Both path renewal and new path creation activities are facilitated by a plethora of supporting organizations that are usually present in well-performing core areas. These range from providers of information about new markets and technologies, organizations offering counseling services, bridging organizations, technology transfer agencies, incubators, science parks, incubators, and so on.

To summarize, organizationally thick and diversified RISs offer strong potentials for endogenous, self-sustaining regional transformation processes. As Martin and Sunley (2006: 420) put it, "Diversity of local industries, technologies, and organizations promotes constant innovation and economic reconfiguration, avoiding lock-in to a fixed structure." Hence one can expect that path renewal and new path creation constitute the typical development pattern in these regions.

3.1.2 DEVELOPMENT CHALLENGES AND POLICY APPROACHES

The development challenges of organizationally thick and diversified RISs are twofold. They face the challenge to sustain their strong capacity to set in motion continuous path renewal and new path creation activities. However, this type of RISs may also need to achieve path extension.

Due to their ideal preconditions—that is, the presence of a heterogeneous industrial mix, institutional variety, and bridging social capital—organizationally thick and diversified RISs are often core centers of continuous change. New path development activities occur on a more or less regular basis. Continuous change, however, might reflect too much exploration and too little exploitation. This might result in a lack of industrial focus; emerging industries and activities may not achieve a critical mass (Boschma, 2014a). What is more, the knowledge and supporting infrastructure of the RIS may not succeed in staying abreast of changes, failing to adapt permanently to newly emerging fields and supporting them by adjustments of research and educational programs and support structures. As Martin (2012: 184), with reference to Setterfield (1998, 2009) and Roland (2004), reminds us, "institutional stability is necessary for economic accumulation, growth and development, but such growth and development may promote change and instability in institutional arrangements. In addition, different institutions and different economic sectors evolve at different rates and with different temporalities."

The challenges sketched out earlier imply that organizationally thick and diversified RISs may benefit from policy interventions that promote path extension. Key tasks of policy-makers comprise the identification of the most promising existing industrial fields that have emerged out of past rounds of regional path renewal and new path creation, support them to get positively locked-in and facilitate their further growth. Path stabilization and path extension to promote exploitation activities in newly created fields should thus be privileged. A key element of such an approach might include measures that promote the adaptation of the institutional setup of the RIS—that is, promotion of research activities, education programs, counseling services, and so on that support innovation and growth along newly established trajectories. Indeed, organizationally thick and diversified RISs may need "more of the same" instead of permanently exploring new things at the cost of exploitation and commercialization of new knowledge.

In the long term, these areas may face the challenge to maintain their capacity to set in motion path branching and new path creation activities.

Even organizationally thick and diversified RISs may be confronted with an erosion of their transformative capacity in the long run, resulting, for instance, from a rigidification of industrial and institutional structures or barriers that prevent related activities to connect. Consequently, an essential policy objective should thus be to sustain the ability of these areas to renew their industrial structures over time. Sound policy actions might include the removal of obstacles that hamper new combinations between industries and knowledge bases (Boschma, 2014a), investment in new research fields, and reconfiguration of the institutional setup to match new industrial requirements.

3.2 Organizationally Thick and Specialized Regional Innovation Systems

3.2.1 Typical Form of Regional Industrial Path Development

Organizationally thick and specialized RISs are characterized by the presence of strong clusters in one or a few industries only and a highly specialized support structure and institutional setup that is strongly adapted to the region's narrow industrial base. Such conditions tend to prevail in old industrial areas (Grabher, 1993; Hassink, 2005; Trippl and Otto, 2009) or in Italian industrial districts (see, for instance, Belussi and Sedita, 2009).

This RIS type exhibits a rather weak capacity for inducing endogenous processes of regional transformation. Organizationally thick and specialized RISs lack the internal diversity of industries, knowledge bases, supporting organizations, and institutional forms that are seen as critically important for developing new regional industrial paths (Asheim et al., 2011; Boschma and Frenken, 2011). The degree of intraregional related variety is low and only a few opportunities for combining or recombining diverse knowledge bases at the regional scale exist (Boschma, 2014a). These areas are often also rich in bonding social capital—that is, regionally oriented, inward looking networks tend to prevail, closing the region off from extra-regional resources and knowledge and reinforcing existing activities at the cost of industrial change.

Organizationally thick and specialized RISs mainly experience innovation along existing regional industrial development paths. Indeed, these areas can be regarded as "core centers of continuity". The strong degree of specialization of a critical mass of firms and support organizations and related Marshallian externalities promote first and foremost continuous incremental innovation activities in existing industries and along prevailing technological pathways. Various forms of positive lock-in effects keep firms on well-established industrial and technological trajectories. Increasing returns and positive externalities reinforce dynamism in existing regional industrial paths (Martin and Sunley, 2006) backed by supporting and institutional structures that are well adapted to the prevailing industrial specialization pattern. Boschma (2014a: 7) points to a negative relation between specialization and renewal capacity, arguing that

> once a region specializes in a knowledge base, this offers opportunities to local firms for further improvements, but regions may also become myopic for opportunities that lay beyond their own development paths, and sunk costs may prevent them from switching to new growth tracks (see also Malmberg and Maskell, 1997; Maskell and Malmberg, 1999).

Path extension is thus the typical form of regional industrial path development that is promoted by organizationally thick and specialized RISs.

This type of RIS, however, is particularly vulnerable to industrial decline. Firms and the whole RIS may lose their capacity to continuously extend established practices. Positive lock-in can turn into negative lock-in, causing the danger of path exhaustion. If changes in the external context conditions require adaptability, novelty, and transformation instead of "more of the same", the lacking potential for endogenous regional industrial renewal that often characterizes organizationally thick and specialized RISs creates major development challenges. The literature on old industrial areas is replete with examples of how negative functional, cognitive, and political lock-in result in stagnation, economic downturn, and decline of industrial paths (see, for instance, Grabher, 1993; Tödtling and Trippl, 2004; Hudson, 2005; Trippl and Tödtling, 2008; Birch et al., 2010; Hassink, 2010; Simmie and Martin, 2010).

3.2.2 Development Challenges and Policy Approaches

Organizationally thick and specialized RISs face major renewal challenges. Existing development paths can become exhausted if positive lock-in turns into negative lock-in (see the aforementioned discussion). As a consequence, policy should focus on avoiding path exhaustion to happen by promoting continuous innovation and upgrading in established industries, or if negative lock-in has set in, stimulating path revitalization, provided that there are enough knowledge assets left that could be used to regain competitiveness in existing industries. At the same time, however, policy interventions to stimulate the extension, upgrading, and revitalization of existing paths are insufficient. Arguably, a key challenge is to move beyond path extension and promote change instead of continuity—that is, to facilitate the development of new industrial paths.

As diversity and related variety are barely present at the regional scale, harnessing exogenous development impulses as a key source for regional transformation should rank high on the policy agenda. Policy options include the promotion of connections to extra-regional knowledge networks to get access to complementary knowledge from abroad and its combination with specialized assets available in the region (Boschma, 2014a). Attraction of foreign direct investment may also be a sound policy approach to support path renewal and new path creation processes in organizationally thick and specialized regions (Trippl and Tödtling, 2008). The success of a policy strategy that builds on the importation of innovative firms from elsewhere, however, is contingent on "the absorption capabilities and competences of the existing industrial base . . ., on the scope for local sourcing of inputs, and the like" (Martin and Sunley, 2006: 423).

Policy-makers can also play a powerful role in activating endogenous sources of new path development by promoting diversification processes of existing companies into new but related fields and supporting new firm formation in entirely new industries. However, such firm- and industry-oriented policy measures need to be complemented by instruments that induce changes in other RIS elements (Trippl and Tödtling, 2008). Investment in new scientific areas, promotion of a reorientation of the support structure, and the formation of new networks should thus be key policy priorities.

3.3 Organizationally Thin Regions

3.3.1 Typical Form of Regional Industrial Path Development

Organizationally thin regions have, by definition, few or none higher education institutions and R&D institutes, none or only weakly developed clusters, and consequently little local knowledge exchange. The regions are often dominated by SMEs operating in traditional and resource-based industries, but also larger, externally owned firms (Tödtling and Trippl, 2005). Traditional industries and a weak knowledge infrastructure mean that SMEs in thin regions are often characterized by the DUI (doing, using, and interacting) mode of innovation (Jensen et al., 2007, Isaksen and Karlsen, 2013). This innovation mode is typically based on experiences and competences acquired on the job as employees face new problems or new customer demands. OECD (2014: 50) also indirectly points to the importance of the DUI mode in rural areas when insisting that innovation in such areas "is grounded in actions of individuals looking for ways to solve specific problems".

The external ownership in some thin RISs may lead to a "branch plant culture", which means that local actors envisage that new jobs are provided by external investors who can hamper local entrepreneurship and innovativeness (Petrov, 2011). A different but not conflicting opinion in the literature is that regions with thin RISs (to the extent that these consist of rural areas) are inward looking and fairly homogenous with regard to knowledge bases and "worldviews". Westlund and Kobayashi (2013) argue that rural areas mostly include bonding social capital, which stimulates cooperation and knowledge exchange, in particular, among well-known, local actors who know the values and norms that hold the networks together.

A recurrent argument in the literature is that "too much bonding social capital becomes negative, creating conformity rather than variety" (Malecki, 2012: 1031). Conformity leads to the opposite of knowledge spillover and interactive learning among actors with a "related variety" of knowledge and technology, which is seen to stimulate innovation in existing industries and the emergence of new industries in a region (Boschma and Frenken, 2011).

The DUI mode of innovation, nearly without R&D activity and a dominance of bonding social capital, leads primarily to incremental changes in products and processes within existing industries in organizationally thin RISs. Such regions therefore often experience path extension and risk falling into negative lock-in and path exhaustion.

3.3.2 Development Challenges and Policy Approaches

Organizationally thin RISs will face problems in renewal of existing and, in particular, in the formation of new regional development paths. Path renewal is, as underlined earlier, triggered by a diverse industrial structure and a variety of firms and knowledge bases in a region (Frenken et al., 2007), which are conditions most often not found in thin RISs. Firms in thin RISs can compensate for a scarce and conformal, local knowledge supply base by 1) internalizing some of the resources that are available external to firms in organizationally thick and diversified RISs (Isaksen, 2014) and by 2) entering into geographic widespread collaboration networks (Herstad and Ebersberger, 2013). The first strategy may not lead to more than path extension if firms build up internal resources to strengthen their already dominant activities. The second strategy points to the fact that firms often use extra-regional knowledge sources and find innovation partners outside their region. This observation seems to be less relevant for rural areas, which are often dominated by bonding social capital. The second strategy then demands to develop new forms of bridging social capital (Westlund and Kobayashi, 2013), which is not a quick fix as the cognitive part of social capital includes historically developed and regional-specific norms and values. One element in a strategy for more extra-regional knowledge links would be to raise the absorptive capacity of regional firms, e.g., through recruiting of more skilled people. This would raise the ability of at least some firms (gatekeepers) in a region to identify and acquire external information, interpret and assimilate it, combine it with existing knowledge, share it with other firms and regional actors, and then apply it to commercial ends (Cohen and Levinthal, 1990; Giuliani and Bell, 2005).

The situation in thin RISs with few technology-related firms and industries means that the universal industry-specific "smart specialization strategies" are less relevant (Monsson, 2014). Rather than focusing on the industry or RIS level, innovation policy in thin RISs should therefore be directed at the firm level. Isaksen and Karlsen (2013) point out that some resourceful firms in thin RISs should act as "door openers" to external knowledge for other local firms, while Monsson (2014) proposes to target high-growth firms from a variety of industries. From these arguments less emphasis is placed on the endogenous development capacities of regions but rather target individual firms that have the ability and will to innovate, to support innovation processes in these, and contribute to diffusion of competence and technology from the "target firms" to other local firms and organizations. The "diffusion strategy" is important to avoid situations in which regions have a few advanced firms with mainly extra-regional knowledge links and innovation partners but which are not really embedded in, and contribute to, the local industrial milieu. Such a situation is quite feasible, as thin RISs have little "local related externalities" to support firms' innovation activities and hence little local knowledge spillovers. Policy tools that compensate for the lack of organically created externalities, for example, technology parks, can be relevant. Firms in core areas have far better access to specialized suppliers, experienced labor, and knowledge organizations nearby and can benefit from local spillovers, while organizationally thin RISs may need help to create such resources through policy.

Following such reasoning, thin RISs may achieve path renewal first of all by adapting resources that initially derive from outside the region, which requires some local organizations with boundary-spanning functions and that aim contributing to knowledge spillovers from resourceful and externally linked firms. Policy recommendations therefore include to link firms to partners and knowledge sources outside and inside the region. Attracting innovative firms and branches of national research institutions or research centers from outside is also put forward as policy recommendations in thin RISs (Tödtling and Trippl, 2005). Such initiatives may demand national initiatives, which point to the fact that path renewal and creation in organizationally thin RISs are potentially more reliant on policy interventions than is the case in particular in thick and diversified regions (Dawley, 2014).

4. CONCLUSIONS

This chapter has investigated conceptually the relation between RIS structures and types of regional industrial path development. It has also discussed how policy can influence the direction of economic development in different types of regions. We have drawn a basic distinction between thick and diversified RISs on the one hand and thin RISs and thick and specialized RISs on the other hand. It has been argued that these RIS types support different forms of regional industrial path development. Favorable conditions for path renewal and path creation exist in thick and diversified RISs for reasons often highlighted in the literature on related variety, knowledge spillovers, and academic entrepreneurship. The two other types of RIS structures promote in particular path extension.

The main development challenge for thick and specialized and thin RISs is then to avoid becoming trapped into path extension, which can also lead to path exhaustion. To some extent, the rather opposite challenge is present in thick and diversified RISs. In these regions, a too strong focus on and use of resources for entrepreneurial start-ups and renewal may result in too little knowledge exploitation. Some of the fragmentation of the RIS in various large cities may reflect frequent transformations of the industrial structure, which means that related knowledge bases and knowledge flow between R&D institutions and important firms and regional clusters may not be developed. Even if significant renewal and path creation occur in thick and diversified RISs, path extension may still be a challenge for this type of RIS.

Based on the investigation of how different RIS structures influence the directions of regional change, we discussed which policy approach is required in each of the three RIS types. We recommend regions characterized by organizationally thin RISs to focus on individual firms rather than industries or "systems" when designing their innovation policy. The policy can, in particular, aim to raise the ability of some firms or organizations to act as "gatekeepers". This includes stimulating the absorptive capacity of some firms or organizations so that they are able to bring in knowledge from external sources and to rework and distribute it to other RIS actors.

Regions characterized by thick and specialized RISs ought to increase diversity of knowledge by utilizing extra-regional development impulses. Relevant policies include helping firms to link to extra-regional knowledge sources and to attract firms, education, or research institutions from outside the region. Policy can also promote diversification processes of existing firms into new but related activities and support new firm formation in entirely new industries.

Thick and diversified RISs will, according to our analysis, benefit from "path extension policies." Important is then to stimulate the positive lock-in of regional industries by use of more or less traditional cluster policy tools such as network building to promote knowledge exchange and development of common input factors for firms within an industry. Policy can also contribute to sustaining the regions' capacity for new path development by removing obstacles that hamper new combinations between industries or knowledge bases and by investing in new research areas.

The conceptual analysis leads to some general lessons. One lesson, which is old and well known, includes that regions and RISs are different; they exhibit distinctive development potentials and challenges. This calls for a differentiated policy approach. In spite of being an old lesson, it may remind us of theoretical reflections of path dependence and new path development directly or indirectly build on the situation in dynamic core regions with organizationally thick and diversified RISs. These reflections may overstate the possibilities to achieve path renewal and path creation by means of endogenous resources.

Instead, a second lesson is that path extension prevails for different reasons in most thin, as well as thick and specialized, RISs. These RISs have little related variety due to few, or closely related, organizations and a predominance of bonding social capital.

A strong path extension may, sooner or later, result in stagnation and job loss due to low adaptability of RISs. A third lesson, however, is that weak path extension may also constrain job growth at the regional level. Positive path extension leads to continual development of competence within specific regional industries and value chains, strengthening of RISs, increased competitiveness, and, in sum, possibilities of job growth. Very dynamic thick and diversified RISs may lose these growth triggers from positive path extension.

A fourth lesson is that endogenously created path renewal and path creation rarely occur outside of thick and diversified RIS. This demands exogenous development impulses, in particular, in thin, and in thick and specialized, RISs. These types of RISs are thus more than core regions reliant on policy interventions and extra-regional investments and knowledge sources.

REFERENCES

Asheim, B. T., Boschma, R. and Cooke, P. (2011). Constructing regional advantage. Platform policies based on related variety and differentiated knowledge bases. *Regional Studies*, 45(7), 893–904.

Asheim, B. T., Bugge, M., Coenen, L. and Herstad, S. (2013). *What does evolutionary economic geography bring to the table? Reconceptualising regional innovation systems.* CIRCLE Working Paper no. 2013/05, Circle: Lund University.

Asheim, B., Cooke, P. and Martin, R. (2006). The rise of the cluser concept in regional analysis and policy: A critical assessment. In B. Asheim, P. Cooke and R. Martin (eds.), *Clusters and regional development. Critical reflections and explorations* (1–29). London/New York: Routledge.

Asheim, B. T. and Isaksen, A. (2002). Regional innovation systems: The integration of local 'sticky' and global 'ubiquitous' knowledge. *Journal of Technology Transfer*, 27, 77–86.

Belussi, F. and Sedita, S. R. (2009). Life cycle vs. multiple path dependency in industrial districts. *European Planning Studies*, 17(4), 505–528.

Birch, K., MacKinnon, D. and Cumbers, A. (2010). Old industrial regions in Europe: A comparative assessment of economic performance. *Regional Studies*, 44(1), 35–53.

Boschma, R. (2014a). Towards an evolutionary perspective on regional resilience. Papers in Evolutionary Economic Geography, No. 14.09, Utrecht University.

Boschma, R. (2014b). Constructing regional advantage and smart specialization: Comparison of two European policy concepts. *Scienze Regionali*, 13(1), 51–68.

Boschma, R. and Frenken, K. (2011). Technological relatedness and regional branching. In H. Bathelt, M. P. Feldman and D. F. Kogler (eds.), *Beyond territory. Dynamic geographies of knowledge creation, diffusion, and innovation* (64–81). London and New York: Routledge.

Boschma, R. and Frenken, K. (2011). The emerging empirics of evolutionary economic geography. *Journal of Economic Geography*. Oxford University Press, 11(2), 295–307.

Boschma, R. and Iammarino, S. (2009). Related variety, trade linkages, and regional growth in Italy. *Economic Geography*, 85(3), 289–311.

Cohen, W. M. and Levinthal, D. A. (1990). Absorptive capacity: A new perspective on learning and innovation. *Administrative Science Quarterly*, 35, 128–153.

Dawley, S. (2014). Creating new paths? Offshore wind, policy activism, and peripheral region development. *Economic Geography*, 90(1), 91–112.

Doloreux, D. and Parto, S. (2005). Regional innovation systems: Current discourse and unresolved issues. *Technology in Society*, 27, 133–153.

Eliasson, K., Westlund, H. and Fölster, S. (2013). Does social capital contribute to regional economic growth? Swedish experiences. In H. Westlund and K. Kobayashi (eds.), *Social capital and rural development in the knowledge society* (113–126). Cheltenham: Edward Elgar.

Frenken, K., van Oort, F. and Verburg, T. (2007). Related variety, unrelated variety and regional economic growth. *Regional Studies*, 41, 685–697.

Garud, R., Kumaraswamy, A. and Karnøe, P. (2010). Path dependence or path creation? *Journal of Management Studies*, 47(4), 760–774.

Giuliani, E. and Bell, M. (2005). The micro-determinants of meso-level learning and innovation: Evidence from a Chilean wine cluster. *Research Policy*, 34(1), 47–68.

Grabher, G. (1993). The weakness of strong ties. The lock-in of regional development in the Ruhr area. In G. Grabher (ed.), *The embedded firm. On the socioeconomics of industrial networks* (255–277). London and New York: Routledge.

Hassink, R. (2005). How to unlock regional economies from path dependency? From learning region to learning cluster. *European Planning Studies*, 13(4), 520–535.

Hassink, R. (2010). Locked in decline? On the role of regional lock-ins in old industrial areas. In R. Boschma and R. Martin (eds.), *Handbook of evolutionary economic geography* (450–468). Cheltenham: Edward Elgar.

Hassink, R., Klaerding, C. and Marques, P. (2014). Advancing evolutionary economic geography by engaged pluralism. *Regional Studies* (forthcoming). http://dx.doi.org/10.1080/00343404.2014.889815.

Henning, M., Stam, E. and Wenting, R. (2013). Path dependence research in regional economic development: Cacophony or knowledge accumulation? *Regional Studies*, 47(8), 1348–1362.

Herstad, S. and Ebersberger, B. (2013). On the link between urban location and the involvment of knowledge-Intensive business service firms in collaboration networks. *Regional Studies*, doi: 10.1080/00343404.2013.816413.

Hudson, R. (2005). Rethinking change in old industrial regions: Reflecting on the experiences of North East England. *Environment and Planning A*, 37(4), 581–596.

Isaksen, A. (2014). Industrial development in thin regions: Trapped in path extension? *Accepted in Journal of Economic Geography*, doi: 10.1093/jeg/lbu026.

Isaksen, A. and Karlsen, J. (2013). Can small regions construct regional advantages? The case of four Norwegian regions. *European Urban and regional studies*, 20(2), 243–257.

Jensen, M. B., Johnson, B., Lorenz, E. and Lundvall, B. Å. (2007). Forms of knowledge and modes of innovation. *Research Policy*, 36, 680–693.

Landabaso, M. (2012). What public policies can and connot do for regional development. In P. Cooke, M. D. Parrilli and J. L. Curbelo (eds.), *Innovation, global change and territorial resilience* (364–381). Cheltenham: Edward Elgar.

Lundvall, B.-Å. (2010). Scope, style, and theme of research on knowledge and learning societies. *Journal of the Knowledge Economy*, 1(1), 18–23.

MacKinnon, D. (2012). Beyond strategic coupling: reassessing the firm-region nexus in global production networks. *Journal of Economic Geography*, 12(1), 227–245.

MacKinnon, D., Cumbers, A., Pike, A., Birch, K. and McMaster, R. (2009). Evolution in economic geography: Institutions, political economy and adaptation. *Economic Geography*, 85, 129–150.

Malecki, E. J. (2012). Regional social capital: Why it matters. *Regional Studies*, 46(8), 1023–1039.

Malmberg, A. and Maskell, P. (1997). Towards an explanation of regional specialization and industry agglomeration. *European Planning Studies*, 5, 25–41

Martin, R. (2010). Roepke lecture in economic geography—Rethinking regional path dependence: Beyound lock-in to evolution. *Economic Geography*, 86(1), 1–27.

Martin, R. (2012). (Re)Placing path dependence: A response to the debate. *International Journal of Urban and Regional Research*, 36(1), 179–192.

Martin, R. and Sunley, P. (2006). Path dependence and regional economic evolution. *Journal of Economic Geography*, 64(4), 395–437.

Maskell, P. and Malmberg, A. (1999). Localised learning and industrial competitiveness. *Cambridge Journal of Economics*, 23(2), 167–186.

Monsson, C. K. (2014). Development without a metropolis: Inspiration for non-metropolitan support practices from Denmark. *Local Economy*, Online First Version, doi: 10.1177/0269094214532903.

Morgan, K. (2013). Path dependence and the state. In P. Cooke (ed.), *Re-framing regional development* (318–340). London and New York: Routledge.

Neffke, F., Henning, M. and Boschma, R. (2011). How do regions diversify over time? Industry relatedness and the development of new growth paths in regions. *Economic Geography*, 87(3), 237–265.

OECD. (2014). *Innovation and modernising the rural economy*. Paris: OECD Publishing. http://dx.doi.org/10.1787/9789264205390-en.

Petrov, A. N. (2011). Beyond spillovers. Interrogating innovation and creativity in the peripheries. In H. Bathelt, M. P. Feldman and D. T. Kogler (eds.), *Beyond territory. Dynamic geographies of knowledge creation, diffusion, and innovation* (168–190). London and New York: Routledge.

Pike, A., Birch, K., Cumbers, A., MacKinnon, D. and McMasters R. (2009). A geographical political economy of evolution in economic geography. *Economic Geography*, 85, 175–182.

Rodríguez-Pose, A. (2013). Do institutions matter for regional development? *Regional Studies*, 47(7), 1034–1047.

Roland, G. (2004). Understanding institutional change: Fast-moving and slow-moving institutions. *Studies in Comparative Institutional Development*, 38(4), 109–131.

Setterfield, M. (1998). *Rapid growth and relative decline: Modelling macroeconomic dynamics with hysteresis*. London: Macmillan.

Setterfield, M. (2009). Path dependency, hysteresis and macrodynamics. In P. Arestis and M. Sawyer (eds.), *Path dependency and macroeconomics* (37–79). London: Palgrave Macmillan.

Simmie, J. (2012). Path dependence and new technological path creation in the Danish Wind Power Industry. *European Planning Studies*, 20(5), 753–772.

Simmie, J. and Martin, R. (2010). The economic resilience of regions: Towards an evolutionary approach. *Cambridge Journal of Regions, Economy and Society*, 3(1), 27–43.

Strambach, S. (2010). Path dependence and path placticity: The co-evolution of institutions and innovation—the German customized business software industry. In R. Boschma and R. Martin (eds.), *The handbook of evolutionary economic geography* (406–431). Cheltenham: Edward Elgar.

Sydow, J., Windeler, A., Miiller-Seitz, G. & Lange, K. (2012). Path constitution analysis: A methodology for understanding path dependence and path creation. *Business Research*, 5(2), 155–176.

Tödtling, F. and Trippl, M. (2004). Like phoenix from the ashes? The renewal of clusters in old industrial areas. *Urban Studies*, 41(5–6), 1175–1195.

Tödtling, F. and Trippl, M. (2005). One size fits all? Towards a differentiated regional innovation policy approach. *Research Policy*, 34(8), 1203–1219.

Tödtling, F. and Trippl, M. (2013). Transformation of regional innovation systems: From old leagacies to new development paths. In P. Cooke (ed.), *Reframing regional development* (297–317). London: Routledge.

Trippl, M. and Otto, A. (2009). How to turn the fate of old industrial areas: A comparison of cluster-based renewal processes in Styria and the Saarland. *Environment and Planning A*, 41(5), 1217–1233.

Trippl, M. and Tödtling, F. (2008). Cluster renewal in old industrial areas. In C. Karlsson (ed.), *Handbook of research on cluster theory* (203–218). Cheltenham: Edward Elgar.

Westlund, H. and Kobayashi, K. (2013). Social capital and sustainable urban-rural relationships in the global knowledge society. In H. Westlund and K. Kobayashi (eds.), *Social capital and rural development in the knowledge society* (1–17). Cheltenham: Edward Elgar.

5 Mechanisms of Innovation-Based Cluster Transformation

Zsuzsanna Vincze and Jukka Teräs

1. INTRODUCTION

Clusters are networks of organizations, and their transformation is a collective social phenomenon. Clusters have been defined as "a set of co-located firms operating in related industries" (Gnyawali and Srivastava, 2013). They are agglomerated configurations of companies and institutions with positive externalities that benefit from specialized labor, productive inputs, and knowledge (e.g., Krugman, 1991; Baptista and Swann, 1998; Porter, 1998; Maskell, 2001; Lorenzen, 2005) on the supply side. On the demand side, firms in clusters may take advantage of strong local demand from related industries. Under certain conditions, firms may also benefit from being located close to rivals due to decreased consumer search cost and learning from key users (Porter, 1998). However, clustering does not provide all of these benefits indefinitely. The limits to gaining these benefits relate to congestion and competition effects that arise from input and output markets (Pouder and St. John, 1996; Baptista and Swann, 1998; Maskell and Malmberg, 2007; Delgado et al., 2014) and other changes in the economic and societal environment. Thus clusters need to change over time.

Although researchers have argued that clusters represent a relatively efficient or competitive form of economic organization, the changes in clusters are not well understood. For cluster transformations, the commonly applied life cycle perspective offers little explanation (Lorenzen, 2005; Martin and Sunley, 2011). Taylor (2010) strongly argues for "deeper and more nuanced, and locally and historically sensitive understanding of the processes of local economic growth." His related argument is that to better understand the nature of interorganizational relationships in geographical locations, we need to recognize the variety of mechanisms firms use to cope with change. Martin and Sunley (2011) encourage researchers to develop alternative approaches for cluster development and change. Beyond the weakening factors of the fashionable cluster growth models specified by Taylor (2010), we can also understand the aforementioned calls from the perspective that organizations in the real world are not in different stages but rather are in constant transition. The foundation of organizational life is change (Tsoukas and Chia, 2002). Stability and change are, in fact, different outcomes of the same dynamics (Feldman and Orlikowski, 2011). Change itself is a requirement in the context of dynamic external and internal forces. At the same time, change should create a new state of stability (cf. Farjoun, 2010), which is necessary to sustain an organization (e.g., a cluster). The elements of stability are necessary for the continuity in an organizational environment, as they provide an anchor for change to become effective.

Since the process of the transformation of a cluster depends on agents' perceptions, decisions, and activities, we consider "transformations" to be when people think differently and do things differently. By defining transformative change in this way, we follow Romanelli and Khessina's (2005) argument that cluster development depends on the perceptions of internal and external cluster agents, and that these perceptions influence all kinds of investments. We then contend that changes in mind-sets and behaviors will manifest in the change of a cluster's boundaries and developmental path in relation to environmental changes. The key questions are thus as follows: Which mechanisms are relevant to bring about such changes so that we can explain the phenomenon of cluster transformation? How does the transformation process develop?

Understanding mechanisms—causally linked events that occur repeatedly in real life if certain conditions apply—is crucial for the development of deeper and more fine-grained explanations of dynamic social phenomena (Astbury and Leeuw, 2010). On various levels of aggregation, cluster transformation may evolve as a consequence of the interaction between mechanisms and other entities operating at different levels of reality.

In the relevant literature on organization, network, innovation, and clusters, we identify several social mechanisms, such as situational and action-formation mechanisms (Hedström and Swedberg, 1998, Hedström and Ylikoski, 2010). Illustrated by the in-depth analysis of the Örnsköldsvik biorefinery and the Oulu information and communication technology (ICT) cluster cases presented in this chapter, we propose various transformational mechanisms (Hedström and Swedberg, 1998, Hedström and Ylikoski, 2010) that help explain the transformation of the two clusters.

This chapter is structured as follows. First, our literature review accounts for elements of mechanisms potentially relevant for explaining cluster transformation. The methodology section briefly describes the empirical data collection and analysis. The following section provides an analysis of two case studies in order to illustrate the proposed transformational mechanisms. The discussion section elaborates on the novel, context-relevant cluster transformation framework.

2. LITERATURE REVIEW

2.1 Applied Typology of Mechanisms

We are aware that the explanation of the complex transformation phenomenon may involve many mechanisms on different levels. Therefore, we adopt the established typology of mechanisms developed by Hedström and

Swedberg (1998). This typology of mechanisms is the most often adopted in social scientific analyses (Mayntz, 2004: 249). We use it here to build up the web of mechanisms in the case of cluster transformations and to interpret how *the macrolevel transformation* can be explained. We focus on explaining the macrolevel transformation as the *explanandum* in the cluster cases. Our prerequisite of explanation is to build up the web of mechanisms relevant to the context rather than summing up from the lower-level mechanisms to the higher-level mechanisms. In applying Hedström and Swedberg's (1998) typology (Figure 5.1), the following definitions are provided for three kinds of mechanisms:

- *Situational mechanisms* (macro-micro, arrow 1 in Figure 5.1) are related to the individual or group of people and the economic and sociocultural conditions that form an individual's beliefs and desires (e.g., time). This definition will guide our literature search for internal and external forces and agents' goals.
- *Action-formation mechanisms* (micro-micro, arrow 2 in Figure 5.1) link the beliefs and desires of individuals with action. For us, this means that we need to link the agents' goals with their actions. In this chapter, we argue for three types of action (exchange, learning, and networking) that are linked with the agents' goals (the micro part of situational mechanisms).
- *Transformational mechanisms* (micro-macro, arrow 3 in Figure 5.1) generate the intended and unintended social outcomes. This chapter focuses on transformational mechanisms. In this study, the social outcome is the transformation of the cluster (as defined qualitatively based on mind-set and behavioral changes), irrespective of whether the transformation is partial or full or intended or not; in other words, whether it is planned or emerged.

We highlight the following three transformational mechanisms: changes in the knowledge base, changes in the business model, and changes in the

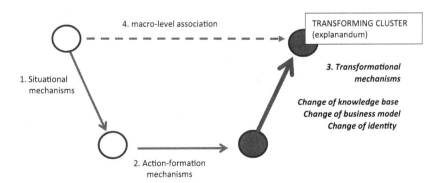

Figure 5.1 Typology of Social Mechanisms

organizational identity. The three transformational mechanisms are based on relevant literature and are empirically examined via in-depth analyses of the two cluster cases.

2.2 Triggers of Change and Situational and Action-Formation Mechanisms

Before focusing on the key issue of this chapter, i.e., transformational mechanisms, we briefly review potential situational and action-formation mechanisms (Hedström and Swedberg, 1998; Hedström and Ylikoski, 2010) in the relevant literature.

Although precisely how clusters change is not well understood, we can still find literature about the triggers of changes in clusters. Triggers of changes may be read interchangeably with the determinants or forces of such changes. They can also be understood as economic and sociocultural conditions that form the beliefs and desires of individuals and/or groups of people. In the literature on clusters, these triggers are either seen by focusing on exogenous factors or on endogenous factors (Lorenzen, 2005). Triggers of changes may be identified in changes in cost structures and technologies (Asheim and Coenen, 2005) that apply across geographical spaces. Cluster change can be triggered by changes in trade flows. Political powers and trade regimes may lock regions into particular trade and development patterns (Grabher 1993, see also Tödtling and Trippl, 2005 and Trippl and Otto, 2009), and they may change as a result of multinational enterprises' (MNE) global movements (e.g., McCann and Arita and Gordon, 2002). The institutional tradition offers various explanations for change based on differences among institutional infrastructures and institutional changes (North, 1997). Although the treatment of entrepreneurial processes and the "chaotic" concept of social capital in cluster models can be criticized (Taylor, 2010), change in clusters may be triggered by the endogenous factors of social capital, entrepreneurs, and strategic alliances (business or institutional/political) that are opting for collective efficiency (Storper and Venables, 2002). Entrepreneurship is essentially linked to cluster development because entrepreneurship provides evolutionary and constructive forces (Sölvell et al., 2003). One of the roles of entrepreneurs is to promote the coordination of activities in complex economic systems (Casson and Della Giusta, 2007).

The results of cluster change are measured quantitatively (e.g., European Cluster Observatory, 2015). Indicators such as the number of companies (entry-exit), turnover, or export of the cluster companies, regional GDP, employment rates, and measures of living standards do not, however, tell much about whether we observe mere incremental or more significant transformational development of clusters. We agree with Lorenzen (2005) in that numbers as outcomes do not help much in explaining the process of transformation. We should understand better *how* companies, institutions, and externalities entering and/or exiting clusters bring about changes of mind-sets and behavior, which will later be apparent in the new boundaries and developmental trajectories of clusters.

In light of Hedström and Swedberg's (1998) definitions of the mechanism categories, these triggers are important for tracing situational mechanisms. The aforementioned exogenous and endogenous forces can be seen as part of situational mechanisms because they may work as the macro part in situational mechanisms. Thinking in terms of the theoretical methodology (section 2.1) mentioned earlier, the intended and emergent outcomes help us to trace the goals of agents. From the aforementioned quantitative measures of cluster change, it is clear that one of the goals has to be concerned with the economic success of the cluster. Other goals may need to be considered in terms of the "triple bottom line." Beyond economic measures, businesses and other organizations need to focus on the environmental and social cost of their actions and evaluate the impact of their environmental and social efforts (Gimenez et al., 2012). Logically, these goals may be included in the micro part of situational mechanisms in Hedström and Swedberg's (1998) typology. As mechanisms always produce something (Pajunen, 2008), the logical starting point of this analysis will be the goals of cluster agents, as their goals come into play over time. This is essentially an exercise to match internal and external factors and members' goals. Based on matching these goals, we argue that we should be able to see the interdependencies of the activities carried out in the action-formation mechanisms.

Forces and outcomes as such do not explain the transformation. We need to search for actions that link the forces to outcomes. Derived from the generally accepted understanding of what clusters are and what they do (section 1), the starting point for this search is that both the economic and the learning aspects of clusters need to be accounted for (Krugman, 1991; Lundwall, 1992; Sorenson, 2003; Asheim and Coenen, 2005; Gnyawali and Srivastava, 2013). The organizations in a cluster are linked by the value chains through exchanges and by the interactive learning processes. There is a general agreement that innovations are the drivers of change and the engines of growth (Schumpeter, 1934, 1942). Innovation is a process that is essentially based on knowledge and networks. Indeed, in the innovation literature, a strong consensus prevails that firms, independent of size and sector, benefit from cooperation with each other. In such a collaborative environment, internal and external resources, knowledge, and competences are combined and re-combined (Ahuja, 2000; Bessant and Tidd, 2007). Firms enter into relationships with partners who possess complementary resources and capabilities. This is particularly important in order to cope with environmental uncertainty and constraints (Gnyawali and Srivastava, 2013). The benefits of networking include increased innovation capacity and performance.

Activities that relate to the agents' goals are the actual action-formation mechanisms (Arrow 2, Figure 5.1). Action-formation mechanisms bring new types of companies, institutions, and positive externalities to clusters such that new cumulative causation will occur. These changes maintain and/or transform cluster boundaries and development paths.

Based on the literature review presented so far, we argue that the situational and action-formation mechanisms can be categorized as follows (Table 5.1).

While we describe (in the empirical section) the similarities and differences in terms of situational and action-formation mechanisms between the Örnsköldsvik and Oulu clusters, a more systematic analysis of why these differences and similarities exist may require further study. Nevertheless, our framework advocates for a tight connection between these two categories of mechanisms through identifiable cluster goals.

Table 5.1   Categories of Situational and Action-Formation Mechanisms

Mechanism categories	Higher-order categories
Situational mechanisms(macro)	Internal forces (social capital, entrepreneurship, and strategic alliance)
	External forces (cost structure, technology, trade flow, political power, MNE, institutions)
Situational mechanisms(micro)	Goals (economic and others)
Action-formation mechanisms(micro)	Goals (economic and others)
Action-formation mechanisms(micro)	Exchange
	Learning
	Networking

2.3 Transformational Mechanisms

In our view, transformational mechanisms have to match with the idea of the duality of change and that both the value chain and interactive learning processes link the organizations to each other. When we look at change as it unfolds, we also need to take into account that change may be essential in order to promote stability and that stability may be essential to bring about change (Tsoukas and Chia, 2002; Farjoun, 2010; Feldman and Orlikowski, 2011). While the lack of change leads to entropy, change pursued by agents also creates stability, which is necessary to sustain a cluster. With these considerations in mind, we highlight three potential transformational mechanisms: change in the knowledge base, change in the business model, and change of identity. The selection of these three transformational mechanisms is supported by the literature as follows.

2.3.1 Change in the Knowledge Base

Innovation is based on the accumulation, flow, and utilization of knowledge; furthermore, it plays a central role in cluster change. We therefore suggest that the action-formation mechanisms need to include the generation and use of new knowledge through exploration and exploitation processes (March, 1991). That is, the change in the knowledge base is essentially a transformational mechanism. Thus answering the question of what kind of knowledge base the cluster relies on over time is a central issue. It can be further argued that innovation will remain latent unless and until the specific innovation can be successfully matched with a suitable business model (Chesborough, 2010, Teece, 2010).

2.3.2 Change in the Business Model

The business model has been described as the link between innovation and value creation (Chesbrough and Rosenbloom, 2002) as well as the cognitive link between entrepreneurial appraisal of an opportunity and its exploitation (Fiet and Patel, 2008). The underlying opportunity and the business model are interconnected, while the business model may be an important link between innovation and organizational structure (George and Bock, 2011). The business model describes the business as a system and examines how all the components of the system fit together. Business models are important in translating resources into economic value. Similarly (Porter, 1990; Richardson, 2008), the questions regarding clusters as a whole are as follows: What value does the cluster propose? How does the cluster create and deliver that value? How does the business model generate revenues and profit? Change in such a value system essentially happens by eliminating players, adding players, and changing the functions of certain players (Magretta, 2002).

We see that the change in the business model may be a relevant transformational mechanism because "a business model depicts the content, structure, and governance of transactions designed so as to create value through the exploitation of business opportunities" (Amit and Zott, 2001: 493). Furthermore, such a change establishes the context and boundaries for activities and processes associated with resource and capability development. Business models can be seen as boundary-spanning activity systems, linking the different components within an organization and shedding light on the dynamics of how this is done (Zott et al., 2011). Taking business models as transformational mechanisms, the focus is on answering the question of how the cluster is organized and doing business over time.

2.3.3 Change of Identity

Organizational identity is a useful concept to establish whether an organization at one point is the same during another point. Identity is deeply embedded and inextricable from organizational routines, practices, knowledge, skills, capabilities, and distinctive competencies. While it is a socially constructed cognitive category, identity helps make sense and explain action as it serves as a perceptual screen or filter that influences how organizational members process and interpret issues (Gioia et al., 2013). Identity is essential to any member of society, including individuals, organizations, and nations. Identity has features that provide continuity over time based on what is central to the organization's character in the eyes of the organizational members. The organization's identity also distinguishes it from other similar organizations (Fiol and Romenelli, 2012; Gioia et al., 2013). It manifests as key values, history, labels, products, services, or practices. Identity codes may parsimoniously describe and maintain cluster boundaries (Romanelli and Khessina, 2005), while influencing the developmental capacities of regions through informing understandings and directing geographical targets of investments. Since we adhere to the duality of change and a dynamic perspective, we thus propose that change in the cluster's identity is a transformational mechanism. Essentially, identity change (as a transformational mechanism) answers the question of what the cluster becomes over time.

Here we propose transformational mechanisms in the form of knowledge base, business model, and identity changes. The three transformational mechanisms and their links to situational and action-formation mechanisms, on the one hand, and their links to changes in mind-set and behavior, on the other, are the focus of the empirical analysis. We believe that with these three suggested transformational mechanisms (Table 5.2), we can explain the changes in mind-set and behavior as they appear in changes of boundaries and developmental paths, i.e., the transformation of a cluster.

Table 5.2   Transformational Mechanisms in Cluster Transformation

Transformational mechanisms (micro)	Higher-order categories Knowledge base Business model Identity
The phenomenon we explain (macro)	Cluster transformation (change of mind-sets and behaviors)

3. METHODOLOGY

Our empirical methodology is a longitudinal case study. The selected regional knowledge-intensive clusters have undergone a period of change long enough to be properly analyzed. The cluster analysis is based on theoretical considerations presented earlier in this chapter. With the case study approach, we adhere to the perspective that cluster transformation is a social process, which is deeply embedded in time and the contexts that produce and are produced by time and context (Pettigrew, 1997; Taylor, 2010).

Complexities are evident in the cluster and its constituting parts (section 4). We focus on the perspective of the cluster management organizations that arguably play an important role in intermediating innovation processes (Lefebvre 2013). From this perspective, the cluster members' individual goals (i.e., other than common cluster goals shared by the cluster members) have to be considered as internal forces. We combine various types of data, which enhance the opportunity to study cluster change (Yin, 1994, Siggelkow, 2007).

We consider two particular clusters in Sweden and Finland that are appropriate for this chapter, because the changes in these regional clusters have been documented extensively. The data are accessible and transparent to enhance rich case description, which is essential for theory development (Eisenhardt, 1989; Langley, 1999, 2009; Eisenhardt and Graebner, 2007).

From 2007 onward, we have collected retrospective and real-time data (Bizzi and Langley, 2012) both in Örnsköldsvik and in Oulu, resulting in more than 300 transcribed pages of interview material and data from focus group sessions with key decision makers from various cluster organizations. The interviews helped in terms of triangulating and assigning meaning to the different objective and subjective realities that influenced the cluster development. We obtained rich secondary data too (i.e., cluster company websites, public presentations, industry analysts, business historians, and journalists). Moreover, we have had numerous meetings with key individuals from the cluster actors in Örnsköldsvik and Oulu. The Swedish biorefinery cluster in Örnsköldsvik has attracted considerable research attention (Arbuthnott et al., 2010; Peterson, 2011; Coenen et al., 2012; Coenen et al., 2013; Nicol, 2013). In Oulu, the ICT cluster has already been studied by several researchers (e.g., Männistö, 2002, Hyry, 2005, Teräs, 2008, Teräs and Ylinenpää, 2012). The earlier research studies are used as references for our work.

Following Van de Ven and Engleman's (2004), Van de Ven and Poole's (2005) and Langley's (2009) methodological considerations for process theory development, the data collected were categorized to account for events within the selected time periods and to identify processes that depart from these events. Based on this type of organization of data, we are able to search for mechanisms of cluster transformation (Table 5.1 in section 2.2 and Table 5.2 in section 2.3.3). The results of this process are reported in the following section, and the insights gained are further discussed in light of the relevance of our propositions and the mechanism-based explanation as a whole.

4. ANALYSIS AND RESULTS

This section provides the analysis of the transforming case study clusters in 2000–2012. First, we describe the Örnsköldsvik and Oulu cases with their specific features, which are relevant in terms of cluster boundaries and the conditions (i.e., the limits) of the mechanisms-based explanations. The aim of these descriptions is also to highlight the overarching transformation in terms of the selected transformational mechanisms. Second, we introduce the key events that provide us with time periods in order to systematically elaborate on the proposed transformational mechanisms in each cluster. This requires the identification of the specific cluster goals and their attainment in light of changing internal and external forces and actions. Our aim is to answer the following questions for each period: Why did the specific goals develop? Which factors forced the development of the new goals (internally and externally)? Which actions were taken to reach the goals? What is happening in terms of the selected transformational mechanisms to drive the changes toward the goals?

4.1 Örnsköldsvik and Oulu Clusters: An Overview

The Örnsköldsvik biorefinery cluster is located on the northeastern coastline of Sweden. Some of the cluster firms have a long history of more than 150 years of industrial and technological change that has influenced their approach to doing business. The process that changed the paper and pulp conglomerate into an evolving biorefinery cluster is the focus of our study. Throughout their history, many of the core firms that are currently part of the cluster were integrated in one corporation. The cluster encompasses different qualities of corporate boundaries and power inequalities (Taylor, 2010): on the one hand, the boundaries and power imbalances are reminiscent of transacting value-chain partners, and on the other hand, they resemble intra-organizational units, which are coordinated by a commonly owned cluster management company (Zettinig and Vincze, 2012). The biorefinery cluster can be classified as a sectoral system of innovation (Malerba, 2004). Firms have wood as common input and their production relies on the core processes in Domsjö Fabriker (DF), but their outputs are heterogeneous. The cluster has changed its market orientation, business models, and structure a number of times during its recent history, while the enduring identity is that of a biorefinery since 2003.

The main products of the Örnsköldsvik site during the 1990s were paper pulp and ethanol. However, the annual production of paper pulp gradually decreased from 150,000 tons in 1990 to 25,000 tons in 2005 and then stopped entirely. During the same period the production of specialty cellulose increased from 100,000 tons in 1995 to 255,000 tons by 2010. Since it was founded in 2000, the lead company, Domsjö Fabriker, has invested a total of Swedish Krona (SEK) 1.5 billion in the expansion of Sweden's first biorefinery for the production of specialty cellulose, lignin, bioethanol, methane, bio-resins, and carbon dioxide (Johard, 2011). Sweden's innovation agency (VINNOVA) provides six million SEK annually through the Biorefinery of the Future project, and regional actors invest an equal amount to match this funding. An extra 12 million SEK per year has been supplied from EU structural funds, member companies, public and private research funds (regional and national), and FP7 and other EU sources (Lindberg and Teräs, 2014). In 2014, the biorefinery cluster association had 21 members. The average yearly turnover of the cluster management organization (SP Processum) has been 23.5 million SEK. All their activities are devoted to bio-refining R&D and cluster development.

As Coenen et al. (2013) noted, the biorefinery initiative relied on the combination of forestry, energy, specialty chemicals, and biotechnology over the past 15 years. In terms of change in the knowledge bases, the paper and pulp and energy industries have long been in close alignment as large-scale process industries that both drew on synthetic knowledge bases and could quickly adopt IT in the 1990s. Biotechnology and specialty chemicals, which rely on the analytic knowledge basis, entered the cluster more recently.

In detecting the proposed transformational mechanism, this overview identifies knowledge base changes as the cluster moved from the paper and pulp industry to biorefinery. The new independence from the large paper and pulp conglomerate, ownership changes, and the new type of coordination by the commonly owned cluster management organization all indicate business model changes at the cluster level. These changes also show the transformation to a new, common cluster identity.

The Oulu ICT cluster is located in North Finland on the east coast of the Gulf of Bothnia. The Oulu ICT cluster experienced extraordinary growth in the 1990s and early 2000s, largely due to the success of the locomotive company Nokia. The number of ICT cluster jobs in the Oulu region rose rapidly up to more than 15,000 jobs in 2000 (City of Oulu Planning Department, 2007). The rapid conversion of the Oulu region from a traditional industrial region into an internationally known center of advanced technologies and world-class companies has been labeled as the *Oulu Phenomenon*. The growth of the ICT cluster stagnated, however, in the 2000s. The previous role of Nokia as the locomotive company in the regional ICT cluster has diminished in the Oulu region, due to Nokia making continuous reductions in the local labor force with further negative effects on the subcontractors.

In the 2000s, the Oulu ICT cluster was led by Nokia heading the local subcontracting network, research institutions (key institutions included University of Oulu, University of Oulu Applied Sciences, and VTT Technical Research Centre of Finland), and public sector actors such as the City of Oulu and the Council of Oulu Region, banks, venture capitalists, and intermediary organizations (e.g., Technopolis technology park). Until the 2000s, the Oulu cluster was propelled by the "Oulu Spirit," which is a sort of solidarity and cooperative willingness across the cluster actors, including strong leadership and Technopolis as the cluster motor. However, the "Oulu Spirit" of cooperation diminished between 2000 and 2010. The role of Technopolis as a cluster motor in Oulu diminished largely due to a strategy change at Technopolis to become a national actor.

The major change in the knowledge base took place in the second half of the twentieth century (i.e., the "Oulu Phenomenon"). There have been recent attempts to diversify from the ICT knowledge base toward other sectors, e.g., environmental technology and mining technology. The changes in the business model of the Oulu ICT cluster are related to both the changes in Nokia and its subcontracting network, and the public-private initiatives to promote, catalyze, and coordinate the cluster development. Changes in cluster identity can be detected with mental mind-set changes and attempts related to, e.g., cluster branding.

4.2 Transformational Mechanisms in the Örnsköldsvik Cluster, 2000–2011

Time Period 1 (2000–2003)

During the first period, the main goal was renewal and securing sustainable businesses in the Örnsköldsvik site. The main events of the first period included, for instance, the change of ownership at the lead company Domsjö Fabriker AB (DF), the establishment of the independent research institute MoRe in 2001, and the Technology Science Park initiative. DF has a very dynamic recent history because of frequent ownership changes. These shifts of ownership have systemic implications for other cluster members and the cluster as a whole. Restructuring of the cluster was possible based on the accumulated experience of 100 years, competences, and passion for searching new and better solutions. Transformation was carried out with restructuring and provided the opportunity to develop new ideas.

Time Period 2 (2003–2009)

During the second period, the main events were the downsizing of the local activities of the Finnish owner in Örnsköldsvik and actually selling the paper and pulp mill. Then portfolio investors came in to save DF, with the idea of rebranding and selling it as soon as possible. Fluctuation of global oil prices regulations affecting renewable energy and sustainable businesses in the country and the EU are constant external forces impacting the Örnsköldsvik cluster. Toward the end of the period, the global decline of cotton production and the financial crisis affected the cluster. An important internal force was DF's new commitment to the production of dissolving cellulose and related products.

The local technology park was in place in 2003. The goals included differentiation from other science parks in Northern Sweden. The focus on member companies and their interest set in motion several processes; for example, assessing external financial resources that enabled a balance between those who can provide viability through exploitation of knowledge-generating revenues (March, 1991), while also engaging in developing a number of new trajectories exploring new knowledge for future opportunities (e.g., cooperation with regional universities). Balancing exploration and exploitation of knowledge is a sign of continuous change in the cluster knowledge base. "Processum," the cluster management organization, assumed a bridging role between the member companies while finding and working on common challenges. The cluster changed its business model (i.e., how it related to companies and other stakeholders) and reformulated its identity from a technology park focused on the process industry to a biorefinery cluster process industry technology park to a biorefinery cluster. The aforementioned new processes affected the perceived boundaries of cluster firms (Zettinig and Vincze, 2012). In terms of changing the common identity from a technology park to the biorefinery cluster initiative, the argument was to avoid competition with neighboring cities, which at that time also pursued the science park hype. The establishment of the cluster management organization was an evident structural change, while it redefined what businesses the cluster was in and assisted in new openings.

Time Period 3 (2009–2011)

By the third period, the global recession had begun to affect the cluster. The cluster was further affected by the fluctuation of crude oil and dissolving cellulose prices and an unfavorable shift of interest in Swedish politics. Internally, the CEO of the cluster management organization had changed; however, the focus on biorefinery development, the active cooperation and growth of the cluster, and the cluster management organization continued. The number of employees in the cluster management organization grew from 4 to 17 and initiated and implemented 130 R&D projects since 2008. The commercialization of research and creation and scaling up the new biorefinery industries were the new objectives during this period. The goal of pursuing open innovation has facilitated closer collaboration and emphasized intrapreneurship in the cluster. A lot of learning in the form of incoming new research projects and networking among the most active cluster member organizations and between external constituents (e.g., politicians) characterize this period.

Time Period 4 (2011 Onward)

In 2009, the DF investors (who took over from the Finnish company) wanted to capitalize on their investment. They realized that their financial capacities were neither sufficient for capturing the booming dissolving cellulose market nor to really benefit from potentially positive long-term developments. Political influences were also at play, thereby increasing uncertainties in the long-term development of producing and marketing alternative energy and fuel. Preparations were made to begin selling DF shares, but the plan changed when an Indian MNE made a winning bid to take over the firm. DF is now again part of an MNE, which requires exploiting the certainties of the MNE (the bulk of dissolving cellulose). While the Indian owner brought in financial security, it caused some uncertainty in terms of the continuation of the biorefinery focus. At the same time, learning processes and networking grew partially with the goal of inspiring the Indian owner to learn the work in a cluster structure and, more specifically, in a Triple Helix model.

4.3 Transformational Mechanisms in the Oulu Cluster, 2000–2011

Time Period 1 (2000–2004)

The number of ICT cluster jobs in the Oulu region increased rapidly to more than 15,000 jobs in 2000 (City of Oulu Planning Department, 2007). However, the first signs of the potential slowdown of the development of the Oulu ICT cluster were also seen at that time. The goal of the ICT cluster was to maintain its strong international position and competitiveness, but some attempts were made to diversify into other technology areas, such as the Oulu Growth Agreement 2002. The indisputable role of Technopolis Science Park as the coordinator of the ICT-driven, high-technology cluster diminished, largely due to Technopolis expanding its activities into other national technology concentrations in Finland. Moreover, the former "Oulu Spirit," a local solidarity and cooperative willingness of the cluster actors, started to gradually dilute. Regarding transformational mechanisms in 2000–2004 in Oulu, there was a consensus on the importance of accumulated knowledge based on wireless technologies and the advanced regional ICT development infrastructure. Local and regional actors appreciated the business model of the Oulu ICT cluster as a forerunner of the structural change in industries, despite the changed role of Technopolis as the central figure. Regarding the cluster identity, it was mentioned by several informants that the practices of former university students taking over business and research in Oulu were changing.

Time Period 2 (2004–2008)

The Oulu region started gradually losing ICT jobs in 2004–2008. The expertise of the Oulu region was, however, still recognized by international experts. A growing number of actors in the Oulu ICT cluster sensed an increasing "satellite-unit-only" attitude toward Oulu, with fewer investments in knowledge bases. It was evident that the locomotive company Nokia decreased its relative importance in Oulu. New regional innovation strategies were launched, such as "Oulu Inspires Innovation Strategy 2007–2013," to promote new entrepreneurship and innovations. Moreover, the Board of the City of Oulu nominated a Triple Helix Committee in 2007 to further develop the innovation system in Oulu. However, the ICT cluster experienced a lack of strong leadership. Regarding the knowledge base, the former indisputable belief in the strength of the ICT expertise inside Oulu showed some signs of weakening despite positive external reviews of the knowledge base of the Oulu ICT cluster. Regarding the business model, the decreased importance of Nokia as the locomotive company in the Oulu ICT cluster resulted in discussion and initiatives to create new businesses and diminish the dependence on only a few companies. However, there was still the belief in the regional innovation system among regional actors, which was created during the "Oulu Phenomenon." According to informants, the identity of the Oulu ICT cluster was questioned by some regional actors in the period 2004–2008, based on critiques that it was staying too long in the comfort zone of former success.

Time Period 3 (2008–2011)

During the period 2008–2011, the previous leading role of Nokia in the ICT cluster in Oulu continued to diminish. Nokia Mobile Phones decreased its number of employees in Oulu from 2,500 to 1,300 in 2009–2011. These job cuts had a negative effect on the ICT subcontractors in the region. The diversification attempts of the region´s expertise into other sectors were not able to start significant new development cycles. A special program referred to as "Bridge" was launched in Oulu in 2011 to help Nokia experts who had lost their jobs in Oulu to find new jobs. According to the informants of this study, both the brain drain of talented ICT experts and the role of the university in building up the future knowledge base were increasingly discussed in the region. The changed role of Nokia had transformed the ICT business model based on a strong ICT company assisted by local subcontractors. Regarding the cluster identity, city branding and high-technology branding started to become a serious issue.

Time Period 2011 Onward

The Nokia-driven era of the ICT cluster in Oulu experienced a big change in 2013 when Nokia announced that it was going to sell the mobile phone unit to Microsoft. Later, Microsoft announced the closure of the unit in Oulu. The NSN Nokia-Siemens Networks Unit in Oulu, however, has since increased its labor force to 2,600 jobs. The Business Oulu, a unit of the City of Oulu, has taken over as the leading actor in promoting Oulu as a high-technology city and in catalyzing new public-private partnerships. New business and start-up programs have been initiated in the last few years to pave the way for a "renaissance" of the "Oulu Phenomenon." Regarding the knowledge base, the former self-confidence of the cluster actors in the excellence of the cluster has diminished. The business model, based on technology developed in Oulu, faced increasing doubts, as did the cluster leadership. Regarding the cluster identity, the critiques of the unwillingness to change have been clearly identified.

5. DISCUSSION AND CONCLUDING REMARKS

The analysis of the Örnsköldsvik and Oulu clusters confirms that the three suggested transformational mechanisms (knowledge base, business model, and identity) were identified in the dynamic evolution of the selected clusters. In both cases, we were able to identify each of the three transformational mechanisms throughout the various periods of the cluster evolution. Based on our analysis, the three suggested transformational mechanisms are able to capture at least the main features of social outcomes, irrespective of whether the transformation is partial or full or if it was intended or unintended. The transformation of our Nordic, technology-oriented clusters' transformation may differ significantly from other clusters especially in terms of lower-level mechanisms (every cluster transforms in its own unique manner).

This chapter does not provide a full explanation of social mechanisms related to cluster change. Some of the key issues that remain to be studied include the following. First, the linkages of transformational mechanisms to situational and action-formation mechanisms need to be revealed. The illustration presented in Figure 5.1 indicates that an "isolated" analysis of transformational mechanisms only is not sufficient as it must be completed with the analysis and linkages related to situational and action-formation mechanisms. Second, the selection of transformational mechanisms requires further effort. Despite the fact that the analysis of case studies in this chapter was able to verify the three transformational mechanisms, the potential existence of additional mechanisms deserves further attention.

In this chapter, we have taken a process perspective (Gioia et al., 2013) and focused on a historically and locally relevant understanding of transformation (Taylor, 2010). Importantly, the three transformational mechanisms suggested in this chapter match the idea of the duality of change (Farjoun, 2010, see section 1) and that the organizations are linked to each other by both the value chain and the interactive learning processes (e.g., Lundvall, 1992). We believe that with this conceptualization, we are able to explain how changes in mind-set and behavior are expressed as changes of boundaries and developmental paths (i.e., transformation of a cluster).

Our approach provides an attempt to complement the analysis of cluster change with mechanisms. The typology of social mechanisms adopted in this chapter to analyze change in regional clusters adds to the relatively few attempts in the literature to understand cluster transformation. The conceptualization, which is based on mechanisms, provides novel insights regarding why and how clusters' agents generate intended and unintended outcomes, while transforming toward more sustainable development. This lays strong foundations for future theoretical and empirical research and also benefits managers and policy-makers in understanding the transformation of clusters. With the novel form of theory building with social and economic mechanisms, we are better able to provide context-relevant explanations of economic and social changes, while avoiding some of the major limitations of the typical policy prescriptions for cluster models.

ACKNOWLEDGMENTS

The authors gratefully acknowledge the funding from the Academy of Finland for the CluTra project (No: 138835) to which this chapter contributes at the Turku School of Economics/University in Turku, Finland.

REFERENCES

Ahuja, G. (2000). The duality of collaboration: Inducements and opportunities in the formation of inter-firm linkages. *Strategic Management Journal*, 21(3), 317–343.

Amit, R. and Zott, C. (2001). Value creation in e-business. *Strategic Management Journal*, 22(6/7), 493–520.

Arbuthnott, A., Eriksson, J. and Wincent, J. (2010). When a new industry meets traditional and declining ones: An integrative approach towards dialectics and social movement theory in a model of regional industry emergence processes. *Scandinavian Journal of Management*, 26(3), 290–308.

Asheim, B. T. and Coenen, L. (2005). Knowledge bases and regional innovation systems: Comparing nordic clusters. *Research Policy*, 34, 1173–1190.

Astbury, B. and Leeuw, F. L. (2010). Unpacking black boxes: Mechanisms and theory building in evaluation. *American Journal of Evaluation*, 31(3), 363–381.

Baptista, R. and Swann, P. (1998). Do firms in clusters innovate more? *Research Policy*, 27, 525–540.

Bessant, J. and Tidd, J. (2007). *Innovation and entrepreneurship*. Chichester: John Wiley & Sons.

Bizzi, L. and Langley, A. (2012). Studying processes in and around networks. *Industrial Marketing Management*, 41, 224–234.

Casson, M. and Della Guista, M. (2007). Entrepreneurship and social capital: Analysing the impact of social networks on entrepreneurial activity from a rational action perspective. *International Small Business Journal*, 25(3), 220–244.

Chesbrough, H. (2010). Business model innovation: Opportunities and barriers. *Long Range Planning*, 43, 354–363.

Chesbrough, H. and Rosenbloom, R. S. (2002). The role of the business model in capturing value from innovation: Evidence from Xerox Corporation's technology spin-off companies. *Industrial and Corporate Change*, 11, 529–555.

City of Oulu Planning Department (2007). Oulun seudun elinkeinorakenne 1996-2006-2020 (In Finnish only). *Oulun kaupunkisuunnitteluvirasto*. Series A187. ISSN0357-8194. Oulu.

Coenen, L., Moodysson, J. and Martin, H. (2013). *Renewal of mature industry in an old industrial region: Regional innovation policy and the co-evolution of institutions and technology*, Paper no. 2013/07, CIRCLE, Lund University, Sweden.

Coenen, L., Moodysson, J. and Westendorf, H. (2012). *Bridging science and traditional industry: Institutional change for emergent biorefinery technologies*. Paper presented at the AAG Annual Meeting, New York, February 24–28.

Delgado, M., Porter, M. E. and Stern, S. (2014). Clusters, convergence, and economic performance. *Research Policy*, 43(10), 1785–1799.

Eisenhardt, K. M. (1989). Building theories from case study research. *Academy of Management Review*, 14, 532–550.

Eisenhardt, K. M. and Graebner, M. E. (2007). Theory building from cases, opportunities and challenges. *Academy of Management Journal*, 50(1), 25–32.

European Cluster Observatory. (2015). www.clusterobservatory.eu.

Farjoun, M. (2010). Beyond dualism; stability and change as a duality. *Academy of Management Review*, 35(2), 202–225.

Feldman, M. S. and Orlikowski, W. J. (2011). Theorizing practice and practicing theory. *Organization Science*, 22(5), 1240–1253.

Fiet, J. O. and Patel, P. C. (2008). Forgiving business models for new ventures. *Entrepreneurship Theory and Practice*, 32(4), 749–761.

Fiol, M. C. and Romanelli, E. (2012). Before identity: The emergence of new organizational forms. *Organization Science*, 23(3), 597–611.

George, G. P. and Bock, A. J. (2011). The business model in practice and its implications for entrepreneurship research. *Entrepreneurship Theory & Practice*, 35, 83–111.

Gimenez, C., Sierra, V. and Rodon, J. (2012). Maximizing the triple bottom line through spiritual leadership. *Organizational Dynamics*, 37(1), 86–96.

Gioia, D. A., Patvardhan, S. D., Hamilton, A. L. and Corley, K. G. (2013). Organizational identity formation and change. *The Academy of Management Annals*, 7(1), 123–193.

Gnyawali, D. R. and Srivastava, M. K. (2013). Complementary effects of clusters and networks on firm innovation: A conceptual model. *Journal of Engineering and Technology Management*, 30, 1–20.

Grabher, G. (1993). The weakness of strong ties: The lock-in of regional development in the Ruhr area. In G. Grabher (ed.), *The embedded firm. On the socioeconomics of industrial networks* (255–276). London: Routledge.

Hedström, P. and Swedberg, R. (1998). Social mechanisms: An introductory essay. In P. Hedström and R. Swedberg (eds.), *Social mechanisms. An analytical approach to social theory* (1–31). Cambridge: Cambridge University Press.

Hedström, P. and Ylikoski, P. (2010). Causal mechanisms in social sciences. *Annual Review of Sociology*, 36, 49–67.

Hyry, M. (2005). *Industrial growth and development in Northern Finland: The case of Oulu 1970–2002*. A thesis for the Degree of Doctor of philosophy. Coventry Business School, Coventry University.

Johard, C. (2011). *Domsjö Fabriker—The success story continues, SPCI*. Stockholm, Sweden.

Krugman, P. (1991). *Geography and trade*. Belgium, Leuven: Leuven University Press and Cambridge, Mass.: MIT Press.

Langley, A. (1999). Strategies for theorising from process data. *Academy of Management Review*, 24(4), 691–710.

Langley, A. (2009). Studying processes in and around organizations. In D. Buchanan and A. Bryman (eds.), *The Sage handbook of organizational research methods* (409–429). Thousand Oaks, CA: Sage.

Lefebvre, P. (2013). Organising deliberate innovation in knowledge clusters: From accidental brokering to purposeful brokering processes. *International Journal Technology Management*, 63(3–4), 212–243.

Lindberg, G. and Teräs, J. (2014). *Bioeconomy and the regional economy: The Örnsköldsvik biorefinery cluster*. Nordregio, News Issue 4.

Lorenzen, M. (2005). Why do cluster change? *European Urban and Regional Studies*, 12(3), 203–208.

Lundwall, B.-Å. (ed.). (1992). *National systems of innovation. Towards a theory of innovation and interactive learning*. London: Pinter Publishers.

Magretta, J. (2002). Why business models matter. *Harvard Business Review*, 80(5), 86–92.

Malerba, F. (2004). Sectoral systems of innovation: Basic concepts. In F. Malerba (ed.), *Sectoral systems of innovation* (9–41). Cambridge: Cambridge University Press.

Männistö, J. (2002). *Voluntaristinen alueellinen innovaatiojärjestelmä (Voluntaristic regional innovation system)*. University of Lapland Acta Universitatis Lapponiensis 46.

March, J. G. (1991). Exploration and exploitation in organizational learning. *Organization Science*, 2(1), 71–87.

Martin, R. and Sunley, P. (2011). Conceptualizing cluster evolution: Beyond the life cycle model? *Regional Studies*, 45(10), 1299–1318.

Maskell, P. (2001). The firm in economic geography. *Economic Geography*, 77(4), 329–344.

Maskell, P. and Malmberg, A. (2007). Myopia, knowledge development and cluster evolution. *Journal of Economic Geography*, 7(5), 603–618.

Mayntz, R. (2004). Mechanisms in the analysis of social macro-phenomena. *Philosophy of the Social Sciences*, 34(2), 237–259.

McCann, P., Arita, T. and Gordon, I. R. (2002). Industrial clusters, transaction costs and the institutional determinants of MNE location behaviour. *International Business Review*, 11, 647–663.

Nicol, C. G. (2013). *Change in the cage, exploring an organisational field: Sweden's biofuel region*. Ph.D. Thesis, Umeå School of Business and Economics, Studies in Business Administration, Series B, No. 84.

North, D. C. (1997). *The contribution of the new institutional economics to an understanding of the transition problem*. UNU-WIDER WIDER Annual Lecture.

Pajunen, K. (2008). The nature of organizational mechanisms. *Organization Studies*, 29(11), 1449–1468.

Peterson, C. (2011). Sweden: From large corporation towards a knowledge-intensive economy. In P. Hull Kristensen and K. Lilja (eds.), *Nordic capitalism and globalization: New forms of economic organization and welfare institutions*, 183–219. Oxford: Oxford University Press.

Pettigrew, A. M. (1997). What is a processual analysis? *Scandinavian Journal of Management* (Special Issue), 13(4), 337–348.

Porter, M. E. (1990). *The competitive advantages of nations*. London: Macmillan Press.

Porter, M. E. (1998). Clusters and the new economics of competition. *Harvard Business Review*, November–December, 77–90.

Pouder, R. and St. John, C. (1996). Hot spots and blind spots: Geographical clusters of firms and innovation. *Academy of Management Review*, 21(4), 1192–1225.

Richardson, J. (2008). The business model: An integrative framework for strategy execution. *Strategic Change*, 17(5–6), 133–144.

Romanelli, E. and Khessina, O. M. (2005). Regional industrial identity: Cluster configurations and economic development. *Organizational Science*, 16(4), 344–358.

Schumpeter, J. A. (1934, 1980). *The theory of economic development*. London: Oxford University Press.

Schumpeter, J. A. (1942, 1975). *Capitalism, socialism and democracy*. New York: Harper & Row.

Siggelkow, N. (2007). Persuasion with case studies. *Academy of Management Journal*, 50(1), 20–24.

Sölvell, Ö., Lindquist, G. and Ketels, C. H. M. (2003). *The cluster initiative greenbook*. Stockolm: Ivory Tower AB.

Sorenson, O. (2003). Social networks and industrial geography. *Journal of Evolutionary Economy*, 13, 513–527.

Storper, M. A. and Venables, J. (2002). *Buzz: The economic force of the city*. DRUID Summer Conf., Copenhagen/Elsinore.

Taylor, M. (2010). Clusters: A mesmerising mantra. *Tijdschrift voor Economische and Sociale Geografie*, 101(3), 276–286.

Teece, D. J. (2010). Business models, business strategy and innovation. *Long Range Planning*, 43(2–3), 172–194.

Teräs, J. (2008). *Regional science-based clusters. A case study of three European concentrations.* Acta Universitatis Ouluensis Publication series C 302. Oulu 2008.

Teräs, J. and Ylinenpää, H. (2012). Regional dynamics in non-metropolitan hi-tech clusters: A longitudinal study of two Nordic regions. In A. Rickne, S. Laestadius, H. Etzkowitz (eds.), *Innovation governance in an open economy. Shaping regional nodes in a globalized world* (69–91. London: Routledge.

Tödtling, F. and Trippl, M. (2005). One size fits all? Towards a differentiated regional innovation policy approach. *Research Policy*, 34, 1203–1219.

Trippl, M. and Otto, A. (2009). How to turn the fate of old industrial areas: A comparison of cluster-based renewal process in Styria and the Saarland. *Environment and Planning A*, 41, 1217–1233.

Tsoukas, H. and Chia, R. (2002). On organizational becoming: Rethinking organizational change. *Organization Science*, 13, 567–582.

Van de Ven, A. H. and Engleman, R. M. (2004). Event and outcome driven explanations of entrepreneurship. *Journal of Business Venturing*, 19(3), 343–358.

Van de Ven, A. H. and Poole, M. S. (2005). Alternative approaches for studying organizational change. *Organizational Studies*, 26(9), 1377–1404.

Yin, R. K. (1994). *Case study research, design and methods.* Applied Social Research Method Series. Thousand Oaks, CA: Sage.

Zettinig, P. and Vincze, Z. (2012). How clusters evolve? *Competitiveness Review, An International Business Journal*, 22(2), 110–132.

Zott, C., Amit, R. and Massa, L. (2011). The business model: Recent developments and future research. *Journal of Management*, 37(4), 1019–1042.

6 What About Disruptions in Clusters? Retaking a Missing Debate

José Luis Hervás-Oliver

1. INTRODUCTION

Radical innovations make existing technological capabilities obsolete and represent clear departures from existing practice (Ettlie, 1983), entailing substantial changes and discontinuities (Tushman and Anderson, 1986). Most of the literature on clusters and industrial districts, however, implicitly assumes circumstances of continuous or sustaining (i.e., nondisruptive) innovation generation, especially when the networks governing clusters[1] are said to be of the traditional or "old" Marshallian district kind (c.f., Robertson and Langlois, 1995; Asheim, 1996; Iammarino and McCann, 2006). With some exceptions, such as references to Silicon Valley (e.g., Adams, 2011), radical innovation and the way its *creative destruction* facilitates transition from old to new paradigms (Schumpeter, 1934) is almost absent in the cluster literature. Despite many attempts to link innovation to its geography (Howells, 2012), the cluster literature has not yet conceptualized discontinuities (Bathelt, 2009). Hence, in the cluster literature, radical or disruptive innovations have been traditionally overlooked and understudied.

In this conversation, radical or disruptive innovation is defined as knowledge new to the industry and to the focal cluster—that is, knowledge outside the thematic focus of the cluster. One of the key points in our framework's argument is that the evolution of clusters corresponds with, and follows from, the technological paradigm of those industries that form their bases in line with Li et al. (2011).

Although we recognize that incremental innovations are a great source of change and advantage in clusters, we also note that it has been shown that their occurrence might result in a kind of cluster myopia (Maskell and Malmberg, 2007) and lock-in (Grabher, 1993), at least in the long term. Therefore, in order to understand why some clusters lock-in while others, in contrast, are able to reinvent themselves (e.g., Grabher, 1993; Hassink and Shin, 2005; Storper, 2011), the study of the sources of disruption in clusters is of utmost importance, being one of the blind spots in the cluster literature (see Garofoli, 1991; Bianchi and Giordani, 1993; Crevoisier, 1994; Asheim, 1996; Gilbert, 2012). As yet, there is neither a comprehensive theoretical framework, nor ample empirical evidence, capable of providing a full description of disruptions in clusters. The chapter unfolds the mechanisms at work fostering the generation of disruptive knowledge in clusters. This work contributes to the field of economic geography by clarifying how *disruptions* are created in clusters.

The chapter is organized as follows. After this introduction, section 2 discusses disruptive innovation and openness in clusters. Section 3 studies the role of technological gatekeepers and their networks and complementary assets in clusters. Section 4 analyzes cognitive inertia in clusters. Finally, section 5 concludes and gives new insights for the development of the cluster evolution topic. Future research avenues are also set out.

2. TECHNOLOGY-DISTANT KNOWLEDGE: SEEKING OPENNESS

Taking into account the concepts of exploitation (refinement of existing technology) and exploration (invention of new ones), as expressed by March (1991) in respect of organizational learning, this chapter builds on that idea and elaborates upon a disentangling of the learning process in clusters and the types of knowledge generated. In doing so, this chapter transfers the concept from the organization unit of analysis to the cluster level and theorizes about learning and knowledge creation in clusters and clustered firms. As March (1991) states, the adaptive processes, by refining exploitation more rapidly than exploration, are likely to become effective in the short run but self-destructive in the long run. Thus the exploitative orientation can be depicted by an organization's learning being focused on the refining of its current competences, while finding it difficult to give them up in order to enter into unexplored and riskier new ways and paths, thereby falling into the so-called "success trap." An excessive focus on exploitation may result in organizational myopia and competency traps (Levitt and March, 1988).

The reason why this occurs, according to the cluster literature, is that bounded rationality and path dependency in clusters (Martin and Sunley, 2006) induce organizations to simply absorb local knowledge available (Maskell and Malmberg, 2007), thereby restricting the acquisition of knowledge choices to just a few (local) potential alternatives. This is due to the enclosing and limiting effect of strong dense networks (Gargiulo and Benassi, 2000; Crespo et al., 2014). Such choices lead to the creation of incremental knowledge related to existing products and technological paradigms. The aforementioned thinking is implicit in most of the ID literature. In this vein, Bianchi and Giordani (1993: 31) point out that IDs can generate innovations by incremental steps. Similarly, Garofoli (1991) also stresses that IDs are better suited to gradual change rather than to disruption. Robertson and Langlois (1995: 42) establish a difference between the innovative networks of Silicon Valley from those Marshallian and Italianate districts just by virtue of the importance and occurrence of disruptive innovation involved.

In contrast, "going beyond local search" (Rosenkopf and Nerkar, 2001) and exploring outside a cluster's core technological focus enables the avoidance of lock-in or myopia. Harrison (1994) argues against the self-sufficiency implicit in industrial districts—that is, the local endogenous model may suffer from lack of openness and for this reason emphasizes the importance of external forces, such as the presence of multinational companies. In this chain of thought, Eisingerich, Bell, and Tracey (2010: 252) find out that high performing regional clusters are underpinned by network strength and also by network openness. Network openness is measured as: we are connected to a range of firms, differing in size, age, capabilities, and industry; this organization readily accepts new members to its network of exchange partners in the cluster; we are well connected with actors outside this cluster; linkages with actors in this cluster are very difficult to reconfigure. Eisingerich et al. (2010) conclude that superior performance in clusters is likely to depend on the diversity of actors, openness to new members, and extent of linkages to organizations operating outside the cluster, facilitating thus the detection of inventions outside the cluster and avoiding lock-in.

In this vein, Menzel and Fornahl (2010: 231) point out that there is a need for the introduction of knowledge from "outside the thematic focus of the cluster" in order for creative destruction in clusters to occur and thus cluster renewal. Put differently, disruptions may arise and established dominant designs may be challenged, thanks largely as a consequence of the introduction of technology-distant knowledge sought out through exploration (Tushman and Anderson, 1986; Anderson and Tushman, 1990). There is some evidence for the aforementioned occurrence. In Montebelluna, in Italy, the ski boot manufacturing industrial district there introduced plastic into the manufacturing process, thereby improving on a patent registered by the Lange company in 1957 in Colorado (USA). The introduction of plastic injection technology for ski boots manufacturing was a major disruption of the cluster's thematic knowledge, traditionally based on leather boots. This pushed the district into a period of high growth and into diversification into alternative shoemaking: including soccer, motorcycle, bicycle, tennis, and after-ski boots, which rejuvenated the cluster (Sammarra and Belussi, 2006). Also, Adams' (2011) description of developments in Silicon Valley showed the effects of disruption innovation brought about by the introduction of technology-distant knowledge, with the cluster evolving from a focus on electronics to expertise in Internet and then semiconductors, computers, and aerospace. Adams (2011: 377) shows how the emergence and consolidation of the Silicon Valley as a formidable high-tech region came about in no small part because of the actions of multilocational firms based elsewhere—that is, due to the openness to attract new firms and knowledge from outside the cluster. In this chain of thought, Gilbert (2012:738) states that, "creative destruction occurs when firm innovative milieus are influenced by other industries." Similarly, Roveda and Vecchiato (2008:824) recognize that in order to renew clusters, in front of new threats from low-cost countries from Asia and for keeping the districts competitive, it is necessary to transfer existing technologies from other sectors or to develop radical innovations.

We can also consider that these potential technologies from other industries, new to the focal cluster, can also be originated from different industries located in the same region where a cluster is located. The debate, therefore, would be more centered around the idea of related variety (e.g., Frenken et al., 2007; Boschma and Frenken, 2011). Thus the process of branching would facilitate the generation or adoption of discontinuous or radical innovation by cluster firms.

3. DISRUPTIVE INNOVATION AND TECHNOLOGICAL GATEKEEPERS: ARE NETWORKS LEARNING CONDUITS OR TRAPS?

3.1 Are TGs Disrupters and Change Agents in Clusters?

The concept of TG is first developed in the organizational studies field, referring to individuals who connect a firm to external knowledge by Allen's (1977). It is also approached as anchor tenants (Feldman, 2003).

The cluster literature posits that technological gatekeepers are essential to cluster learning processes because they access external (to the cluster) knowledge and then carry out a conversion process, which deciphers the external knowledge and turns it into something locally understandable and useful (Becattini and Rullani, 1996). The most prominent type of firms in clusters are recognized to be the technological gatekeepers (TGs) or anchor tenants, referred to as large, local R&D-intensive firms that channel new knowledge to the cluster (Agrawal and Cockburn, 2003; Lorenzoni and Lipparini, 1999). The TGs are said to have orchestrating networks in clusters, attracting investments, providing a vision for directing innovation, and supplying technological knowledge to local start-ups (Agrawal and Cockburn, 2003; Baglieri et al., 2012). These large, leading firms, with high absorptive capacities and high R&D expenditures, shape a cluster's learning process (e.g., Lorenzoni and Lipparini, 1999; Morrison, 2008). For instance, Lorenzoni and Lipparini (1999: 321–332) established that these firms possess distinctive competencies and there is a broad recognition in the organizational community of their status and leading role in the relationship sets in which they are embedded, shaping interfirm networks and representing a structure-reinforcing competence. These firms are committed to invest in creating interactive platforms with selected partners in which knowledge and information are generated and transferred. This learning process in the network prevents the entrance of unconnected competitors. Over time, repeated transactions and trust building potentially lead to lower transaction costs, thus lowering the overall production costs of the network. Similarly, Munari, Sobrero, and Malipiero (2012) say that inventive activity in the industrial district is strongly concentrated in and fostered by a few large worldwide players, who dominate patenting activity and innovation production, while the remaining firms mainly access district knowledge that is facilitated or mediated by those focal firms.

The cluster literature, however, does not explicitly address the issue of radical innovation. In fact, it is assumed that incumbent TGs are more engaged in making incremental improvements (Asheim, 1996; Adams, 2011; Gilbert, 2012; Munari et al., 2012) to existing products and designs (in the sense of Tushman and Anderson, 1986; Baumol, 2004), and they oppose any threat of disruptive knowledge in order to maintain the status quo and their central positions in the cluster's networks (e.g., Gargiulo and Benassi, 2000; Allarakhia and Walsh, 2010). Disruptive technologies can threaten established markets (Bower and Christensen, 1995), and incumbent TGs do not wish new technologies to destroy the value of their existing assets, nor their complementarities with other firms and industries, and so threaten their control and orchestration of networks and markets. Consequently, incumbents do not consider investments in disruptive technologies (Tellis, 2006). Rather, they prefer to generate competence-enhancing knowledge related to their existing core technological focus.

When addressing clusters, this reluctance to disrupt and change status quo is markedly manifested, indeed. As Roveda and Vecchiato stated about industrial districts in Northern Italy (Como and Lecco) (2008: 822–823):

> its fragmentation in a large number of firms . . . . is the essential condition for the continuous enrichment and evolution of the knowledge underlying the current technologies of the district; on the other hand, it turns out to be the hardest obstacle to the diffusion and adoption of radically new technologies. . . . What really matters is the need to convince these firms that the new technology will not force them to give up the position they have in the local socio-economic system and to which they are used; what really matter is to convince these firms of the possibility of fully grasping the new technology, and therefore of shaping it, so being able to still play a relevant role in the continuous knowledge creation process.

Put differently, incumbent TGs are mostly reluctant to change. Glasmeier (1991) described the effects of disruption on wristwatch technology in the Jura region in Switzerland. In this case, incumbents did not show any inclination to switch to new electronic technologies. As Glasmeier (1991: 478) states (words into brackets mine), "industry leaders were often skeptical about the viability of new proposals [about different technologies], particularly if they implied a radical reorientation." Even when new technologies, originally developed in the Jura cluster by Swiss firms in order to counteract

Japanese (electronics) disruptions, the reluctance was extraordinarily manifested. Following Glasmeier (1991: 479), this is recognized: "But neither did
any single manufacturer have an incentive to switch technologies." In fact,
that reluctance to change was so deeply rooted, that even when one Swiss
company disrupted with the *tuning fork* (a transition technology between
the traditional mechanical and the quartz crystal), the idea was only successfully commercialized in the USA:

> This skeptical complacency proved costly when Hetzel, the Swiss inven-
> tor of tuning fork technology was ignored by Swiss watch manufac-
> turers. After he successfully commercialized his new technology in the
> United States, the Swiss were forced into a defensive position just to
> gain access to the new technology.
>
> (Glasmeier, 1991: 478)

Another example illustrates this idea. Cho and Hassink (2009) state that:

> Local networks of dominant industrial production become so narrowly
> focused on a particular type of retrogressive economic activities that is
> unable to shift into a new restructuring track. When being locked into
> rigid trajectories, the existing networks face increasing costs, due to
> reluctance and resistance, to replace old with new networks.
>
> (p. 1185)

3.2 TGs and Network Structures: Weak or Strong Ties?

External linkages (Bathelt et al., 2004) are supposed to increase knowledge
variety, avoiding myopic search (e.g., Ahuja and Katila, 2004; Maskell and
Malmberg, 2007). Thus external linkages usually go together with weak ties
and both will favor discontinuous knowledge generation, whereas strong
ties orchestrated by incumbent TGs are based on local buzz and redundant
knowledge that facilitate the generation of incremental knowledge.

Burt (1992, 1997), on the one hand, proposes that sparse networks with
many structural holes provide access to a wide range of nonredundant
information sources. Coleman (1988, 1990), on the other hand, argues that
the enclosure of actors in strong networks facilitates the exchange of tacit
knowledge. Sparse networks rich in structural holes generate opportunities
to grasp new knowledge (Burt, 1992) but pose an action problem, because
the unconnected units around the structural holes make for a difficulty for
the coordination and application of new ideas (Burt, 2004). On the contrary,
dense networks made up of strong ties, which usually occur in local spaces,
hinder the generation of new ideas because of the redundancy of information circulating but nevertheless present optimal conditions for applying the
knowledge exchanged (e.g., Burt, 2004). In particular, radical (or disruptive) innovation may result from novel information available in sparse (non-
dense) networks, while dense networks can be more related to incremental

innovation (Obstfeld, 2005: 123). In this vein, the disruptive or radical innovation coming out of sparse networks may be associated with exploratory learning (in the sense of March, 1991), while incremental innovation within dense networks is more related to exploitative learning. In addition, sparse networks require access to external (to the cluster) information and knowledge, while dense networks allow recombinations of existing knowledge without the necessity to access external (to the cluster) sources of knowledge and can thus minimize the active search for external (to the cluster) linkages. In this sense, incumbent TGs maintaining the status quo and orchestrating networks will be more interested in exploitative learning based on strong ties, which may generate incremental or competence-enhancing knowledge. The reason for this is that, as Tushman and Anderson (1986) and Anderson and Tushman (1990) propose, competence-enhancing discontinuities are improvements that build on previous knowledge, increase the efficiency of the existing dominant design, and are initiated by existing firms.

Lastly, as Obstfeld (2005: 102) argues, innovation requires the joining of people in both sparse and dense networks in order to produce the coordinated action that leads to innovation, a fact confirmed by Rost (2010). Commenting on this controversy about the pros and cons of weak and strong ties, Hansen (1999) found evidence that weak ties help a team search for knowledge but impede the transfer of complex knowledge, which tends to require a strong tie between the two parties to a transfer. Rost (2010) comes to a similar conclusion and says that weak ties leverage the strength of strong ties when it comes to the creation of innovation—implying that weak network architectures have no value without strong ties, whereas strong ties have some value without weak network architectures but are leveraged by this type of structure. In the case of clusters, the new technology-distant knowledge requires insertion into the cluster' existing networks orchestrated by TGs; therefore, in order to translate the new knowledge to the cluster existing networks, strong ties are also required with TGs and their networks. Again, this also implies reinforcing status quo.

3.3 TGs and their Complementary Assets

One of the reasons to understand networks' and TGs' reluctance is a network's role as a complementary asset. *Complementary assets* are defined as assets, infrastructure, or capabilities needed to support the successful commercialization and marketing of a technological innovation, other than those assets fundamentally associated with that innovation (Teece, 1986). TGs will not actively consider destroying the status quo and will be less effective than new entrants in introducing radical or disruptive innovations that threaten their own product portfolio. Following Arrow (1974) and Henderson and Clark (1990), the established incumbents or TGs have their architectural knowledge embedded in channels, filters, and strategies that handicap the development of new assets due to a legacy of irrelevant architectural knowledge. Additionally, Christensen (1997) links incumbent failure to resource dependency theory (Pfeffer and Salancik, 1978) in the sense that incumbents are embedded in value networks (including suppliers, customers, complementary products providers, and communities), which new technologies can replace. In clusters, the TGs are said to seek to maintain stable and high-quality linkages (Lorenzoni and Lipparini 1999; Giuliani, 2011: 1339–1340) with other firms in order to avoid potential technological disruptions that could alter the status quo. Hence TGs are more interested in the creation of less disruptive incremental technology-related knowledge (Glasmeier, 1991; Gargiulo and Benassi, 2000; Roveda and Vecchiato, 2008; Allarakhia and Walsh, 2010), thus favoring the creation of competence-enhancing knowledge (Anderson and Tushman, 1990), which is built on TGs existing assets. Incumbent TGs are embedded in routines and channels that may become inert and difficult to change and which are unable to adapt to a type of innovation (radical or disruptive) that challenges organizations' technical capabilities (Nelson and Winter, 1982; Abernathy and Clark, 1985).

Madhavan, Koka, and Prescott (1998) elaborate on this by pointing out that dominant players with high centrality in the current networks benefit when nondisruptive knowledge enhances and strengthens existing bases of competition. In all, the current cluster literature, however, does not address this fact. Even dynamic and longitudinal approaches take for granted that TGs persist and endure over time, assuming that no disruptions are expected.

4. COGNITIVE INERTIA FROM EXISTING TGs AND NETWORKS: THE PROBLEM OF STATUS QUO

The phenomenon of spatial industry concentration also presents disadvantages, provided that geographic proximity facilitates cluster members to be more prone to inertia than organizations outside clusters (Glasmeier, 1991; Pouder and St. John, 1996; Porter, 1998: 243), lock-in or myopia (Martin and Sunley, 2006; Maskell and Malmberg, 2007). The biased models of local managers oriented toward imitating other local managers triggers this process. As Pouder and St. John (1996: 1207) posit:

> Mental models based primarily on local competitors will be biased toward those competitors; at the same time they will direct attention away from outside competitors. Consequently, as local competitors increasingly dominate the perceptions of managers in the hot spot, competitors outside of the industry will be subject to less rigorous scrutiny.

This intuition is supported by Porac and colleagues (1987: 74–75), who, in a study of retailers, noted that their

> competitive moves will be primarily aimed at countering the tactics of firms within the same [competitive] category rather than firms in

categories not scanned. [The competitive] focus of attention [is] locked in by the cognitive structuring effect of the business category so defined.

An excessive focus on existing knowledge and technology in clusters due to an excessive reliance on the combination of existing local knowledge (Martin and Sunley, 2006) and a manifested reluctance to change, specially observed among leading incumbents (Glasmeier, 1991; Sull, 2001) may result in lock-in and decline. Similarly, the idea of organizational inertia (Hannan and Freeman, 1977, 1984) also reflects this reluctance, due to the fact that organizations have committed internal investments, such as the making of sunk costs in plant and equipment and personnel, or that they may have developed valuable exchange relationships with other organizations connected together through networks. Firms could be trapped in their own success or failure (Ahuja and Lampert, 2001; Leonard-Barton, 1992; Levitt and March, 1988). According to Levinthal and March (1993: 105), organizations become trapped in one or more of several dynamics of learning that self-destructively lead to excessive exploration or excessive exploitation. As Leonard-Barton (1992) shows, disruptions transform core capabilities into core rigidities, making obsolete the incumbents' resources and technologies.

The latter is well exemplified in clusters, following Glasmeier (1991: 478):

> The tightly articulated network surrounding watch manufacturing strengthened the status quo. Regional institutions were interwoven into the fabric of the industry. Educational institutions were steeped in watchmaking tradition, turning out skilled workers who spent up to four years learning to make watches from start to finish. Banking institutions were deeply implicated in the fortunes of the watch industry. In the early 1970s regional banks were known to have as much as 50 percent of their loanable funds invested in family-run watch-related enterprises. And the industry made heavy investment in collective R&D laboratories. The complicated web of watch manufacturing permeated the core of the region's social, political and economic institutions.

The complementary assets reflected in the previous subsection are also identified in Glasmeier's work. This study showed how complementary assets were also embedded in the distribution and marketing network. As Glasmeier (1991: 481) posits:

> The Swiss also had to contend with a centuries-old distribution system built around the watch as a piece of jewelry. Mechanical watches were traditionally distributed through jewelry stores, and jewelers made steady profits on repair. But quartz technology threatened to change all that. Swiss distribution outlets initially balked at the quartz watch . . . . watch distributors effectively stalled the introduction of Swiss quartz analog watches in defense of their own market for watch repair. Quartz watches were more accurate and relatively unbreakable compared with mechanical watches.

This inertia is also well manifested by Hall (1997), who elaborates on how the steel TGs in the US Pittsburgh cluster face great difficulties in responding to mini-mill production technology. Similarly, Sull (2001) offers a description referring to the Akron tire cluster in Ohio, detailing how the cluster evolved from a community of innovation to a community of inertia and showing how the cluster was unable to change to the new radial tire technology developed by the French competitor Michelin.

As Pouder and St. John (1996: 1210) point out, during the convergence phase,[2] clusters manifest a transition toward homogeneity, supported by managers' biased models oriented toward imitating local firms, and they show a decline in the collective level of innovation. Sull (2001: 11) sticks to this idea when describing the *active inertia* displayed by Akron-based tire (based on bias technology) companies facing the change from bias to radial design, stating that,

> The Akron-based tire companies did not ignore the radial tire, nor did they respond slowly. Rather they responded to the new technology quickly, but did so in a manner consistent with the models of competition prevailing within Akron. Goodyear responded to radial tire in 1967 by futher extending the core bias tire design.

The latter shows how incumbents invest more than new entrants, but in their existing competences, not in the new technology. Thus the research efforts of TGs trying to adapt to respond to the new technologies is just centered on their existing capabilities and designs (competence enhancing), trying not to adopt the new technologies but refining theirs (almost obsolete). The same was observed in the Jura cluster in Switzerland, well described by Glasmeier (1991).

This evidence reflects the idea that competence-enhancing discontinuities are improvements that build on previous knowledge, increase the efficiency of the existing dominant design, and are initiated by existing firms (Tushman and Anderson, 1986; Anderson and Tushman, 1990), promoting, in the long term, a negative lock-in in clusters (Martin and Sunley, 2006; Maskell and Malmberg, 2007). In all, TGs dislike competence-destroying or radical innovations.

Then the question to be answered comes up: How can clusters be renewed? The obvious question is that for this purpose, the renewal of actors, networks, and technologies is a must, especially for fostering competence-destroying disruptions that introduce knowledge heterogeneity in clusters. Incumbent technology gatekeepers may not be the players triggering that change, but new firms. We have also evidence of this actor and technology renewal. As Hervás-Oliver and Albors-Garrigos (2014) show in the Castellón ceramic tile cluster, a new spin-off disrupted the ceramic tile industry in the early 2000s by developing a new tile decoration technology based on printing technology. Similarly, Baglieri et al. (2012) find out, by researching two nanoelectronics clusters in France and Italy, that cluster rejuvenation comes from scientific and technological diversity, competition for orchestration, overlap among networks, and the ability of sleeping anchor tenant organizations to renew actors and technologies. They showed that as soon as the process of specialization (asset specificity, network specificity, and technology speciation) starts, competition for orchestration stimulates new anchor tenant organizations to influence new research avenues within the cluster and shape new networks within and outside the cluster, as Eisingerich et al. (2010) point out. From the network perspective, Crespo et al. (2014) show how new knowledge comes from the periphery, meaning that strong TG-led and closed networks do not facilitate the entrance of new knowledge but promote the circulation of existing ones (*assortativity*). Thus network and cluster renewal both require a certain level of *disassortativity*. The latter indicates a high level of connections between the core and the periphery so that information and knowledge can circulate through many structural bridges between the core and the periphery, allowing new knowledge circulation and explorative innovations to move more easily from periphery to core members. Again, cluster literature, with the exception of Silicon Valley and other like studies (e.g., Saxenian, 1994), poorly addresses the debate on the potential new firms but focuses mainly on the incumbents TGs.

5. CONCLUSIONS

The goal of this study has been to elaborate and reflect on radical innovation in clusters. In other words, our aim has been to understand disruptive knowledge in clusters. Our analysis of the role of incumbents in clusters and the potential problem of cognitive inertia and lock-in enlarges the repository of knowledge and understanding of why clusters cannot evolve through processes of radical innovation or creative destruction. Constructing a multidisciplinary theoretical framework that draws on both organizational studies and economic geography literatures, this chapter has extended theory on cluster evolution. Also, this chapter has contributed to the evolutionary economic geography literature by adding a change perspective to the somewhat continuity-based path dependency approach, presenting a new framework that captures radical innovation in clusters.

We developed the following propositions to be empirically tested in clusters:

- Cluster renewal by radical innovation requires exploration in technologically distant areas outside the thematic focus of the cluster
- Incumbent TGs are more likely to search in technology-related areas within the thematic focus of the cluster with the aim to prevent disruptive shocks altering their network centrality
- Cognitive inertia in clusters, due to the strong networks orchestrated by established TGs and the dominant normative structure within the local community, prevent the adoption of radical innovations

The view of the regional anchor firm as having a significant role in cluster development is confirmed (Feldman, 2003). In this view, regions and clusters are said to be technologically influenced by anchor (leading) firms from which knowledge is spilled over to the benefit of other enterprises, thereby contributing to increases in entrepreneurial activity as well as to geographic concentration and agglomeration. Put differently, through established networks, the incumbent TGs provide the necessary milieu or environment in which new knowledge can flourish. This development and knowledge generation capability is a predominantly exploitative and competence-enhancing one, and even focuses on incremental innovations. Besides, the rigidity of the complementary assets committed to the old technology turn those assets into core rigidities when in front of disruptions and thus prevent the entrance and development of exploratory and radical knowledge. Therefore, it is explicitly recognized as the manifest limitation of the TGs' ability or propensity to introduce disruption into clusters. This limitation is founded on the fact that TGs' strong and dense networks are based on a preexisting dominant design and technology, which reinforce status quo and foster cognitive inertia or lock-in in the long run.

Lastly, the aforementioned conclusions have helped us develop an evolutionary framework that enriches the cluster literature. This framework contributes to a better understanding of the characteristics of cluster networks (e.g., Eisingerich et al., 2010; Crespo et al., 2014), adding the key network distinction of type of knowledge (radical) exchanged, something not previously addressed in the cluster field. In addition, the theoretical framework enriches cluster life-cycle literature. Particularly, it has added to Menzel and Fornahl's (2010) framework of cluster evolution and their predictions about a missing actor and its role in the renewal of clusters: new firms. Lastly, the chapter's framework also contributes to the understanding of mechanisms and constructs related to lock-in and path dependence in clusters.

Overall, we believe that the cluster literature is strengthened by the provision of new knowledge about the understanding of disruption, a subject long overlooked by scholars. For future studies, there is a need for greater elaboration of the distinction between continuous and noncontinuous knowledge generation in clusters and its implications for cluster evolution. Also, there are unsolved questions that need to be addressed in future empirical studies; for example, are TGs resilient in the face of disruptions? Who are new entrants surpassing TGs and promoting radical change in clusters? Lastly, empirical evidence on this framework is crucial.

ACKNOWLEDGMENTS

I am thankful for financial support from the Spanish Ministry of Economics (ECO2010–17318) Innoclusters Project.

NOTES

1 We focus on both Marshallian industrial districts and other cluster types and use the terms interchangeably throughout the chapter. However, following Becattini (1979), we recognize the role of intensive social capital processes said to be typical of the industrial district model.
2 Refer to the fact that agglomerations are mature and the positive externalities decrease, similar to a mature stage of a cluster life cycle in which knowledge heterogeneity decrease and there are not new technological trajectories.

REFERENCES

Abernathy, W. J. and Clark, K. B. (1985). Innovation: Mapping the winds of creative destruction. *Research policy*, 14(3), 3–22.

Adams, S. B. (2011). Growing where you are planted: Exogenous firms and the seeding of Silicon Valley. *Research Policy*, 40, 368–379.

Agrawal, A. K. and Cockburn, I. (2003). The anchor tenant hypothesis: Exploring the role of large, local, R&D-intensive firms in regional innovation systems. *International Journal of Industrial Organization*, 21, 1227–1253.

Ahuja, G. and Katila, R. (2004). Where do resources come from? The role of idiosyncratic situations. *Strategic Management Journal*, 25, 887–907.

Ahuja, G. and Lampert, C. M. (2001). Entrepreneurship in the large corporation: A longitudinal study of how established firms create breakthrough inventions. *Strategic Management Journal*, 22, 521–543.

Allarakhia, M. and Walsh, S. (2010). Managing knowledge assets under conditions of radical change: The case of the pharmaceutical industry. *Technovation*, 31(2–3), 105–117.

Allen, T. J. (1977). *Managing the flows of technology: Technology transfer and the dissemination of technological information within the R&D organization.* Cambridge Mass.: MIT Press.

Anderson, P. and Tushman, M. L. (1990). Technological discontinuities and dominant designs: A cyclical models of technological change. *Administrative Science Quarterly*, 35(4), 604–633.

Arrow, K. (1974). *The limits of organization.* New York: Norton.

Asheim, P. (1996). Industrial districts as «learning regions». *European Planning Studies*, 4, 379–400.

Baglieri, D., Cinici, M. C. and Mangematin, V. (2012). Rejuvenating clusters with sleeping anchors: The case of nanoclusters. *Technovation*, 32(2), 1320–1335.

Bathelt, H. (2009). Re-bundling and the development of hollow clusters in the East German chemical industry. *European Urban and Regional Studies*, 16(4), 363–381.

Bathelt, H., Malmberg, A. and Maskell, P. (2004). Clusters and knowledge: Local buzz, global pipelines and the process of knowledge creation. *Progress in Human Geography*, 28, 31–56.

Baumol, W. J. (2004). Entrepreneurial enterprises, large established firms and other components of the free-market growth machine. *Small Business Economics*, 23(9–21), 310–342.

Becattini, G. (1979). Dal 'settore' industriale al 'distretto' industriale. Alcune considerazioni sull'unità d'indagine dell'economia industriale. *Rivista di economia e politica industriale*, 1, 7–21.

Becattini, G. (1990). The Marshallian industrial district as a socio-economic notion. In F. Pyke, G. Becattini, and W. Sengenberger (eds.), *Industrial districts and*

118   *José Luis Hervás-Oliver*

interfirm cooperation in Italy (37–51). Geneva: International Institute for Labour Studies.

Becattini, G. and Rullani, E. (1996). *Local systems and global connections: The role of knowledge.* In F. Cossentino, F. Pyke and W. Sengenberger (eds.), *Local and regional response to global pressure: The case of Italy and its industrial districts* (159–174). Geneva: Iils.

Bianchi, P. and Giordani, M. G. (1993). Innovation policy at the local and national levels: The case of Emilia-Romagna. *European Planning Studies*, 1, 25–41.

Boschma, R. and Frenken, K. (2011). Technological relatedness and regional branching. In H. Bathelt, M. P. Feldman and D. F. Kogler (eds.), *Dynamic geographies of knowledge creation and innovation* (64–81. Routledge: Taylor and Francis.

Bower, J. L. and Christensen, C. M. (1995). Disruptive technologies: Catching the wave. *Harvard Business Review*, January–February, 73(1), 43–53.

Burt, R. S. (1992). *Structural holes: The social structure of competition.* Cambridge, Mass.: Harvard University Press.

Burt, S. R. (1997). The contingent value of social capital. *Administrative Science Quarterly*, 42(2), 339–365.

Burt, R. S. (2004). Structural holes and good ideas. *American Journal of Sociology*, 110, 349–399.

Cho, M.-R. and Hassink, R. (2009). The limits to locking-out through restructuring: The textile industry in Daegu, South Korea. *Regional Studies*, 42, 1183–1198.

Christensen, C. M. (1997). *The innovator's dilemma: When new technologies cause great firms to fail.* Cambridge, Mass.: Harvard Business Press.

Clark, K. B. (1985). The interaction of design hierarchies and market concepts in technological evolution. *Research Policy*, 14, 235–251.

Coleman, J. S. (1988). Social capital and the creation of human capital. *American Journal of Sociology*, 94, 95–120.

Coleman, J. S. (1990). *Foundations of social theory.* Cambridge, Mass.: Belknap Press of Harvard University Press.

Crespo, J., Suire, R. Y. and Vicente, J. (2014). Lock-in or lock-out? How structural properties of knowledge networks affect regional resilience. *Journal of Economic Geography*, 14, 199–219.

Crevoisier, O. (1994). Book review (of Benko, G., A. Lipietz (eds.), Les regions qui gagnent, Paris-1992-. *European Planning Studies*, 2(2), 258–260.

Eisingerich, A., Bell, S. J. and Tracey, P. (2010). How can clusters sustain performance? The role of network strength, network openness, and environmental uncertainty. *Research Policy*, 39, 239–253.

Ettlie, J. E. (1983). Organization policy and innovation among suppliers of food processing sector. *Academy of Management Journal*, 26, 27–44.

Feldman, M. (2003). The locational dynamics of the US biotech industry: Knowledge externalities and the anchor hypothesis. *Industry and Innovation*, 10(3), 311–328.

Frenken, K., Van Ort, F. and Verburg, T. (2007). Related variety, unrelated variety and regional economic growth. *Regional Studies*, 41(5), 685–697.

Gargiulo, M. and Benassi, M. (2000). Trapped in your own net? Network cohesion, structural holes and the adaptation of social capital. *Organization Science*, 11(2), 183–196.

Garofoli, G. (1991). Local networks, innovation and policy in Italian industrial districts. In E. M. Bergman, G. Maier and F. Tödtling (eds.), *Regions reconsidered* (119–140). London: Mansell.

Gilbert, X. (2012). Creative destruction: Identifying its geographic origins. *Research Policy*, 41(4), 734–742.

Giuliani, E. (2011). Role of technological gatekeepers in the growth of industrial clusters: Evidence from Chile. *Regional Studies*, 45(10), 1329–1348.

Glaeser, E. L., Kallal, H. D., Scheinkman, J. A. and Shleifer, A. (1992). Growth in cities. *Journal of Political Economy*, 100, 1126–1152.

Glasmeier, A. (1991). Technological discontinuities and flexible production networks: The case of Switzerland and the world watch industry. *Research Policy*, 20(5), 469–485.

Grabher, G. (1993). The weakness of strong ties: The lock-in of regional development in the Ruhrarea. In G. Grabher (ed.), *The embedded firm: On the socioeconomics of industrial networks* (255–278). London: T.J. Press.

Hall, C. G. L. (1997). *Steel Phoenix: The fall and rise of the U.S. steel industry*. New York: St. Martin's Press.

Hannan, M. and Freeman, J. (1977). The population ecology of organizations. *American Journal of Sociology*, 82(5), 929–964.

Hannan, M. and Freeman, J. (1984). Structural inertia and organizational change. *American Sociological Review*, 49(2), 149–164.

Hansen, Morten T. (1999). The search-transfer problem: The role of weak ties in sharing knowledge across organization subunits. *Administrative Science Quarterly*, 44, 82–111.

Harrison, B. (1994a). *Lean and mean: The changing landscape of corporate power in the age of flexibility*. New York: Basic Books.

Harrison, B. (1994b). Concentrated economic power and Silicon Valley. *Environment and Planning A*, 26(2), 307–328.

Hassink, R. and Shin, D.-H. (2005). The restructuring of old industrial areas in Europe and Asia. *Environment and Planning A*, 37(4), 571–580.

Henderson, R. M. and Clark, K. B. (1990). Architectural innovation: The reconfiguration of existing product technologies and the failure of established firms. *Administrative Science Quarterly*, 35(1), 9–30.

Hervás-Oliver, J. L. and Albors-Garrigos, J. (2014). Are technology gatekeepers renewing clusters? Understanding gatekeepers and their dynamics across cluster life cycles. *Entrepreneurship and Regional Development*, 26(5–6), 523–559.

Howells, J. (2012). The geography of knowledge: Never so close but never so far apart. *Journal of Economic Geography*, 12, 1003–1020.

Iammarino, S. and McCann, P. (2006). The structure and evolution of industrial clusters: Transactions, technology and knowledge spillovers. *Research Policy*, 35, 1018–1036.

Leonard-Barton, D. (1992). Core capabilities and core rigidities: A paradox in managing new product development. *Strategic Management Journal*, 13, 111–125.

Levinthal, D. A. and March, J. G. (1993). The myopia of learning. *Strategic Management Journal*, 14, 95–112.

Levitt, B. and March, J. G. (1988). Organizational learning. *Annual Review of Sociology*, 14, 319–340.

Li, P.-F., Bathelt, H. and Wang, J. (2011). Network dynamics and cluster evolution: Changing trajectories of the aluminium extrusion industry in Dali, China. *Journal of Economic Geography*, 12, 127–155.

Lorenzoni, G. and Lipparini, A. (1999). The leveraging of interfirm relationships as a distinctive organizational capability: A longitudinal study. *Strategic Management Journal*, 20(4), 317–338.

Madhavan, R., Koka, B. and Prescott, J. E. (1998). Networks in transition: How industry events (re)shape interfirm relationships. *Strategic Management Journal*, 19, 439–459.

March, J. (1991). Exploration and exploitation in organizational learning. *Organization Science*, 2(1), 71–87.

Martin, R. (2010). Rethinking regional path dependence: Beyond lock-in to evolution. *Economic Geography*, Vol. 86 (1), 1–27. Martin, R. and Sunley, P. (2006). Path dependence and regional economic evolution. *Journal of Economic Geography*, 6(4), 395–437.

Martin, R. and Sunley, P. (2011). Conceptualizing cluster evolution: Beyond the life cycle model? *Regional Studies*, 45(10), 1299–1318.

Maskell, P. and Malmberg, A. (2007). Myopia, knowledge development and cluster evolution. *Journal of Economic Geography*, 7, 603–618.

Menzel, M. and Fornahl, D. (2010). Cluster life cycles- Dimensions and rationales of cluster evolution. *Industrial and Corporate Change*, 19(1), 205–238.

Morrison, A. (2008). Gatekeepers of knowledge within industrial districts: Who they are, how do they interact? *Regional Studies*, 42(6), 817–835.

Munari, F., Sobrero, M. and Malipiero, A. (2012). Absorptive capacity and localized spillovers: Focal firms as technological gatekeepers in industrial districts. *Industrial and Corporate Change*, 21(2), 429–462.

Nelson, R. R. and Winter, S. G. (1982). *An evolutionary theory of economic change*. Cambridge, Mass.: Harvard University Press.

Obstfeld, D. (2005). Social networks, the Tertius Iungens orientation, and involvement in innovation. *Administrative Science Quarterly*, 50, 100–130.

Pfeffer, J. and Salancik, G. R. (1978). *The external control of organizations: A resource dependence perspective*. New York: Harper & Row.

Porac, J., Thomas, H., and Emme, B. (1987). Understanding strategists' mental models of competition. In G. Johnson (ed.), *Business strategy and retailing* (59–79). New York: Wiley.

Porter, M. E. (1998). *On Competition*. Boston: Harvard Business School Publishing.

Pouder, R. and St. John, C. H. (1996). Hot spots and blind spots: Geographical clusters of firms and innovation. *Academy of Management Review*, 21(4), 1192–1225.

Robertson, P. L. and Langlois, R. N. (1995). Innovation, networks, and vertical Integration. *Research Policy*, 24, 543–562.

Rosenkopf, L. and Nerkar, A. (2001). Beyond local search: Boundary-spanning, exploration, and impact in the optical disk industry. *Strategic Management Journal*, 22(4), 287–306.

Rost, K. (2010). The strength of strong ties in the creation of innovation. *Research Policy*, 40(4), 588–604.

Roveda, C. and Vecchiato, R. (2008). Foresight and innovation in the context of industrial clusters: The case of some Italian districts. *Technological Forecasting & Social Change*, 75, 817–833.

Sammarra, A. and Belussi, F. (2006). Evolution and relocation in fashion-led Italian districts: Evidence from two case-studies. *Entrepreneurship & Regional Development*, 18(6), 543–562.

Saxenian, A. L. (1994). *Regional Advantage: Culture and Competition in Silicon Valley and Route 128*. Cambridge, MA: Harvard University Press.

Schumpeter, J. A. (1934). *The theory of economic development*. Cambridge, Mass.: Harvard University Press.

Storper, M. (2011). Why do regions develop and change? The challenge for geography and economics. *Journal of Economic Geography*, 11, 333–346.

Sull, D. N. (2001). From community of innovation to community of inertia: The rise and fall of the U.S. Tire Industry. *Academy of Management Proceedings*, BPS, L1.

Teece, D. J. (1986). Profiting from technological innovation: Implications for integration, collaboration, licensing and public policy. *Research Policy*, 15(6), 285–305.

Tellis, G. J. (2006). Disruptive technology or visionary leadership. *The Journal of Production and Innovation Management*, 23, 34–38.

Tushman, M. L. and Anderson, P. (1986). Technological discontinuities and organizational environments. *Administrative Science Quarterly*, 31(3), 439–465.

Part II
Business Innovation

7 Building High-Tech Clusters? The Case of the Competitiveness Cluster "Secure Communicating Solutions" in the French Provence-Alpes-Côte d'Azur Region

Christian Longhi

1. INTRODUCTION

Areas where clusters of new high-technology firms are to be found attract attention as potential breeding grounds for future industry. Because of the potential in terms of wealth and job creation, there is considerable interest in explaining how these high-tech centers develop and can be encouraged. They have often been considered as an embodiment of the knowledge-based economies that govern the evolution of our societies and overcome the continuous waves of obsolescence of knowledge and technology (Foray, 2009).

The role of clusters, i.e., localized concentration of horizontally and vertically linked firms, to create and sustain competitive advantage has been definitively imposed by Porter (1989) and acknowledged by the literature (Porter, 1998; Malmberg and Maskell, 2002; Martin and Sunley, 2003). Clustered firms have been shown to grow and innovate faster than non-clustered ones (Audretsch and Feldman, 1996). But these processes are neither straightforward nor automatic.

Knowledge is far from "being in the air" in existing clusters (Cassi and Plunket, 2013); it is increasingly agreed upon that it cannot be assumed beforehand that all firms in a cluster are involved in local networks of collective learning (Breschi and Lissoni, 2001, Bell and Giuliani, 2005, Giuliani, 2005, ter Wal, 2013). Some firms can be excluded from the processes of collective learning because of competition, some others can simply lack the absorptive capacity (Cohen and Levinthal, 1990, Lazaric et al., 2008) necessary to enter in these processes. Geographical proximity is neither a necessary or sufficient condition to access knowledge; other dimensions of proximity, organizational or cognitive, have been developed (Boschma, 2005, Torre and Rallet, 2005), which can account even more than co-location. Many studies have shown that the creation of knowledge is less and less an isolated process internal to individual firms but a collaborative process involving networking of heterogeneous organizations (Caloffi et al., 2012).

The pace of innovation and technological progress going with the global-ized knowledge-based economy deepens the basic role of these networks. Powell et al. (1996) have evidenced that the R&D intensity and level of technological sophistication of industry are positively correlated with inter-firm alliances. These alliances have grown rapidly since the mid-1980s, especially those aimed at technological learning and knowledge creation (Nooteboom, 1999; Nooteboom et al., 2005); they enable established firms limited in their pursuit of opportunities by their existing capabilities and experience to combine heterogeneous resources, renewing the economy over time (Penrose, 1959; Garnsey, 1998). The locus of innovation is thus to be found in networks of interorganizational relationships (Powell et al., 1996).

Clusters can trigger externalities leading to economic performance (Por-ter, 1989; Krugman, 1991) or innovation, knowledge creation, learning as processes of social interaction between individuals or firms in networks (Saxenian, 1994; Boschma, 2006; Fleming and Frenken, 2006). But clusters and networks do not necessarily coincide. As ter Wal (2013) clearly states following Visser (2009: 168–169),

> clusters refer to spatial concentration processes involving a related set of activities in which context firms may but need not cooperate. Conversely, networks refer to cooperation in the form of knowledge exchange between firms and other actors that may but need not develop these links at the local or regional level.

Furthermore, the relations between clusters and networks have not a deterministic optimal form. A basic seminal reference to capture the impli-cations of networks on clusters remains Markusen (1996). The nature and intensity of interactions are not associated with physical proximity but with the organizational structure that governs these interactions (local and exter-nal) between firms and institutions. A clear, relevant taxonomy for cluster configurations is derived from the nature of interactions that can also serve as a basis for analyzing localized knowledge-creation processes.

Clusters and networks have thus to be tackled together. The relevant issue this chapter will attempt to address is the local collective learning net-works working in clusters.

"Cluster" and "competitiveness" are among the most popular buzz-words of our time, the first being implicitly a solution for the second. At least as much as researchers, policy-makers have thus turned to be interested in clusters and networks. The implementation of cluster policies as relevant for firms to cope with the challenges of the knowledge-based economy as well as the growing complexity of technology management has been pro-moted worldwide. Cluster policies, cluster strategies, cluster development programs, etc., have been actively developed (Giuliani and Pietrobelli, 2011; Uyarra and Ramlogan, 2012) "to promote economic development by form-ing and strengthening inter-organizational networks."

After the Inter-Ministerial Committee for Spatial Planning and Development of September 14, 2004, this policy has taken a specific form in France that was referred to as "Poles of Competitiveness." [1] The French policy consists of "increasing top-down pressures on regions or local areas to position themselves" (Kiese, 2006), i.e., to build projects of development based on their technological capabilities or knowledge bases, the definition and governance of the projects being entrusted to firms and research institutes, and the heterogeneous actors involved in the processes of creation of knowledge and innovation.

The chapter focuses on a specific pole located in the French region of Provence-Alpes-Côte d'Azur (PACA), the "Secure Communicating Solutions" (SCS) pole. The pole is particularly interesting for our purpose related to clusters and collective knowledge networks dynamics. It is indeed a matter of bringing together complementary skills in order to create new synergies between different kinds of partners, between different clusters, and between different types of technologies. The aim in microelectronics is to merge skills from "the silicon to uses" to address the markets, to reduce or resolve organizational and cognitive distances.

Section 2 presents the policy and the clusters supporting the pole SCS. The pole aims to foster collective R&D networks of heterogeneous agents and produces basic sources of information on these processes. The chapter does not intend to evaluate the policy as such. It builds on the R&D networks identified through the pole to characterize the specific organizational forms of knowledge creation and the collective learning processes at work in the clusters. Section 3 presents the relevant database resulting from the working of the pole and the methodology implemented in the related empirical analysis. Section 4 implements a social network analysis of this database to characterize the organizational forms promoted by the firms and embedded in the clusters. Section 5 focuses on proximity issues and identifies the different types of learning networks in the clusters. Section 6 concludes the chapter.

2. INNOVATION IN POLICY

2.1. The "Poles of Competitiveness" Renaissance

In the French context, the policies aiming at competitiveness have taken and still take a specific form, referred as "Poles of Competitiveness." They are embedded in the French tradition of economic analysis, as they can be linked to the works of François Perroux. "Poles of Competitiveness" policies were used at the end of the seventies to facilitate the emergence and development of "strategic" sectors regarding the international division of labor and presided the definition of industrial policies. It is important to notice that in this conception, the poles are defined according to a strict sectoral approach without any territorial dimension (Longhi and Rainelli, 2010).

The reference to the poles has disappeared from the eighties with the decline of industrial policies. They reappeared in a renewed form in 2004 in the French public policy in line with the cluster strategies promoted by the European Union. These new Poles of Competitiveness have been defined as the new French industrial policy, aiming at reinforcing the specializations of the economy, strengthening the attractiveness of the territory, and favoring the emergence of new activities via synergies between research and industry. They are defined as

> "The combination on a given geographic space of firms, training institutions and public or private research centres engaged to generate synergies in the execution of shared innovative projects. The partnerships can be oriented towards a market objective or a scientific and technological domain".
>
> (Interministerial Delegation for Territorial Competitiveness and Attractiveness, 2005)

The key words of the definition of the poles are "collaborative innovative projects" entailing heterogeneous actors. The poles are not financed directly by the public policy; their members are only financed when the R&D projects they propose to dedicated calls are selected. The policy aims thus basically to provide incentives to foster local interactions, cooperation, to strengthen the performance of the clusters regarding innovation and creation of knowledge.

Interestingly, the SCS pole is built on two existing clusters resulting from the old French industrial and regional policies of the last century, the microelectronics activities in the "Bouches du Rhône *département*," along an axis running from the town of Rousset to the town of Gémenos, and the high-tech activities of the "Alpes-Maritimes *département*," broadly centered on the technology park of Sophia-Antipolis. They were both created ex nihilo, but in different ways. The former originated in the context of various plans intended to develop a technology sector, in this case, microelectronics. The latter originated in the context of regional policy, supported by a public policy of decentralization and public investment in telecommunications infrastructure, but without any specific technology project.

These exogenously generated public creations rooted in the territories either gave rise to endogenous processes or they disappeared. In the case of the PACA region, two clusters with local endogenous dynamics emerged; but as we shall see, they had very different organizational structures, based on (to quote Markusen, 1996) the *hub-and-spoke* and the *satellite platform* forms respectively. The Pole of Competitiveness, product of contemporary public policies, is meant to "bridge" elements of a value chain dispersed in the two clusters. Geographical, organizational, and cognitive proximities issues (Boschma, 2005; Torre and Rallet, 2005) will have thus to be tackled.

2.2. Public Policy Constructed Clusters: Rousset and Sophia-Antipolis

The microelectronics cluster in the town of Rousset is a pure product of the traditional French industrial policy, which was centralized and made up of plans implemented by "national champions." The plans led to the creation from scratch of the company Eurotechnique in the industrial area of Rousset in 1979 to build and develop the industry, followed by the government-led location of Thomson-EFCIS, Nanomask (later Du Pont Photomasks), a different merging that gave rise to the group SGS-Thomson Microelectronics, called STMicroelectronics, and the development of a dense cluster of subcontractors (Daviet, 2000, 2001; Rychen and Zimmermann, 2000; Garnier and Zimmermann, 2004; Mendez et al., 2008). The founding of the company Gemplus, now Gemalto, and the emergence of an innovative industrial web between Rousset and the neighboring town of Gémenos, where Gemplus was located, characterized a second phase. Gemplus has been created as a spin-off of Eurotechnique-Thomson Components based on a radical innovation, the design and production of cards. It has triggered a movement of endogenous development based on local capabilities. The area grew as a hub-and-spoke cluster in the Markusen taxonomy, large firms surrounded by a dense set of specialized subcontractors.

Nevertheless, the microelectronics industry still experienced crises and threats of large companies that had to close down. These crises led to the founding of various associations with the aim of consolidating activities. In particular, the creation of active industrial associations CREMSI (Regional Centre of Studies for Micro-electronics and Interactive Systems), which later became ARCSIS (Association for Research on Materials and Integrated Security Systems), PROMES (Lab for PROcesses, Materials and Solar Energy), etc., which were founded by the management of the large companies with the aim of creating linkages between industry and science, including SMEs, and seeking and obtaining public support for the implementation of projects (Zimmermann, 2000). These actions were coupled with the creation of large research institutes, gathering elements that had until then been disparate. At the time the cluster policy was implemented, there was thus already a well-designed structure for interactions in the Rousset-Gémenos cluster.

Sophia-Antipolis is the core of the pole area based on the Alpes-Maritimes. It is the result of regional policies promoting the creation of high-value-added activities implemented in the context of spatial planning. This project was born in a region without any industrial or academic tradition; its only resources were linked to its main activity at the time, tourism. The success of the project was determined by the involvement of Pierre Laffitte of France Télécom, which gave Sophia-Antipolis an advanced telecommunication infrastructure and an important international airport (Longhi, 1999). Up to the beginning of the 1990s, Sophia-Antipolis grew through the accumulation of external resources. The project benefited from the French policy of decentralization, with the IT centers of large French firms that moved there and from the "multinationalization" of the 1970s and 1980s, when American companies set facilities in the European market. On these bases, Sophia-Antipolis took off through companies being attracted by the quality of the available (telecom) infrastructures to set up and manage their European markets or their global telecommunication networks. In addition, the project attracted education and research centers, which contributed to the emergence of a qualified labor market.

The project grew as a satellite platform in the Markusen sense: a system of rich exterior relations (albeit poor in local interactions) led from outside for external markets. Resources were fundamentally internalized within the companies, the absence of local resources or their strategies having led them to build self-contained ensembles. The growth slowed considerably at the beginning of the 1990s, with the economic crisis that struck the computer science activities. But basically the factors of success of Sophia-Antipolis, a platform endowed with efficient infrastructures to develop markets or activities, were at odds with the new phase of globalization. Another organizational form had to be built.

Industrial associations played a considerable role to face the crisis and favor the emergence of collective processes in Sophia-Antipolis. In particular, the association Telecom Valley grouped together all the telecommunications and microelectronics actors, including large and small companies and research centers. To face the risks of delocalization, it aimed at highlighting the skills that were specific to Sophia-Antipolis and its indisputable importance at the European level. Finally, the emergence of mobile technologies and the Internet led to a revival of the cluster, with these technologies originating within a number of local companies, making Sophia-Antipolis a key location in the European high-tech industry. The establishment of facilities by large corporations no longer took place by means of huge investments and transfers of human resources, but through knowledge-led strategies, the establishment of small units that took advantage of the skills, and qualified resources produced or already available locally.

3. THE POLE SCS: DEFINITION AND RELEVANT DATABASE

The pole SCS draws on resources from both of the clusters described earlier. Relations between them were relatively underdeveloped, but organizational linkages have begun to be formed through the establishment of platforms (CIM PACA—Integrated center for Microelectronics of the Province of Alps and Cote d'Azur) in microelectronics financed by the region and the *département* of Alpes-Maritimes. The platforms aimed at making available software components by world leaders based in Sophia-Antipolis to firms and research institutes. ARCSIS and SAME (Sophia Antipolis MicroElectronics forum), the microelectronics associations of each of the two clusters, promoted this operation. With the French government's call for tenders for Poles of Competitiveness, the idea of creating a broader project that brought together all the actors in the region arose, still under the influence of the associations, ARCSIS, SAME, Telecom Valley, and crystallized as the SCS pole.

The pole was created around the idea of bringing together the leaders in microelectronics, telecommunications, and software to cover the entire value chain from silicon to its uses on the markets and take advantage of the convergence of these various industrial sectors. It groups together local actors in two clusters located in areas of the "*départements*" of Bouches du Rhône [13] and Alpes-Maritimes [06].[2] Needless to say, the pole does not involve all the *départements* as such. Its boundaries are discontinuous and endogenous. It does not cover the areas of administrative units but rather the agglomerations of resources ("R&D zones") that make up the project.[3] The territory is endogenous as its frontiers are defined with the project of development it supports, which matches the resources involved.

The pole does not also gather all the firms and institutions of the areas it covers. It has the institutional form of French "association" acting for its members; one has to formally join the association, to pay fees, to be involved. The pole has involved around 600 members over its history, some (the large firms, the research institutes) are permanent members, others (the SMEs) enter and exit depending on their R&D projects, for an annual average of roughly 250. The members benefit from the governance body of the pole, which fosters the emergence of innovative, collaborative projects; supports the participation of SMEs in projects; and assists the members and their projects up to labeling and involvement in a call.

The core of the activity of the Poles of Competitiveness is made up of R&D projects. These projects do not cover entirely the formal interfirm R&D alliances or even the informal local network relationships related to knowledge, learning, and innovation in the clusters. They are a specific subset of the collective learning networks, with a form imposed by the rules of the games of the poles and the call addressed, usually partnerships involving necessarily SMEs and research institutes, rules some firms consider restrictive enough not to compete for public research subsidies. Nevertheless, a lot of R&D relationships are today mediated through the poles, which provide reliable information on previously unknown collaborative activities. The projects labeled by the governance system of the pole forms thus a good proxy to grasp the local R&D activity, the nature of local interactions and local collective learning networks, as well as linkages with external partners.

The pole has labeled 447 R&D projects during the period 2005–2014 under analysis, which indicates a sizable amount of activity. This database is the basic information used to highlight the collective learning networks running in the pole. It gathers the main characteristics of the projects: the nature of the call addressed, basically calls specifically aimed at poles and financed by an inter-ministerial fund (FUI), calls by the Regional Council (CR), and calls by the National Research Agency (ANR) dedicated to more basic research; the location and nature of the project leader (industrial group, SME, academic institute, association); the location and nature of the partners involved in the project (industrial group, SME, academic institute, association); and the status of the labeled project, selected (financed) or not, in the call addressed.

4. THE SCS COLLECTIVE LEARNING NETWORKS

The 447 R&D projects implemented in the pole SCS have involved 760 different partners: 22.2% for [13], 13.6% for [06], and 64.2% are external to the clusters! Nevertheless, many partners belong to one project, some are involved in dozens, defining 2,378 project-partner relations. The "effective" shares of the different clusters are as follows: 29.5% for [13], 21.3% for [06], and 49.2% for external partners, whose roughly 20% belongs to the region "Ile de France"! This significant portion of external project leaders testifies to the acknowledgment the clusters have earned in specific skills. As we will see, the local leaders also build important external partnerships to access remote knowledge. The literature has emphasized this last issue through the concept of "gatekeepers of knowledge" (Allen, 1977; Rychen and Zimmermann, 2006; Morrison, 2008). But regarding the high-tech cluster another way is similarly relevant; namely, the access to local-specific knowledge by distant partners and its insertion in external clusters or learning networks.

The selection process related to the calls has been favorable for the partners involved: 44% were selected on the whole, but in a very imbalanced form, from 48% for [13] to 43% for [06] and 42% for [0], or from 61% for the FUI call to 29% for the ANR, or from 54% for the large groups to 39% for the academics involved in projects. The unselected projects are obviously important to consider, as they account for a part of the informal interactions between the different firms, the institutes of research. Even if not exhaustive, the projects provide a relevant proxy of the formal and informal interactions and alliances governing the collective learning networks feeding knowledge creation and the organizational forms of the clusters.

The database of these projects allows us to approximate the collective learning networks running in the pole SCS. The properties of the networks can be derived from a social network analysis according to the following methodology. The R&D projects database forms a bipartite network linking the projects to the partners involved, with the partners being large groups, SMEs, and academics. The different partners associated in a project are supposed to form a complete undirected graph, as they are involved in a collaborative process. A one-mode network of the partners can be derived from the original bipartite network; a node will represent a partner and the links connecting pairs of nodes their involvement in a common collaborative project or collaborative learning process. Some links can thus have a heavy weight, as the same partners can be associated in many different projects. Some partners can also be involved in various projects, but not necessarily with the same actors.

The large number of labeled projects has led to numerous interactions within the SCS cluster. The collective learning networks related to the R&D

projects of the pole result in 760 nodes and 4,787 edges, i.e., 4,787 "part-nerships" relations. The graphs of the networks and the analysis of the associated centrality measures give interesting insights on the clusters. Figure 7.1 presents these graphs of the pole SCS using the Fruchterman-Reingold visualization algorithm, which displays the most interconnected nodes close to each other. The following conventions have been adopted for the nodes attributes: nodes representing partners located in [13] are black, in [06] grey, and in [0] white. The size of a node is proportional to its degree, i.e., the number of nodes that the node is connected to, the width of an edge to its weight. Figure 7.1 shows the networks of the partners involved in the labeled project and in the financed projects for all the SCS projects and for the FUI projects respectively.

SCS R&D labelled projects

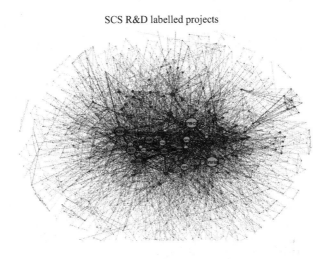

FUI R&D selected projects

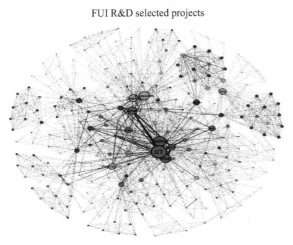

Figure 7.1 SCS Collective Learning Networks

The graphs show core-periphery structures, i.e., groups of highly inter-connected nodes, the core of the partnership networks, connected with peripheral nodes. These last nodes are strongly connected to the core, but not much interconnected, as the analysis *infra* of the distribution of degrees will confirm. These core-periphery networks have often been considered as efficient for learning processes and viability of the high-tech clusters. They allow for spreading information quickly (Borgatti, 2006). These networks are a condition of the resilience of the clusters (Crespo et al., 2013), the firms or institutes of research involved in strong ties in the core access to weak ties in the periphery to renew knowledge bases and sustain the innovative processes. The notion of periphery does not refer to geographic distance but to the properties of the networks and often cognitive distances.

As already emphasized, the partners external to the regional clusters play an important role; they are in the periphery of the graphs and involved in the process of renewal of the knowledge base and also in the core of the networks. The graphs of the labeled projects and even more the one of the financed ones highlight different organizational forms of the clusters. The core of [13] is made of dense and balanced interconnected relations of large firms (STMicroelectronics, Gemalto), research institutes (ENSMSE, IM2NP, AMU) and some related SMEs, when [06] is mostly restricted to institutes of research, with the exception of Orange, in fact, the research center of Orange located in Sophia-Antipolis. The large groups of Sophia-Antipolis,[4] Texas Instrument, IBM, Amadeus, etc., are not present in the core of the pole, even if active in industrial associations and permanent members of the pole. Most are international groups. Nevertheless, path dependency linked to the organizational form of the satellite platform on which the cluster has grown is certainly part of the explanation. Figure 7.2 presents some centrality measures derived from the analysis of the SCS network.

Different centrality measures have been used to characterize the involvement of the partners in the collective learning network, degrees and weighted degrees (i.e., first the number of nodes that a node is connected to and second the number of nodes that a node is connected to weighted by the weights of the edges), and betweenness centrality displayed in Table 7.1. The degree distribution of R&D networks is highly skewed; the weighted one would be even more. Some firms or organizations appear central in the network, working as brokers. The shape of the distributions recalls the preferential attachment of Barabási and Albert (1999), some nodes attracting entrants. The log-log plot in Figure 7.2 shows a nearly linear negative trend in the log frequency as a function of the log degree after degree 2, and an important tail of low-frequency nodes, highlighting a very heavy skewness.

Beyond the degree distribution, it is important to understand how nodes of different degrees are linked with each other. The last plot of Figure 7.2 represents the average degree of the partners of a given partner in the collaborative learning network. It figures the assortativity of the network, i.e., the correlation between the centrality of a partner and the centrality of all its partners. As the quadratic form of the cloud evidences, the partners of

Log-Log Degree Distribution

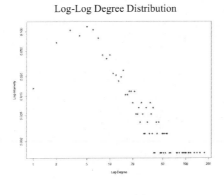

(Dis)Assortativity

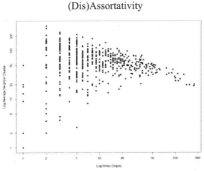

Figure 7.2   Centrality Measures

lower degree tend to link partly with partners of lower degree but mainly of higher degree, and the partners with higher degrees with lower ones. The network is disassortative, as in many technological cases (Newman, 2003), the core and the periphery are better connected. As explained in Crespo et al. (2013), the core is more open and peripheral actors holding new or disruptive knowledge can link and benefit from the well-established core partners to find opportunities of knowledge combinations to address new markets. The governance of the pole helps also to spin new linkages and supports SMEs.

Table 7.1 presents those partners that make up the core of the network, ordered according to their weighted degrees. It emphasizes the characteristics of the clusters supporting the pole; for example, [06] is deeply involved with research institutes when the core of [13] is well balanced between important central industrial and research partners. Interestingly, an external partner appears as the sixth most important actor of the pole, all calls mixed. It disappears when the analysis is restricted to selected FUI.

Another measure of centrality, betweenness centrality, is worth considering. The index measures how often a partner appears on the shortest paths between all others partners of the network. Knowledge exchanges within

Table 7.1   Centrality Measures

| SCS Collective Learning Network | | | | |
Partner	Cluster	Degree	Weighted Degree	Betweenness Centrality
Eurecom	Lab	6	176	344	39028.8
ST	LG	13	141	306	20000.5
IM2NP	Lab	13	154	300	28585.8
Inria	Lab	6	178	299	37965.9
CEA	Lab	13	116	235	12390.7
Thales	LG	0	101	229	11460.8
ENSMSE	Lab	13	110	222	12868.6
Gemalto	LG	13	100	186	11322.4

| FUI Collective Learning Network | | | | |
Partner	Cluster	Degree	Weighted Degree	Betweenness Centrality
ST	LG	13	92	181	10928.4
ENSMSE	Lab	13	67	122	4687.3
IM2NP	Lab	13	73	111	5064.6
Gemalto	LG	13	60	105	5102.9
Eurecom	Lab	6	69	103	8460.2
Orange	LG	6	56	88	6082.8
AMU	Lab	13	64	83	5563.9
CEA	Lab	13	43	79	1846.2

Source: SCS and own calculation

the network are likely to flow through the high betweenness partners. They can perform brokering roles across the clusters as they connect otherwise disconnected partners. In the case of the SCS pole, this role can be played within a cluster, between the clusters of the pole, or toward the clusters external to the pole. The main institutes of research of the pole are central and connect otherwise disconnected large and small firms. Two large cohesive firms, STMicroelectronics and Gemalto also play a pivotal role to bridge the different elements of the pole, heterogeneous actors and clusters.

The restriction of the exhaustive database of the R&D projects to the FUI projects provides a proxy of the learning networks feeding knowledge creation in the industrial system. From the creation of the poles, the FUI organizes twice-a-year calls devoted to supporting R&D collaborative projects dedicated to firms, large and small, and research institutes belonging to at least one pole. The pole SCS has labeled 107 FUI projects, of which 60 have been financed.

Figure 7.1 shows the graphs of the selected FUI learning networks. Regarding our clusters, different main features emerge from inspection of the graphs. The existence of a strong and balanced core in [13], gathering heterogeneous actors, firms, and research institutes, which appears robust after the selection process. In [06], a similar core does not emerge; a salient feature being the shortage of firms there, with the exception of Orange. The pivotal partners from [06] are indeed close to the partners of [13], which make the core of the network. Another important actor of [06], INRIA, is disconnected from the core and inserted in a dense set of external relationships. Table 7.1 shows the pivotal role of [13] in the core of the learning network. STMicroelectronics stands as the highest betweenness partner, followed by Eurecom and Orange. These members are brokers connecting disconnected elements of knowledge and drawing bridges across the clusters.

5. PROXIMITIES

The aim of the Pole of Competitiveness policy has been to trigger R&D networks to reinforce clusters, and in the case of SCS to create in some sense a new cluster in terms of cognitive and organizational proximities, merging the technologies and knowledge bases of heterogeneous actors from the prevailing clusters, building value chains to address the markets starting from R&D and innovation. The analysis of the SCS pole highlights the forms of the networks that have endogenously emerged. In fact, it appears that several levels have to be tackled to capture the whole induced processes at work:

—within cluster networks, the organizational form emerging between the local partners involved in the collective learning processes;

—in-between clusters networks, the bridges between Rousset-Gémenos and Sophia-Antipolis, to take advantage of weak ties (Granovetter, 1973) and structural holes (Burt, 1992), eventually to trigger the emergence of in-between strong ties and recompose the core;

—distant clusters networks. Finally, clusters are open, evolving complex systems (Garnsey and Longhi, 2004), local and global linkages of the firms are pivotal to their resilience and their involvement in innovative networks.

Just as firms form more and more R&D alliances (Powell et al., 1996, Nooteboom et al., 2005), clusters create mutual external links as different knowledge bases have to be merged. Intra-cluster strong ties, high levels of embeddedness, can trigger lock-in effects in declining technological paths and question the resilience of the cluster (Crespo et al., 2013). The existence of weak ties to access remote knowledge can fuel the learning process. "Knowledge pipelines" (Storper and Venables, 2003, Bathelt et al., 2004) have to be built to renew and reinforce the local buzz, the adaptation of the core to changes. Nevertheless, regarding high-technology clusters, pipelines also have to allow external partners to reach the local knowledge bases to feed their own learning process with nonredundant, distant knowledge.

A balanced exchange of inflows and outflows of knowledge has to be maintained to secure the viability and growth of the high-tech clusters.

In the SCS pole case, the prevalence of disassortative learning networks linking cores and peripheries as well as the huge involvement of distant partners seems to be a sign of the renewal of the knowledge bases and of the acknowledgment of the local capabilities. These dynamics are seemingly well rooted in the two clusters considered, but despite the existence of brokers like ST, Eurecom, or Orange, the ties between them are perhaps limited compared to the potential bridges.

Beyond the centrality measures, the weights of the different edges linking the partners gives important information on the structure of the cores of the pole and the clusters, the cohesiveness of the related networks. The distribution of the weights is highly skewed, confirming the core—periphery structure of the networks. Indeed 80% of the edges are of weight 1 and 16% of weight 2 in the SCS learning network. Table 7.2 presents the most weighted edges for the SCS network and then for the FUI related one, the industrial learning network.

Symbolically, the heavier edge of the networks links Eurecom [06] and a distant partner located in the region, Ile de France, attesting to the involvement of the pole in global innovation networks. Incidentally, Ile de France is very close and deeply inserted in the pole learning networks. This link is associated with ANR projects, as it disappears in the FUI network. The edges related to [06] involve indeed mostly research institutes, with a pivotal role of Eurecom, which stands as some kind of hub. Orange again is the most involved industrial partner.

The case of [13] is very different; a core of cohesive partners emerges, linking strongly industrial and research partners in a balanced way, with equally heavier edges linking industrial firms together, research institutes together, and firms and research institutes as well. When considering the edges of the FUI learning network, the same core of [13] emerges and gather the same heterogeneous partners, when [06] links mainly research institutes with research institutes. The industrial learning network of the pole is clearly located in [13]. With the exception of Thales, the heavier weighted edges link partners of the same clusters, in-between significant edges link Eurecom, Gemalto, and ST—the main brokers of the pole. The in-between links fill the periphery of the networks and could be considered to feed the innovativeness of the core.

Finally, the intra, inter, and distant links have been addressed building three different networks: the one made of projects whose leaders belong exclusively to [06], the one made of projects whose leaders belong to [13], and the one led by distant partners. The larger network, [13], consists of 342 different partners, against 285 for [06]. They are obviously eventually involved in different projects, with rates of selected partners involved in 45.5% for [13] against 34.5% for [06].

The percentages of partners from intra, inter, and distant cluster partners in these networks highlight the nature of the proximities. The intra share is 58.5%

Table 7.2 Short Heads of the Edges Weight Distribution

SCS Network			FUI Network		
Partner 1	Partner 2	Weight	Partner 1	Partner 2	Weight
Eurecom [06]	Thales [00]	19	CEA [13]	ENSMSE [13]	10
CEA [13]	ENSMSE [13]	18	CEA [13]	Gemalto [13]	9
IM2NP [13]	ST [13]	17	ENSMSE [13]	Gemalto [13]	9
CEA [13]	Gemalto [13]	16	ENSMSE [13]	ST [13]	9
Eurecom [06]	ParisTechSA [06]	16	IM2NP [13]	ST [13]	8
ENSMSE [13]	ST [13]	16	Gemalto [13]	ST [13]	7
CEA [13]	ST [13]	14	CEA [13]	ST [13]	6
ENSMSE [13]	Gemalto [13]	13	Eurecom [06]	Gemalto [13]	6
Eurecom [06]	Orange [06]	12	AMU [13]	ST [13]	5
3Roam [06]	Eurecom [06]	10	Atmel [06]	ST [13]	5
CEA [13]	IM2NP [13]	10	Eads [00]	Orange [06]	5
Eurecom [06]	Inria [06]	10	Eurecom [06]	Orange [06]	5
Gemalto [13]	ST [13]	10	Eurecom [06]	ParisTechSA [06]	5
CEA38 [00]	IM2NP [13]	9	3Roam [06]	Eurecom [06]	4

Source: SCS and own calculation

when the leaders belong to [13] and 46% for [06], the inter shares being 15 and 20. Interestingly, the shares of distant partners are 26.5 and 34% respectively. For [06], the shares of intra and distant partners are quite important, the one of inter cluster being less significant. The cluster is then very open to its distant environment. The share of intra partnerships prevails in projects led by [13]. Nevertheless, the basic feature to notice is the very important involvement of distant clusters in the pole, with the relative shares of distant partners being larger than the in-between relations whatever the leader considered [06] or [13], but particularly for [13].

When the leader is distant, the partners are also obviously distant; the share of [13] in this network is 16% when the one for [06] is 9%. Contrary to often preconceived ideas, the share of [13] is important, the specificities of the local knowledge bases of the cluster appear largely acknowledged, as are the ones for [06]. The pole has certainly contributed to this increased visibility of the local capabilities. The insertions of [06] and [13] are also very different, 20 and 33% respectively in FUI projects, 72 and 62% for

ANR, with the partners involved being 14 and 17% respectively for large firms, 18 and 34% for SMEs, and 67 and 48% for institutes of research. One is clearly academic research oriented when the other is more balanced and significantly industry oriented.

Summing up the different features highlighted from the analysis of the collective learning networks, the organizational forms of the clusters appear somewhat different. Paradoxically, to infer from the Markusen taxonomy (1996), one has a core and periphery organizational form; when the other is somewhat more hub-and-spoke oriented, the edges linking the hubs are lighter.

6. CONCLUSION

The Pole of Competitiveness policy has targeted the development of collaborative network relations in selected clusters and basically produced detailed information on these R&D networks of heterogeneous actors. This information can be considered as a good proxy of the informal and formal alliances implemented by the firms. The chapter has allowed for characterizing the organizational forms of the clusters from the emerging structure of the collective learning networks. The results are in line with the seminal work of Markusen (1996) and the works on proximity: different forms of cluster emerge, even in the same pole. Path dependency of the local and external forms of interactions is very robust; the history of the clusters and the specificities of their emergence can be found in the characteristics of the R&D networks at work. Diversity is a pervasive characteristic of the clusters.

Knowledge, learning, innovation, and clusters are considered keys for the competitiveness of firms and local industrial systems. The diversity of the learning networks revealed in this chapter questions the policy built on the mode "one size fits all" (Todtling and Trippl, 2004; Crespo et al., 2015). The industrial groups of Sophia-Antipolis are not deeply involved in the pole. Paradoxically, these firms are not standing alone, they are historically open and involved in distant knowledge networks, such as the research institutes, but are certainly more oriented toward international alliances and not organized around a strong cohesive core of large heterogeneous actors as in Gémenos–Rousset. The chapter has confirmed, if necessary, that clusters and networks have to be analyzed together. The characterization of the collaborative learning networks structures precisely shows the strategies and behaviors developed by the firms to build their knowledge bases and innovative processes and the way these processes govern the working of the clusters.

Knowledge spillovers are not "in the air" but very specific of the learning networks and clusters to which they belong. The project of the Pole of Competitiveness SCS, which aims to merge distinct knowledge bases born from distinct collective learning networks embedded in distinct clusters, raises difficult obstacles to unlock. The pole has nevertheless supported the financing of many collective learning networks, gathered heterogeneous partners, strengthened the core and cohesive actors of the clusters, and increased in-between knowledge relationships.

NOTES

1 "Pôles de Compétitivité" is the French name of the policy, translated here as "Poles of Competitiveness." "Competitiveness Clusters" is another translation, more often used in the litterature.
2 These numbers refer to the French *départements* units nomenclature. Hence [06] Sophia-Antipolis (Alpes Maritimes) and [13] Rousset-Gémenos (Bouche du Rhône). For the sake of simplicity, we will use *département* numbers to refer to the clusters, speaking of [06] or [13] projects or partners, or [0] when an external partner is involved in a project.
3 The map of the discontinuous areas defined by the pole SCS is given here: http://competitivite.gouv.fr/documents/commun/Les_Poles_en_mouvement/ Poles_de_competitivite_mondiaux/cartes-zonage/Zonage_3718_mep.pdf.
4 http://www.sophia-antipolis.org/index.php/sophia-antipolis/les-entreprises.

REFERENCES

Allen, T. J. (1977). *Managing the flows of technology: Technology transfer and the dissemination of technological information within the R&D organization.* Cambridge, Mass.: The MIT Press.
Audretsch, D. B. and Feldman, M. P. (1996). R&D spillovers and the geography of innovation and production. *The American Economic Review*, 86(3), 630–640.
Barabási A.-L., and Albert, R. (1999). Emergence of scaling in random networks. *Science*, 286, 509–512.
Bathelt, H., Malmberg, A. and Maskell, P. (2004). Cluster and knowledge: Local buzz, global pipelines and the process of knowledge creation. *Progress in Human Geography*, 28(1): 31–56.
Bell, M. and Giuliani, E. (2005). The micro-determinants of meso-level learning and innovation: Evidence from a Chilean wine cluster. *Research Policy*, 34(1), 47–68.
Borgatti, S. (2006). Centrality and network flows. *Social Networks*, 27(1), 55–71.
Boschma, R. (2005). Proximity and innovation: A critical assessment. *Regional Studies*, 39, 61–74.
Boschma, R. A. (2006). Does geographical proximity favour innovation? *Economie et Institutions*, (6–7), 111–127.
Breschi, S. and Lissoni, F. (2001). Knowledge spillovers and local innovation systems: A critical survey. *Industrial and Corporate Change*, 10(4), 975–1005.
Burt, R. S. (1992). *Structural holes. The social structure of competition.* Cambridge, Mass.: Harvard University Press.
Caloffi, A., Rossi, F. and Russo, M. (2012). What networks to support innovation. *DRUID 2012*, Copenhagen, Denmark, June 19–June 21.
Cassi, L. and Plunket, A. (2013). Research collaboration in co-inventor networks: Combining closure, bridging and proximities. *Regional Studies*, 1–19. doi:10.10 80/00343404.2013.816412.

Cohen, W. and Levinthal, D. (1990). Absorptive capacity: A new perspective on learning and innovation. *Administrative Science Quarterly*, 35, 128–152.

Crespo, J., Amblard, F. and Vicente, J. (2015). Simulating micro behaviours and structural properties of knowledge networks: Toward a "one size fits one" cluster policy. *Papers in Evolutionary Economic Geography*, 15.03, Utrecht University.

Crespo J., Suire R., Vicente J., (2013), Lock-in or lock-out? How structural properties of knowledge networks affect regional resilience, *Journal of Economic Geography*, 14(1), 199–219.

Daviet, S. (2000). Émergence et structuration d'une multinationale européenne du semiconducteur, le cas de STMicroelectronics. *Les Annales de Géographie*, 612, 132–151.

Daviet, S. (2001). Mondialisation et ancrage territorial chez STMicroelectronics. *Rives méditerranéennes*, 9, 67–81. http://rives.revues.org/index16.html.

Fleming, L. and Frenken, K. (2006). Evolution of inventor networks in the Silicon Valley and Boston Regions. Papers in Evolutionary Economic Geography, 06.09.

Foray, D. (2009). *L'économie de la connaissance*. Paris: La Découverte.

Garnier, J. and Zimmermann, J. B. (2004). L'Aire métropolitaine marseillaise et les territoires de l'industrie. Working Document no. 2004–35, GREQAM.

Garnsey, E. (1998). A theory of the early growth of the firm. *Industrial and Corporate Change*, 7, 523–556.

Garnsey, E. and Longhi, C. (2004). High technology locations and globalization: Converse paths, common processes. *International Journal of Technology Management*, 28(3), 336–355.

Giuliani, E. (2005). Cluster absorptive capacity: Why some clusters forge ahead and others lag behind? *European Urban and Regional Studies*, 12(3), 269–288.

Giuliani, E. and Pietrobelli, C. (2011). *Social network analysis methodologies for the evaluation of cluster development programs*. IDB Publications 3978, Inter-American Development Bank, Washington, DC.

Granovetter, M. (1973). The strength of weak ties. *American Journal of Sociology*, 78(6), 1360–1380.

Interministerial Delegation for Territorial Competitiveness and Attractiveness (2004). Les poles de compétitivité. *Dossier de presse*. Paris: Matignon.

Kiese, M. (2006). Cluster approaches to local economic development conceptual remarks and case studies from Lower Saxony, Germany. In U. Blien and G. Maier (eds.), *Clusters—wonder tool of regional policy?* Forthcoming.

Krugman, P. (1991). *Geography and trade*. Leuven and Cambridge: Leuven University Press and MIT Press.

Lazaric, N., Longhi, C. and Thomas, C. (2008). Gatekeepers of knowledge versus platforms of knowledge: From potential to realized absorptive capacity. *Regional Studies*, 42(6), 837–852.

Longhi, C. (1999). Networks, collective learning and technology development in innovative high-technology regions: The case of Sophia-Antipolis. *Regional Studies*, 33(4), 333–342.

Longhi, C. and Rainelli, M. (2010). Poles of competitiveness, a French dangerous obsession? *International Journal of Technology Management*, 49(1–23), 66–92.

Malmberg, A. and Maskell, P. (2002). The elusive concept of localization economies: Towards a knowledge based theory of spatial clustering. *Environment and Planning A*, 34(3), 429–449.

Markusen, A. (1996). Sticky places in slippery spaces: A typology of industrial districts. *Economic Geography*, 72(3), 293–313.

Martin, R. and Sunley P. (2003). Deconstructing clusters: Chaotic concept or policy panacea? *Journal of Economic Geography*, 3(1), 5–35.

Martin, R. and Sunley P. (2006). Path dependence and regional economic evolution. *Papers in Evolutionary Economic Geography*, 0606, March, Utrecht University.

Mendez, A. et al. (2008). *Quelle articulation entre les pôles de compétitivité et les tissus productifs régionaux?—Une mise en perspective de quatre pôles en Provence-Alpes-Côte d'Azur.* Research report commissioned by the PACA regional government, France.

Morrison, A. (2008). Gatekeepers of knowledge within industrial districts. Who they are, how they interact. *Regional Studies*, 42(6), 817–835.

Newman, M. E. J. (2003). Mixing patterns in networks. *Physical Review*, E 67, 026126.

Nooteboom, B. (1999). *Interfirm alliances: Analysis and design.* London: Routledge.

Nooteboom, B., Vanhaverbeke, W., Duysters, G. M., Gilsing, V. A. and van den Oord, A. (2005). *Optimal cognitive distance and absorptive capacity*, ECIS working paper 06–01.

Penrose, E. (1959). *The theory of the growth of the firm.* Oxford: Oxford University Press.

Porter, M. E. (1989). *The competitive advantage of nations.* New York: Free Press.

Porter, M. E. (1998). Clusters and the new economy of competition. *Harvard Business Review*, 76, 77–90.

Powell, W. W.; Koput, K. W. and Smith-Doerr, L. (1996). Interorganizational collaboration and the locus of innovation: Networks of learning in biotechnology. *Administrative Science Quarterly*, 41(1), 116–145.

Rallet, A. and Torre, A. (2005). Proximity and localization. *Regional Studies*, 39(1), 47–60.

Rychen, F. and Zimmermann, J. B. (2000). Du bassin houiller de Gardanne au pôle micro-électronique provençal: reconversion ou mutation? *Rives méditerranéennes* 4, 47–60. Accessed from: http://rives.revues.org/index75.html.

Rychen, F. and Zimmermann, J. B. (2006). Clusters in the global knowledge based economy: Knowledge gatekeepers and temporary proximity. *Regional Studies*, 42(6), 767–776.

Saxenian, A. (1994). *Regional advantage: Culture and competition in Silicon Valley, and Route 128.* Cambridge, Mass.: Harvard University Press.

Storper, M. and Venables, A. J. (2003). *Buzz: Face-to-face contact and the urban economy.* London: Centre for Economic Performance, London School of Economics, December.

Ter Wal, A. L. J. (2013). Cluster emergence and network evolution: A longitudinal analysis of the inventor network in Sophia-Antipolis. *Regional Studies* 47: 651–668.

Tödtling, F. and Trippl, M. (2004). *One size fits all? Towards a differentiated policy approach with respect to regional innovation systems.* SRE—Discussion Papers, 2004/01, WU Vienna University of Economics and Business, Vienna.

Uyarra, E. and Ramlogan, R. (2012). *The effects of cluster policy on innovation.* Nesta Working Paper No. 12/05.

Visser E. J. (2009). The complementary dynamic effects of clusters and networks. *Industry and Innovation* 16: 167–195.

Zimmermann, J. B. (2000). Comment naissent les firmes allogènes? L'exemple de Gemplus Card. In M. Delapierre, J. P. Moati, and E. M. Mouhoud (eds.), *Connaissance et Mondialisation.*Paris: Economica.

8 The Role of Open Innovation-Oriented Strategies in the Innovation Performance of Mechanical Engineering Start-Up Firms in Northern Italy

Silvia Rita Sedita and Roberta Apa

1. INTRODUCTION

The aim of this work is to investigate the role of open innovation strategies in explaining firms' innovation performance. We explore how differences in firms' collaboration-finding strategies influence their ability to achieve higher levels of novelty in their innovative activities. Many studies have analyzed the impact of openness on innovation but, to our knowledge, none have focused on start-up companies. Our research attempts to fill this gap.

Laursen and Salter (2006) take the merit for first applying a methodological approach to open innovation studies (Chesbrough, 2003), measuring the innovation performance of UK manufacturing firms. We build upon their work by analyzing how the breadth and depth of external search strategies affect the innovation capacity of start-up firms, starting from the idea that the capacity to establish multiple collaboration networks is particularly important for start-up firms needing to cope with the well-known liability of newness (Stinchcombe, 1965). Their relationships with clients, suppliers, industrial partners, consultants, universities, and public research organizations are worth analyzing in this respect. We also add to previous research on the topic by identifying the role of distance in shaping the open innovation strategies of start-up firms. We conduct a three-level analysis, investigating the occurrence and spatial distribution of the most often used innovation collaborations on a regional, national, and international level, following in the footsteps of Dahlander and McKelvey (2005) and Belussi et al. (2010).

This study examines the innovation performance of a sample of 188 start-up firms operating in the mechanical engineering sector in Northern Italy. We considered firms established between 2004 and 2009, measuring their innovation performance in 2012. Our data on their innovation performance and search strategies come from a survey conducted in 2013 using CAWI (computer-assisted web interviewing) and CATI (computer-assisted telephone interviewing) methods. Information on turnover was drawn from the AIDA database, which provides economic and financial indicators for

Italian firms. Innovation performance is measured in terms of the proportion of the firms' turnover deriving from products that are new to the world market. The number of formal collaborative links established with different external sources for the purpose of developing innovation provides a measure of the breadth of the firms' search; and the number of such links that are used intensively provides an indication of the depth of their search.

Our work sheds light on an important but still underdeveloped aspect of start-up performance, namely open innovation strategy. Findings on the geography of the innovation-oriented ties that start-up firms establish tend to reflect the outcome of previous studies conducted on established companies, underscoring the importance of distant sources of knowledge and information for innovation. The main novelty of our research lies in the relative importance of the breadth and depth of start-up firms' search strategies in shaping their innovative output: the breadth of their portfolio of collaborations emerges as a crucial element, whereas the intensity of their usage seems to be irrelevant. The managerial and policy implications of our results are discussed mainly in relation to the potential for innovative entrepreneurship.

2. OPEN INNOVATION: OPPORTUNITIES FOR START-UPS

Traditionally, investment in R&D has been regarded as one of the key strategies to secure technological potential and consequent innovation and economic growth (Trajtenberg, 1990). R&D investments increase the chances of achieving higher standards of technology in firms and regions that would enable them to introduce new, superior products and/or processes, resulting in higher levels of income and growth (Bilbao-Osorio and Rodríguez-Pose, 2004).

Despite the established key role of R&D expenditure in enhancing the likelihood of introducing innovation, there is a body of literature that speaks of this role being in decline, as in Chesbrough's "open innovation" model (Chesbrough, 2003a, 2003b), according to which many innovative firms now spend little on R&D but innovate successfully by drawing on the knowledge and expertise of a wide range of external sources (Chesbrough, 2003a).

A special issue edited by Joel West, Ammon Salter, Wim Vanhaverbeke, and Henry Chesbrough was recently published by Research Policy to celebrate the tenth anniversary of Chesbrough's seminal publication on the open innovation model (Chesbrough, 2003a), and it clearly asserted the maturity and validity of the concept of open innovation. In his well-known book, Chesbrough (2003a) made the point that organizations resorted increasingly to open innovation strategies to augment the variety and speed of knowledge flows essential to innovation, and the author suggested that the old, closed innovation model focusing on internal R&D, which had dominated most of the twentieth century, was becoming obsolete.

The acknowledged ever-increasing importance of inbound and outbound knowledge flows for innovation was threatening the closed model. Judging from recent field research work conducted by Chesbrough and Brunswicker (2013), open innovation practices have been extensively used by large corporations, especially to establish new partnerships, to explore new technological trends, and to identify new business opportunities. To our knowledge, little research has been done to explore how open innovation practices influence the innovative output of SMEs and start-ups.

In the closed innovation model, SMEs are at a disadvantage because they are clearly unable to invest heavily in R&D. Such firms cannot be innovative by counting on their internal knowledge alone; they have to build fruitful relationships with other organizations, taking a network perspective. Crossing the firm's boundaries and cooperating with external actors (research labs, institutions, customers, suppliers, external consultants, and other industrial partners) gives them a chance to multiply their learning opportunities. This is particularly true of start-up firms, which carry the liability of newness and smallness.

Stinchcombe (1965) was the first to introduce and analyze the phenomenon of the liability of newness, investigating its underpinnings and identifying four crucial aspects regarding newborn businesses: 1) new organizations operate inefficiently until people have learned their roles; 2) and until their organizational routines have been developed; 3) "new organizations must rely heavily on social ties among strangers" (p. 149), and their consequent lack of confidence can become an additional source of organizational inefficiencies; and 4) the construction of a stable portfolio of customers takes time, during which customer-producer ties are still very fragile. The real existence of the liability factors identified by Stinchcombe justifies the broad and lasting support for his theory (Abatecola et al., 2012) and explains why new ventures have a higher mortality rate than older companies. New ventures need to access and mobilize resources in order to catch up, contacting and creating relationships with resource providers that can supply the complementary assets that start-ups need to be able to afford the first stages of their development.

Studies on industrial spin-offs (i.e., separate, new ventures created by one or more employees from firms in the same industry) have emphasized the role of knowledge inheritance in moderating the effect of the liability of newness. In these cases, the emerging entrepreneurs use the parent company as a sort of incubator, gaining a good deal of information that helps them to reduce the duration of their exposure to the liability of newness (Klepper, 2001; Klepper and Sleeper, 2005). Start-ups, by definition, have no such hereditary links with incumbent firms (Helfat and Lieberman, 2002),[1] but those housed in a business incubator may have a better chance of successfully addressing the challenges of the early stages of development—especially if the business incubator does not simply provide affordable office space and shared administration services (as in the simplest incubator formula) but also plays a more complex part as moderator of the liability of newness (Bøllingtoft and Ulhøi, 2005).

The liability of newness concerns the early stages of an organization's life cycle, but newborn firms are also often born small. Elaborating on the "liability of newness" principle, Freeman et al. (1983) examined the importance of size and introduced the "liability of smallness" principle. Being small implies having difficulty accessing the tangible, intangible, and human resources needed to compete with incumbent firms. One way to be resilient despite such "dwarfism" is to invest heavily in opening up the start-up's innovation processes, as in the case of the SMEs described by Keupp and Gassmann (2007) and van de Vrande et al. (2010). Gassmann et al. (2010) claimed that many SMEs do not embark on open innovation practices, despite their smallness, because they lack the resources needed to conduct knowledge exploration and selection activities.

The firms that succeed in developing open innovation practices can be expected to reduce the negative effects of the liability of newness and smallness, thereby improving not only their chances of survival but also their innovative performance.

We identify three crucial aspects of the external collaborations that start-ups may deploy to open up their innovation processes: 1) breadth, 2) depth, and 3) spatial distribution. External sources represent an opportunity for "learning at the boundaries" that is rooted in a firm's ability to enrich its knowledge by means of a network of interactions with external partners (suppliers, customers, research and market institutes—see Belussi et al. 2007; Belussi et al. 2010). Knowledge flows are made easier by the increasing use of an internationally shared language and ICT infrastructure (Castells, 2000), with a consequent increase in the availability of sources of innovation for the purpose of creating new processes and productive inputs, favoring economies of variety, and enhancing the heterogeneity of firms. Another important and often underestimated factor influencing the innovative performance of a company concerns the ability to commercialize valuable innovations. This applies particularly to small and start-up firms. Following this line of research, we consider the open innovation strategy as a lever for improving start-up innovation performance. A start-up that adopts an open innovation strategy combines internal and external R&D resources efficiently.

After the seminal contribution from Laursen and Salter (2006), several empirical works quantitatively measured firms' open innovation strategies by describing the breadth and depth of their inbound information flows and/or innovation collaborations (e.g., Van der Meer, 2007; Frenz and Ietto-Gillies, 2009; Grimpe and Sofka, 2009; Leiponen and Helfat, 2010; Love et al., 2011). The main thread of our investigation here concerns the impact of the breadth and depth of start-up firms' search strategies on their innovation performance.

The geography of a firm's innovation ties is an important variable characterizing the variety of its search strategy portfolio: some firms rely more heavily on local collaborations, some on more distant links, and some combine local and distant knowledge flows (see, among others, Bathelt et al., 2004; Gittelman, 2007; Trippl et al., 2009; Belussi et al., 2010; Belussi and Sedita, 2012; Fitjar and Rodríguez-Pose, 2014). We expected to find a variable impact of the geography of these ties on a start-up's innovation performance.

The type of innovation partner can also make a difference, depending on its distance/proximity. The main references here are studies on regional innovation systems (RISs), which have provided evidence of the geographical dimension of innovation collaborations of firms located within a RIS. While the traditional approach to RIS mainly emphasized the importance of local sources of innovation (Cooke, 1992; Asheim, 1995), more recent studies have underscored the crucial role of accessing knowledge and innovation from elsewhere (Asheim and Isaksen, 2002; Bathelt et al., 2004; Asheim and Gertler, 2005; Gertler and Levitte, 2005; Boschma and ter Wal, 2007; Belussi et al., 2010).

Our main research questions here are: Is it preferable to cooperate intensively with local or remote partners? Which partners is it best to keep close at hand? Following on the work by Dahlander and McKelvey (2005), we analyze the occurrence and spatial distribution of innovation-oriented research collaborations developed by start-up firms.

3. METHOD

The data for our analysis were drawn from an original survey focusing on new ventures, conducted between February and June 2013. For the purpose of this analysis, we considered all the companies inserted in the business register of the Italian Chambers of Commerce that had started up between 2005 and 2009 and were still active in 2012. This enabled us to concentrate on the "successful" new ventures, i.e., firms that had survived for at least three years. We chose firms located in Northern Italy, within any of the following regions: Emilia-Romagna, Friuli-Venezia Giulia, Trentino Alto-Adige, and Veneto (in the northeast) and Liguria, Lombardia, Piemonte, and Valle D'Aosta (in the northwest). The firms specialized in medium- to high-tech mechanical industries (Ateco 2002 codes: 29, 31, 34, and 35 [excluding 35.1]) according to the European classification of industries. This sector is interesting, partly because of its relevance on other industries, given that its output (be it a service or product) supports the innovativeness and performance of its clients. In particular, mechanical engineering firms (Ateco 2007 C28; source ISTAT, 2012) account for 6% of all Italian manufacturing firms and their employees account for 12% of the total manufacturing workforce. The mechanical sector is important for the Italian economy because it produces 14.3% of the manufacturing industry's overall added value. It is also worth noting that 50.6% of mechanical engineering firms are exporters, and their total exports make up 51.4% of their turnover (as opposed to a mean 32.2% for manufacturing firms generally), while the intensity of their importing activities for intermediate goods and services is 21.3% (34% for manufacturing firms generally).

From this sector, we obtained a stratified sample based on industry specialization and geographical location (by region). From among the 638 firms initially contacted, we collected 188 valid responses from mechanical engineering firms. A specialized agency conducted interviews with the aid of CATI and CAWI procedures, targeting each firms' entrepreneurs. A questionnaire, six pages long, was administered, which included questions about the firms' structural features and marketing strategies, the founders' characteristics and motives, and the firms' competences, innovation, and networking activities, both at the time of its foundation and in the years that followed. To ensure that the companies had first been established during the years considered, and excluding from the analysis any older firms that had registered with the Italian Chambers of Commerce in years after they had actually started operating (due to name changes, changes in legal status, mergers, acquisitions, and the like), a specific filter question was administered to respondents at the beginning of the interview. Information on the financial performance of the firms being sampled was obtained from the AIDA Bureau Van Dijk and the Chambers of Commerce databases.

4. MAIN FEATURES OF THE SAMPLED FIRMS

In terms of their geographical distribution, 52.66% of our 188 firms are located in Northeastern Italy (21.28% in Emilia-Romagna, 5.32% in Friuli-Venezia Giulia, 1.60% in Trentino Alto-Adige, and 24.47% in Veneto), and 47.34% in the northwestern part of the country (1.60% in Liguria, 37.23% in Lombardia, and 8.51% in Piemonte). As for their age, 30.32% of the firms were born in 2005, 30.32% in 2006, 32.98% in 2007, 5.32% in 2008, and only 1.06% in 2009. So most of the firms sampled were around six years old at the time of our survey. We were particularly interested in seeing whether their relationships with external agents have contributed positively to their innovative capacity, thereby shaping their further development. The companies in our sample are not only young but also small: 76% of them had up to 10 employees in their first year of activity, 23% had up to 50 employees, and only 1% had more than 50 on the payroll. As of 2012, their employee growth rate stood at about 49%, however, denoting a good growth for these firms. These companies also revealed quite a high degree of internationalization: even though 44% of them operate mainly on their local market (where they achieve >50% of their turnover) and 21.7% on the Italian domestic market, 34.3% sell mainly abroad.

Generally speaking, two or three founders linked by previous business activities or by kinship established the sample firms. These founders are generally not very young, averaging around 45 years of age; this is rather counterintuitive, but fairly typical of the Italian start-up scenario. Even the youngest founder in our sample was 39 years old (much older than the 20- to 25-year-olds we might expect to see founding new start-ups). This goes to show that there are still high barriers to entry for young entrepreneurs in the mechanical industry, especially in terms of the initial level of knowledge and expertise required: 48% of the entrepreneurs interviewed said they had decided to create a new venture to take advantage of previous work experience, and 22% of them were driven by the chance to implement innovative ideas that they could not develop in their previous jobs.

Our firms are mainly "pure" start-ups (75%); only 25% of them are corporate spin-offs. The founders started their new businesses mainly to operate in an existing market and to provide products or services that were slightly better (in 59% of cases) or less costly (15%). Only 14% of our overall sample was truly innovative firms that had introduced new products or services to an emerging, as yet unconsolidated, market.

As concerns the firms' sources of funding, 90% are supported by capital provided by friends and family, which accounts for a mean 84% of their entire company capital. The second most often used source is bank loans (chosen by 36% of the firms). Alternative funding sources, such as private equity, seed and venture capital, and business angels, have a very marginal role or none at all. The firms claim that their competitive advantage is mainly a matter of quality (45%), followed by customization (23%), and reliability (17%); they are therefore strongly customer oriented, focusing more on quality and on satisfying their customer's needs than on the costs of their products and services.

Various sources of information are used, to a variable degree, to gain knowledge of the market. In particular, the firms report gathering useful information mainly from their industrial partners (94%), and also from the Internet (75.5%), i.e. blogs, newsletters, websites, and social networks and from participation in conferences and exhibitions (74.5%).

In our sample, 74% of the firms had never taken part in a business incubation program, while 26% were initially supported by private business incubators (85%) and science parks (15%), i.e., infrastructures that provide tenant companies with facilities ranging from office space and capital to management support and knowledge. Some particular types of "networked" business incubators (Hansen et al., 2000) are able to increase the chances of a start-up firm finding partners for its innovation schemes, helping it to become involved in a larger network of innovation actors revolving around the incubator's management (Sedita and Grandinetti, 2014). The creation of external relationships through the intermediation of such an infrastructure may improve the start-up's innovation capacity.

Turning now to the firms' innovation strategies, we identified a number of variables: R&D expenditure, frequency of use of different collaborations in the innovation process, type and frequency of use of means to protect innovations, number of innovations introduced to the market—and number of "green innovations," and the percentage of turnover deriving from products new to the market. In our analysis, we use the last of these variables as an indicator of innovation performance, focusing particularly on investigating the role of open innovation strategies in explaining a firm's innovation performance.

In more detail, 73% of the start-ups allocated a mean 24% of their turnover to R&D activities in their first year. By 2012, there were more firms (80%) investing in R&D, but to a lesser degree (allocating a mean 22% of their turnover). The mechanical engineering firms mainly develop product innovations (about 68%), while 19% are process innovations, and organizational and marketing innovations are poorly developed (6% and 7%, respectively). In our sample, 52% of the firms take steps to protect their innovations, the most widespread solutions being patents (28%) and trademarks (20%), while industrial design rights and trade secrets are rarely used (6%). The preference for the first two solutions is justified by the type of protection they afford. Patents protect firms' technological knowledge, while trademarks protect their marketing assets. Patents and trademarks both embody an exclusive right and provide an incentive for the firm to invest in innovation and marketing activities, respectively (Greenhalgh and Rogers, 2010). Patents and trademarks can also be considered as an indication of firms' commitment to introducing new products or entering new geographical markets. There are also some important differences between patents and trademarks: most of the investment protected by a patent is undertaken before the patent has been granted, while this is not necessarily the case for trademarks, since a large share of the marketing investment is only undertaken after the trademark has been granted (Sandner and Block, 2011).

The firms in our sample seem to pay great attention to the so-called "green innovations": between 2010 and 2012, 46% of these firms produced an average of two innovations for reducing the environmental impact of their manufacturing processes; for these firms, green innovations account for about 20% of their turnover.

As for the firms' endowment of competences, they generally start their activities already in possession of a medium-high level of technological expertise—which is hardly surprising since they are mechanical engineering firms. The competence in which they are weakest is in marketing, but they tend to improve considerably during the first three years of the firm's life (+32.0%). Other competences also improve, with management competences increasing by 24.4%, ICT competences by 20.8%, and technological competences by 19%. The competence-building process takes place exclusively within the firm in one in two cases, while 40% of the firms have both internal and external development patterns, and 10% follow an exclusively external growth path.

5. MAPPING THE SAMPLED FIRMS' COLLABORATION NETWORKS

One of the most important components of an open innovation strategy is investment in external collaborations. Figure 8.1 shows the network of the innovation collaborations most often used by the firms in our sample. We can identify six different strategies (A to F, Figure 8.1) adopted by our sample of mechanical start-ups, as follows:

A. Regional collaborations: this is the most common strategy, used by 49% of the firms interviewed. These firms appear to operate within regional innovation systems, where relationships within a small geographical area are the preferred sources of inbound knowledge flows.
B. National collaborations: 21% of the firms cooperate with actors located in Italy. These firms cannot rely on local knowledge flows alone, so they extend their search strategies beyond the boundaries of their own regions.
C. International collaborations: 11% of the firms prefer to cooperate with partners outside Italy and with foreign customers in particular. The regional embeddedness of these firms is very limited.
D. Regional and national collaborations: 10% of the firms cultivate innovative relationships with partners located in their own regions or in other Italian regions. The geography of their collaborations is circumscribed but still large enough to avoid the lock-in phenomena typical of locally bounded firms.
E. Regional and international collaborations: a small proportion (6%) of the firms in our sample show a tendency to leverage on local knowledge flows, while being open to distant collaborations.
F. National and international collaborations: only a small minority (3%) of the firms do not rely on regional resources at all but orient their search strategies on the national and international level.

The radar (Figure 8.2) shows the most intensively used collaborations, which are clearly those with regional actors, reinforcing the conviction that RISs are likely to host new ventures and sustain them with the aid of regional knowledge flows and policies. A RIS can serve as a fertile environment that reduces the liability of newness and smallness. Customers are the main actors with which companies collaborate in innovation processes on regional, national, and international levels. The mechanical engineering firms pay a great deal of attention to the quality of their products and to ascertaining their customers' needs so that they can offer personalized products and services. This improves their chances of developing successful, marketable innovations. The second most often used type of collaboration is with suppliers on regional, national, and international levels. Then it is the turn of industrial partners, with an intermediate intensity of use, while collaborations with private consultants and universities are rarely used.

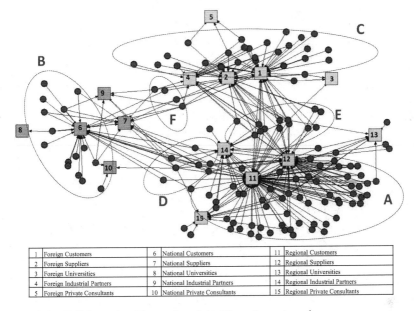

1	Foreign Customers	6	National Customers	11	Regional Customers
2	Foreign Suppliers	7	National Suppliers	12	Regional Suppliers
3	Foreign Universities	8	National Universities	13	Regional Universities
4	Foreign Industrial Partners	9	National Industrial Partners	14	Regional Industrial Partners
5	Foreign Private Consultants	10	National Private Consultants	15	Regional Private Consultants

Figure 8.1   Collaboration Networks of the Firms Interviewed

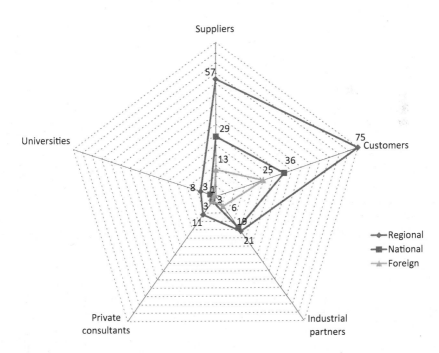

Figure 8.2   Spatial Distribution of Firms' Collaboration Networks

6. MEASURES

Dependent Variable

Innovation performance is often studied using indicators such as number of patents or patent citations. Such measures can be seen as a good proxy of the commitment to innovation of a technology-intensive start-up. Not all inventions are patented (or patentable), however, and there may be large differences across industries and firms (see, for example, Cohen et al., 2000). For our study, we therefore use the proportion of a firm's turnover deriving from products new to the market (INNO_PERF) as an indicator of its innovation performance (Laursen and Salter, 2006; Schneider and Veugelers, 2010). This measure is cross-sectoral (bearing in mind that mechanical engineering firms belong to different subsectors) and comes closer to the real value that a company gains from its commitment to innovation.

Independent Variables

As in Laursen and Salter (2006), we introduce two variables reflecting the openness of firms' external collaboration strategies.

The variable called BREADTH was constructed by combining five types of collaboration for the purposes of innovation (suppliers, clients, industrial alliances, consultants, and universities and other public research organizations). As a starting point, each of these five types of collaboration were coded as a binary variable, where not using or using is given a partner score of 0 or 1, respectively. Then the five types of collaboration can simply be added together so that firms score 0 if they have no collaborations in place and 5 if they use all the aforementioned types of collaboration. The assumption is that firms using a greater variety of collaborations adopt more "open" external collaboration strategies.

The DEPTH variable was constructed using the same five types of collaboration, each scoring 1 in this case if firms reported exploiting collaboration intensively and 0 if they made only a moderate or limited use of a given collaboration. The sum of the scores thus meant that firms scoring 0 used none of their external collaborations intensively, while firms scoring 5 made abundant use of all the various types of collaboration.

We also consider the firms' appropriability strategy, i.e., how they prevent their knowledge from being copied by others and thus retain the added value deriving from their innovations. As Laursen and Salter (2014) demonstrated, an appropriability strategy is an important prerequisite for a firm's absorptive capacity. Based on their econometric analysis of data from a UK innovation survey, they found a concave relationship between firms' breadth of external search and formal collaboration for the purposes of innovation and the strength of the firms' appropriability strategies. We consider the number of protective measures adopted by firms by introducing the

PROT variable, which is constructed by combining four types of protection (patents, trademarks, industrial design rights, and trade secrets). First of all, each of the four types was coded as a binary variable, scoring 0 if a given protection was not used and 1 if it was. Then the sum of the scores meant that a firm scoring 0 used no such means to protect its interests, while a firm scoring 4 used all four means to do so.

Finally, we consider the firms' R&D expenditure (R&D_EXPENDITURE) in terms of the proportion of a firm's turnover invested in R&D activities during the year 2012. This indicator is a proxy of a firm's in-house innovation effort, and it can also be interpreted as a firm's ability to absorb and integrate the knowledge it has gathered from outside.

Finally, we consider the origin of the actors with which firms collaborate for the purposes of innovation, distinguishing between regional, national, or international collaborations. The REGIONAL, NATIONAL, and FOREIGN variables identify the location of the most intensively used collaborations. Each variable expresses a percentage of the total, so the sum of the three variables amounts to 100%. These last variables enable us to see whether our firms operate within a RIS or an open regional innovation system (see Belussi et al., 2010).

Control Variables

Since different geographical areas provide different institutional and industrial settings that can influence firms' innovation performance, we include a GEO control variable that scores 1 for firms located in the northwest of Italy and 0 for those in the northeast. The AGE variable indicates when the company was founded and spans from three to seven years (because it was calculated in 2012), with the oldest firms having been established in 2005 and the youngest in 2009. Our sample consists of small and medium enterprises (SMEs) and, to control for their size, we introduced the SIZE variable indicating the number of active founders and employees at the company in 2012. New ventures are usually classified as start-ups, academic, or corporate spin-offs. Adopting this classification, we also introduced the TYPE variable, which takes a value of 1 if the company is a spin-off, and 0 otherwise.

6. RESULTS OF A PROBIT REGRESSION MODEL

Since our dependent variable is far from being normally distributed, we can calculate an ordered probit model to investigate the tendency of firms' innovation performance to be affected by their innovation strategies. An ordered logit or a probit are both appropriate econometric models to use for this purpose. An ordered probit with known thresholds can also be used, since the boundaries between each category are known. The two methods

Table 8.1 Descriptive Statistics

Variable	Obs	Mean	Std. Dev.	Min	Max
GEO	188	0.4734	0.5006	0	1
AGE	188	5.8351	0.9587	3	7
DIM	168	11.4286	10.3730	1	81
TYPE	184	0.2446	0.4310	0	1
DEPTH	187	1.5882	1.1199	0	5
BREADTH	187	3.0802	1.2044	0	5
PROT	188	1.0479	1.2636	0	4
R&D	164	18.5854	22.4319	0	100
REGIONAL	151	52.1854	40.7850	0	100
NATIONAL	151	30.2782	35.4663	0	100
FOREIGN	151	17.5364	29.9149	0	100
INNO_PERF	163	36	35.4925	0	100

generate essentially identical results, with only a few marginal differences that are insignificant for the purpose of our analysis. The estimation method is that of the maximum likelihood (MLE), which provides the means for choosing an asymptotically efficient estimator for a set of parameters (for details of the properties of ML estimators, see Greene, 1997: 129).

Table 8.2 shows that the breadth of external collaborations positively affects the innovation performance of our start-ups. It seems to be more important for firms to engage in multiple relationships with numerous actors (BREADTH) than for them to have a few very intensive relationships (DEPTH). The firms' appropriability strategy is also relevant to their innovation performance: the more types of protection they use, the higher their chances of a better innovation performance. As expected, higher levels of R&D expenditure also positively affect innovation performance, contributing to a firm's absorptive capacity. As for the geography of the most intensively used collaborations, we can see that firms with collaboration networks reaching beyond the boundaries of their own regions or, better still, of their countries, are more likely to achieve a better innovation performance.

7. CONCLUSIONS

The aim of this work was to investigate the role of open innovation strategies in explaining firms' innovation performance. The empirical evidence emerging from our study comes from analyzing a sample of mechanical engineering start-up firms located in the north of Italy. Our results shed some light on what drives the innovation performance of such start-ups,

Table 8.2 Determinants of Firms' Innovation Performance

	Robust coef.	Std. error	Std. coef
Dependent variable INNO_PERF			
Independent variable			
DEPTH	0.0965	0,1460	0,0813
BREADTH	0.2647*	0,1218	0,2232
PROT	0.1706**	0,0827	0,1438
R&D	0.0090†	0,0050	0,0076
NATIONAL	0.0064†	0,0035	0,0054
FOREIGN	0.0095*	0,0038	0,008
Control variable			
GEO	0.1236	0,2224	0,1042
AGE	−0.0174	0,1256	−0,0147
DIM	−0.0068	0,0064	−0,0057
TYPE	0.0408	0,2460	0,0344
No. of observations	100		
Wald chi2(10)	30,44		
Prob>chi2	0,0007		
Pseudo $R^{2(1)}$	0,062		
Log pseudolikelihood	−234,26886		

1 This is McFadden's pseudo R-squared. Logistic regression does not have an equivalent to the R-squared found in OLS regression, though many people have tried to devise one. There is a wide variety of pseudo R-squared statistics that can generate contradictory conclusions. This statistic does not mean the same thing as R-squared in OLS regression (the proportion of variance for the response variable explained by the predictors), so we suggest interpreting this statistic with great caution.

* $p < .05$.

** $p < .01$.

*** $p < .001$.

† $p < .10$.

contributing to the literature on innovation and entrepreneurship. While the role of open innovation strategies on firms' performance is generally well known and has been empirically demonstrated, there is a lack of evidence concerning start-up firms. To fill this gap, we analyzed three main aspects of interorganizational collaborations, i.e., their breadth, depth, and spatial distribution. A probit regression model enabled us to measure the impact of these three aspects of collaborations on start-up firms' innovation performance, measured in terms of the proportion of their turnover deriving from products new to the world market.

The breadth of a firm's external collaborations (the number of the various types of innovation-oriented ties established by the start-up company) appears to be crucial in order to diversify their innovation inputs and reduce the risk embedded in the innovation process.

The depth of their collaborations (the number of intensively used ties) proved instead to be irrelevant in shaping the start-ups' innovation performances. This might be inherently related to the specificities of newborn firms, which initially need to explore a variety of partnerships to discover which ones work best and are worth developing further. This initial exploration of a broad portfolio of collaborations seems to mitigate the liability of newness.

Unlike the depth of a start-up firm's ties in general, what does affect its capacity for innovation is the geographical distribution of the ties it uses most intensively. This element proved relevant in explaining the differentials in terms of innovation performance. In particular, although the majority of the start-ups' partners were located in the same region, their most important ties were more remote and mainly located abroad.

Our results confirm the conviction that a RIS sustains the early stages of a firm's development, but it is not enough to guarantee a positive innovation performance. Distant collaborations contribute positively to increasing the innovative capacity of start-ups, alongside an open regional innovation system approach (Belussi et al., 2010). This finding is consistent with the picture seen for established companies. A firm's competitiveness is often threatened by local competitors, so it is plausible for companies to try to distinguish themselves from the others by selecting appropriate, exclusive distant collaborators with whom they can develop innovation processes that are difficult to imitate (on the local level). Our empirical findings show that distant innovation-oriented ties are built mainly with global suppliers and clients, which help start-up companies to better connect with new markets and new technologies developed abroad. This is particularly useful for the purpose of customizing technological solutions in the mechanical engineering field. It is common knowledge, and easy to see from the national statistics, that the competitiveness of Italian firms in this sector rests more on their ability to deploy differentiated sources of competitive advantage than on their ability to establish economies of scale and scope.

Our analysis should provide managers of start-ups with some useful suggestions on how to increase their firms' innovation performance. First, they should broaden their portfolio of potential partners. Second, they should identify which of their more distant external collaborations might drive internationally appropriate innovation solutions. By doing so, they will increase their chances of working on globally marketable technological products.

The scarce knowledge of the market typical of start-up companies might thus be overcome.

Policy-makers should acknowledge the importance of linking newborn companies to a regional innovation system capable of assuring them access to local and international resources. One way to develop an efficient RIS for start-ups is to sustain the development of local agencies that can provide a network of possible innovation-oriented ties, such as business incubators or science parks. University-industry collaborations should also be strengthened on the regional level, because this can make it easier for new, small firms to benefit from the extensive research networks of the best-performing universities. Our research has shown that such ties have been scarcely developed by our sample of firms, but—given the potential benefits of such relationships—we recommend encouraging matching between firms and universities.

This work offers an original contribution on an emerging, hitherto insufficiently studied, field of research, i.e., the relationship between the openness of start-up firms' collaboration-finding strategies and their innovation performance. Our empirical evidence comes from a particular industry (one of the most important in the present-day Italian economic scenario); however, the research would need to be extended to other industries or countries, by means of comparative studies, before any generalizations can be drawn from our results.

NOTE

1 According to Helfat and Lieberman (2002, p. 730), start-ups are a type of new entry on a market or new venture "whose founders have no previous employment ties to other firms in the industry".

REFERENCES

Abatecola, G., Cafferata, R. and Poggesi, S. (2012). Arthur Stinchcombe's "liability of newness": Contribution and impact of the construct. *Journal of Management History*, 18(4), 402–418.

Asheim, B. T. (1995). Regionale innovasjonssystem—en sosialt og territorielt forankret teknologipolitikk. *Nordisk Samhällsgeografisk Tidskrift*, 20, 17–34.

Asheim, B. and Gertler, M. (2005). *The geography of innovation.* In J. Fagerberg, D. Mowery and R. Nelson (eds.), *The oxford handbook of innovation* (291–317). Cheltenham: Elgar.

Asheim, B. T. and Isaksen, A. (2002). Regional innovation systems: The integration of local 'sticky' and global 'ubiquitous' knowledge. *The Journal of Technology Transfer*, 27(1), 77–86.

Bathelt, H., Malmberg, A. and Maskell, P. (2004). Clusters and knowledge: Local buzz, global pipelines and the process of knowledge creation. *Progress in Human Geography*, 28, 31–56.

Belussi, F., Pilotti, L. and Sedita, S. R. (2007). Learning at the boundaries for industrial districts between exploitation of local resources and exploration of global

158 *Silvia Rita Sedita and Roberta Apa*

knowledge flows. In R. Leoncini and S. Montresor (eds.), *Dynamic capabilities between firm organization and local systems of production* (181–215). London: Routledge.

Belussi, F., Sammarra, A. and Sedita, S. R. (2010). Learning at the boundaries in an "Open Regional Innovation System": A focus on firms' innovation strategies in the Emilia Romagna life science industry. *Research Policy*, 39(6), 710–721.

Belussi, F. and Sedita, S. R. (2012). Industrial districts as open learning systems: Combining emergent and deliberate knowledge structures. *Regional Studies*, 46(2), 165–184.

Bilbao-Osorio, B. and Rodríguez-Pose, A. (2004). From R&D to innovation and economic growth in the EU. *Growth and Change*, 35(4), 434–455.

Bøllingtoft, A., and Ulhøi, J. P. (2005). The networked business incubator: Leveraging entrepreneurial agency? *Journal of Business Venturing*, 20(2), 265–290.

Boschma, R. A. and Ter Wal, A. L. J. (2007). Knowledge networks and innovative performance in an industrial district: The case of a footwear district in the South of Italy. *Industry and Innovation*, 14, 177–199.

Castells, M. (2000). *The rise of the network society* (2nd ed.). Cambridge, Mass.: Blackwell.

Chesbrough, H. (2003a). *Open innovation: The new imperative for creating and profiting from technology.* Boston: Harvard Business School Press.

Chesbrough, H. W. (2003b). The era of open innovation. *MIT Sloan Management Review*, 44(3), 35–41.

Chesbrough, H. W. and Brunswicker, S. (2013). *Managing open innovation in large firms.* Open innovation Executive Survey, Fraunhofer Verlag.

Cohen, W. M., Nelson, R. R. and Walsh, J. P. (2000). *Protecting their intellectual assets: Appropriability conditions and why US manufacturing firms patent (or not)* (No. w7552). National Bureau of Economic Research.

Cooke, P. (1992). Regional innovation systems: Competitive regulation in the new Europe. *Geoforum*, 23(3), 365–382.

Dahlander, L. and McKelvey, M. (2005). The occurrence and spatial distribution of collaboration: Biotech firms in Gothenburg, Sweden. *Technology Analysis & Strategic Management*, 17, 409–431.

Fitjar, R. D. and Rodríguez-Pose, A. (2014). The geographical dimension of innovation collaboration: Networking and innovation in Norway. *Urban Studies*, 51(12), 2572–2595.

Freeman, J., Carroll, G. R. and Hannan, M. T. (1983). The liability of newness: Age dependence in organizational death rates. *American Sociological Review*, 48(5), 692–710.

Frenz, M. and Ietto-Gillies, G. (2009). The impact on innovation performance of different sources of knowledge: Evidence from the UK Community Innovation Survey. *Research Policy*, 38(7), 1125–1135.

Gassmann, O., Enkel, E. and Chesbrough, H. (2010). The future of open innovation. *R&D Management*, 40(3), 213–221.

Gertler, M. S. and Levitte, Y. M. (2005). Local nodes in global networks: The geography of knowledge flows in biotechnology innovation. *Industry and Innovation*, 12, 487–507.

Gittelman, M. (2007). Does geography matter for science-based firms? Epistemic communities and the geography of research and patenting in biotechnology. *Organization Science*, 18(4), 724–741.

Greene, W. H. (1997). *Econometric Analysis.* Upper Saddle River, N.J.: Prentice-Hall.

Greenhalgh, C. and Rogers, M. (2010). *Innovation, intellectual property and economic growth.* Princeton, N.J.: Princeton University Press.

Grimpe, C. and Sofka, W. (2009). Search patterns and absorptive capacity: Low- and high-technology sectors in European countries. *Research Policy*, 38(3), 495–506.

Hansen, M. T., Chesbrough, H. W., Nohria, N. and Sull, D. N. (2000). Networked incubators. Hothouses of the new economy. *Harvard Business Review*, 78 (5), 74–84.

Helfat, C. E. and Lieberman, M. B. (2002). The birth of capabilities: Market entry and the importance of pre-history. *Industrial and Corporate Change*, 11(4), 725–760.

Keupp, M. M. and Gassmann, O. (2007). The competitive advantage of early and rapidly internationalising SMEs in the biotechnology industry: A knowledge-based view. *Journal of World Business, Special Issue: The Early and Rapid Internationalisation of the Firm*, 42(3), 350–366.

Klepper, S. (2001). Employee startups in high-tech industries. *Industrial and Corporate Change*, 10(3), 639–674.

Klepper, S. and Sleeper, S. (2005). Entry by spinoffs. *Management Science*, 51(8), 1291–1306.

Laursen, K. and Salter, A. (2006). Open for innovation: The role of openness in explaining innovation performance among UK manufacturing firms. *Strategic Management Journal*, 27(2), 131–150.

Laursen, K. and Salter, A. J. (2014). The paradox of openness: Appropriability, external search and collaboration. *Research Policy*, 43(5), 867–878.

Leiponen, A. and Helfat, C. E. (2010). Innovation objectives, knowledge sources, and the benefits of breadth. *Strategic Management Journal*, 31(2), 224–236.

Love, J. H., Roper, S. and Bryson, J. R. (2011). Openness, knowledge, innovation and growth in UK business services. *Research Policy*, 40(10), 1438–1452.

Sandner, P. G. and Block, J. (2011). The market value of R&D, patents, and trademarks. *Research Policy*, 40(7), 969–985.

Schneider, C. and Veugelers, R. (2010). On young highly innovative companies: Why they matter and how (not) to policy support them. *Industrial and Corporate Change*, 19(4), 969–1007.

Sedita, S. R. and Grandinetti, R. (2014). *Relationships at work in a networked business incubator: The case of H-Farm*. Working Paper No. 190–2014, Dipartimento di Scienze Economiche e Aziendali, Università degli Studi di Padova.

Stinchcombe, A. L. (1965). Social structure and organizations. In J. C. March (ed.), *Handbook of organizations* (142–193). Chicago: Rand McNally.

Trajtenberg, M. (1990). A penny for your quotes: Patent citations and the value of innovations. *The RAND Journal of Economics*, 21(1), 172–187.

Trippl, M., Toedtling, F. and Lengauer, L. (2009). Knowledge sourcing beyond buzz and pipelines: Evidence from the Vienna software sector. *Economic Geography*, 85(4), 443–462.

Van De Vrande, V., Vanhaverbeke, W. and Gassmann, O. (2010). Broadening the scope of open innovation: Past research, current state and future directions. *International Journal of Technology Management*, 52(3), 221–235.

Van der Meer, H. (2007). Open innovation—the Dutch treat: Challenges in thinking in business models. *Creativity and Innovation Management*, 16(2), 192–202.

West, J., Salter, A., Vanhaverbeke, W. and Chesbrough, H. (2014). Open innovation: The next decade. *Research Policy*, 43(5), 805–811.

9 Firm Collaboration and Modes of Innovation in Norway[1]

Rune Dahl Fitjar and
Andrés Rodríguez-Pose

1. INTRODUCTION

There has traditionally been a strong dividing line in the research looking at the sources of innovation. This dividing line has been fundamentally
determined by the value different strands of research awarded to science and
technology as the key element for the generation, diffusion, and assimilation
of innovation. Researchers on innovation have, over the years, tended to
place themselves on either side of the dividing line. On one side of the line,
the linear model of innovation (Bush, 1945; Maclaurin, 1953) and research
on knowledge spillovers (Audretsch and Feldman, 1996; Cantwell and Iammarino, 1998; Sonn and Storper, 2008) have looked at innovation from a
scientific and technical perspective. This has led to the use of research and
development (R&D), patenting, information and communication technology (ICT) expenditures, and the level of education and training of the labor
force as the main proxies of, as well as the key factors behind, the development and assimilation of innovation. Other researchers have, by contrast,
been profoundly skeptical about the relevance of R&D, patenting and ICT
expenditure as sources of innovation relevant to the firm (Cooke, 2001).
These researchers on the other side of the dividing line have tended to place
the greatest emphasis on institutions, interactions, networks, and informal relationships that facilitate the generation and exchange of knowledge
(Lundvall, 1992). This strand has given rise to a blooming literature which,
under different definitions and names—e.g., "neo-Marshallian industrial
districts" (Becattini, 1987), "innovative milieu" (Aydalot, 1986), "learning regions" (Morgan, 1997), or "regional innovation systems" (Cooke
et al., 1997; Cooke and Morgan, 1998)—regards innovation as a territo-
rially embedded phenomenon, determined by the social and institutional
conditions in a given territory (Iammarino, 2005).

A number of scholars have tried to bridge the gap between linear
approaches to innovation and those more concerned with institutions and
interactions, often putting the capacity to assimilate external knowledge at
the heart of the process of innovation. Von Hippel (1976), for example, focused
on how user-supplier relationships shaped innovation in the production of

scientific instruments. Cohen and Levinthal (1990) introduced the concept of absorptive capacity in the firm, making it not only dependent on the firm's prior related knowledge and R&D expenditure but also on a firm's interdependence with rivals and history—and path dependent. Chesbrough (2003) has put forward the idea of open innovation, which has propelled to the fore the view that innovation—in contrast to prior paradigms, which emphasized the benefits of in-house innovation closed to external influences—is increasingly the result of a combination of ideas from both internal and external sources. Other attempts have adopted a more macro approach, using regions and metropolitan areas as their unit of analysis (e.g., Crescenzi et al., 2007; Rodríguez-Pose and Crescenzi, 2008).

One of the most prominent recent attempts to connect internal R&D-based and external, institutional- and interaction-based innovation has been that of Jensen et al. (2007). These authors identify two fundamental modes of firm learning: "science, technology, and innovation" (STI) and "doing, using, and interacting" (DUI). The STI mode of innovation refers to the use of scientific knowledge in the development of new technologies that form the basis of new products or processes within the firm. The DUI mode refers to on-the-job problem solving based on the exchange of experiences and know-how, through which firms find solutions to various problems that arise. These processes typically involve a large component of tacit knowledge (Jensen et al., 2007: 62–64). According to Jensen et al. (2007), the STI and DUI modes of innovation have used different approaches, techniques, and proxies to explain and measure how innovation at the level of the firm is generated. The STI mode has generally relied on deductive approaches and quantitative techniques, employing R&D, patenting, ICT, and the formal education of the workforce as the key indicators. The DUI mode of innovation is somewhat more diverse, although inductive and qualitative approaches have tended to prevail. Despite the increasing importance of quantitative analyses focusing on Community Innovation Surveys (CIS), these authors consider that quantitative methods based on survey data have still played a relatively small role in DUI mode approaches: "The vast majority of quantitative survey-based studies of innovation simply had little to say about the relation of DUI mode learning to innovative performance" (Jensen et al., 2007: 681). This is partly a result of the difficulty in operationalizing the complex institutional and relational factors at the base of DUI mode approaches to innovation but also a consequence of a general belief that processes such as learning-by-doing and using are best analyzed through in-depth case studies. Jensen et al. apply latent class analysis to data from 1,643 Danish firms and uncover that the two modes of innovation are complementary. Firms that combine STI and DUI innovation are more likely to introduce new products and services than those specialized in either of the modes (Jensen et al., 2007).

While making a pioneering and important contribution to our knowledge, one of the potential downsides of Jensen et al.'s analysis is that the classification of firms into four clusters according to the intensity of use of STI and DUI modes of innovation by each firm creates a rather crude division, which represents the variables of interest in the logistic regression analysis on which the key conclusions are based. This implies a significant loss of information about STI and DUI modes of learning at the level of each firm.

In this chapter, we aim to make a contribution to this debate by analyzing to what extent STI and DUI modes of innovation are related to firm-level innovation in Norway. We use a specifically tailor-made survey of 1,604 firms with more than ten employees in the five major Norwegian city-regions. The survey measures the different types of interactions that these firms engage in. We classify the interactions with different partner types into STI-interaction types and DUI-interaction types. STI-interaction types include connections with universities, research institutes, and consultancy firms. DUI-interaction types encompass linkages with other firms in the conglomerate, suppliers, customers, and competitors. DUI-type interactions are, in turn, divided into those that fall within the regular supply chain (interactions with suppliers and customers), and those that do not (interactions with competitors).

The main contributions of this chapter lie in four areas. First, in the use of different measures of innovation. In contrast to previous work, which tends to differentiate between product and service innovation (Jensen et al., 2007; Kirner et al., 2009), we distinguish, on the one hand, between product and process innovation, defined as the introduction of new products or processes in the firm over the last three years and, on the other, between incremental and radical innovation. This gives us a classification of four types of innovation, which may be affected by different patterns of collaboration at the level of the firm. The fourfold classification allows for much greater nuance in the explanation of how different forms of firm partnerships may affect different types of innovation. Second, rather than classifying firms according to their innovation practices, we use the different interaction linkages of each firm individually as our independent variables of interest, dividing, in turn, DUI-type interactions according to whether they are conducted within the supply chain or not. Third, we pay specific attention to the often neglected topic of the geographical dimension of the different partnerships of the firm and how they influence innovation. STI and DUI mode interactions are frequently conducted at different geographical scales, and this may significantly affect the capacity of firms to produce different types of innovation. We therefore distinguish between interactions conducted in close geographical proximity, i.e., at the level of a locality or region, and those that are conducted with partners located in distant cities or abroad. Last, but not least, we apply the analysis to a broad sample of firms across different industries in the five largest city-regions of Norway using a tailored survey specially designed for the purpose of this research. By contrast, earlier studies of the DUI and STI modes in Norway have focused on individual industries in smaller regions (e.g., Isaksen and Karlsen, 2010).

The chapter is structured into five further sections. In the theoretical section following this introduction, we briefly look at the role of the sources of knowledge and innovation, focusing later on the geography of STI and DUI modes of innovation. We then present the case and describe the data in section 3. The following section deals with the empirical analysis linking partner types with innovation outcomes. Section 5 examines the geographical dimension of partnerships and how it is related to innovation. The conclusions and some indications for future research are presented in section 6.

2. THE ROLE OF SOURCES OF KNOWLEDGE IN INNOVATION

The scholarly literature about where firms get the knowledge to generate and implement innovation has tended to be divided between two camps: a) a larger camp, which posits that firm-level innovation is the consequence of advances in science and technology (S&T), driven by investment in R&D and by human capital (the STI mode of innovation) and b) a smaller, but growing camp putting the emphasis on learning-by-doing and using (the DUI mode of innovation) (Jensen et al., 2007).

For those placed in the STI camp, innovation in firms is the result of investments in R&D and S&T and interaction with centers producing new knowledge—mainly research centers and universities, but also consultancies, scientific brokers, and foundations for the diffusion of scientific research—which generate the codified and explicit knowledge that can be used by the firm to produce new innovations. The capacity to generate and adopt new innovations will also be largely dependent on the human capital available in the firm and on the level of training of employees. As pointed out by Jensen et al. (2007: 681), in STI-type analyses, "there is a tendency to expect that the increasing reliance on science and technology in the 'knowledge-based economy' will enhance the role played by formal processes of R&D requiring personnel with formal S&T qualifications." Hence STI-type research has, by and large, resorted to investment in R&D, level of education of the workforce, and cooperation with research centers as the key indicators behind the analysis of innovation and the economic outcomes linked to innovation (e.g., Rodríguez-Pose and Crescenzi, 2008).

For those in the DUI camp, innovation is not about putting resources into R&D or pumping up the formal qualifications of employees (Hansen and Winther, 2011); innovation in the firm is mostly generated by the capacity of managers and employees to find solutions to existing problems and to respond to the challenges made by suppliers, customers, and the market. Innovation is therefore about markets and organizations (Caraça et al., 2009) and the result of a combination of learning-by-doing and using, which requires a huge amount of mainly informal interaction between people, both within and outside the firm (Lundvall, 1992; Storper and Venables, 2004; Barge-Gil et al., 2011). Constant and repeated interaction generates the tacit knowledge that facilitates the response to user demands and, ultimately, drives innovation within the firm (Jensen et al., 2007).

Although interaction facilitates innovation by fostering learning processes through the sharing of knowledge and information (Tracey and Clark, 2003), the STI and DUI modes of innovation are linked to different forms of interaction both within the firm and with the environment of the firm (Jensen et al., 2007). Using Lundvall and Johnson's (1994) classification, the STI mode of innovation requires interaction that leads to "know-what" and "know-why" types of knowledge. These are types of knowledge that, despite also having an informal interaction component, tend to be associated with formal relationships. The fundamental channels of transfer of this type of knowledge are either through universally accessible sources of knowledge, such as books, scientific articles, or the Internet, or by the establishment of formal relationships with the organizations that produce this knowledge, such as universities and research centers. The DUI mode of innovation, by contrast, tends to rely on "know-how" and "know-who" types of knowledge. These are types of knowledge that are obtained through repeat, mainly informal, interaction. Imitation and learning-by-doing are the main sources of "know-how." Social capital and local buzz provide the main sources of "know-who."

Hence different types of relationships and interactions are at the base of the STI and the DUI modes of innovation. The "know-what" and "know-why" types of knowledge that fuel STI are generated through often purpose-built engagement by the firm with external agents. These external agents include universities, research centers and institutes, and consultancy firms. The "know-how" and "know-who" needed for a DUI mode of innovation are obtained through informal and formal exchanges internal to the firm, but also with suppliers, customers, and competitors. However, not all of these DUI type of interactions lead to similar forms of "know-how" and "know-who." Within the DUI mode, a distinction can be made between interaction within the supply chain and outside it. Interactions within the supply chain—mainly with suppliers and customers—are fundamentally formal and aimed at improving the delivery of products in order to boost their competitiveness in the market. Innovation is thus one of the main purposes behind the exchanges. Interaction outside the supply chain, mainly with competitors (Porter, 1986), tends to be more informal, leading to knowledge spillovers that are more an unintended consequence of the relationship than its main purpose, as firms try to avoid direct transfer to rivals but cannot control indirect transfer (von Hippel, 1987: 295).

2.1 The Geography of STI and DUI Modes of Innovation

One aspect that has attracted very little attention in the literature about STI and DUI modes of innovation is that the types of interactions that are linked to STI or DUI modes of innovation, respectively, may have very different geographical dimensions. Because of the more formal nature of STI links, geographical proximity may not necessarily be essential for the generation of this type of innovation (Tracey and Clark, 2003).[2] The codified analytical and synthetic knowledge of the sort that dominates within the STI mode is assumed to be universal and can be shared across cultural contexts and geographical distance. STI mode innovation implies a capacity of firms to reach out to universities or research institutes, or vice versa, or for firms to hire management consultants that can serve as bridges between the firm and producers of scientific knowledge. This entails not only intent, but greater pecuniary and time costs (cf. Laursen and Salter, 2006). Because of the higher costs, firms will try to maximize their value for money and look for the best partners for the transmission of knowledge. This would generate links close to what Bathelt et al. (2004) have denominated as "global pipelines"—that is, purpose-built connections between a given local firm and partners in the outside world (see also Maskell et al., 2006: 999). The building of pipelines implies some sort of cognitive—sharing a similar knowledge base (Boschma, 2005)—or organized—part of an organization that facilitates interaction (Torre and Rallet, 2005)—type of proximity. However, this will not necessarily mean geographical proximity, as the best research institutes, universities, or consultancy firms with knowledge that can be readily used by the firm may not necessarily be located in the firm's immediate vicinity. As a consequence, it is likely that STI-mode innovation will rely on a strong nonlocal and non-regional dimension, with local components being particularly relevant only in those cases such as Oxford (Lawton-Smith, 1998), Silicon Valley (Saxenian, 1996), or large urban agglomerations (Feldman, 1999; Glaeser and Gottlieb, 2009) where top research centers coincide with dynamic and innovative firms.

DUI modes of innovation, by contrast, require cooperation with partners that share the same practical problems and experiences. This means that the knowledge that is transferred in the DUI mode of innovation tends, as a general rule, to be more tacit and maybe more frequent in industries with synthetic or symbolic knowledge bases, which rely on local understandings and cultural context (Asheim and Gertler, 2005; Moodysson et al., 2008). But even within the DUI mode of innovation, there are significant differences between relationships within and outside the supply chain. In the former, depending on the location of the suppliers and customers, these relationships can be of two kinds: a) interaction at a distance, when customers and suppliers are not located nearby, which means a lack of geographical proximity but strong cognitive, organizational, and, most likely, social and institutional proximity (Boschma, 2005) and b) interaction at close quarters, when different agents in the production chain share the same location, adding geographical proximity to all the other types of proximity.

DUI mode relationships with competitors will, in all likelihood, be much more constrained geographically. The ad hoc and informal nature of the interaction, the feeling that "something is in the air" (Gertler, 2003), means that firms, in order to benefit from the tacit knowledge linked to DUI mode relationships outside the supply chain, have to "be there" (Gertler, 1995). This necessarily represents face-to-face contacts and geographical proximity to be able to reap the spillovers and the tacit knowledge generated from local buzz (Storper and Venables, 2004).

In order to capture these different relationships and interactions, we distinguish between regional and non-regional cooperation across the three categories considered in this chapter: STI-mode relationships, DUI-mode relationships within the supply chain, and DUI-mode relationships outside the supply chain. In brief, partnerships within the STI mode of innovation are likely to be based on more universal knowledge that can be transferred across large geographical distances, meaning there is less value added in cooperating with locally based scientific partners. Thus there may be more to be gained from sourcing science-based knowledge from global nodes of excellence rather than restricting oneself to local partners. In contrast, DUI mode of innovation relationships—particularly outside the supply chain—can be expected to rely more on geographical proximity, as local partners will be more accessible than faraway ones for this type of learning.

3. CASE DESCRIPTION AND DATA

In order to answer the questions of whether and in which way different types of STI and DUI partnerships and their geographical dimensions affect different types of innovations, we conducted a survey in the spring of 2010 of firms located in the five largest urban agglomerations of Norway: Oslo, Bergen, Stavanger, Trondheim, and Kristiansand. Combined, these city-regions make up about half of the population of Norway. The survey was based on a questionnaire incorporating questions from the Community Innovation Surveys (CIS). Data collection was administered by Synovate, a survey firm specialized in innovation management, and took the form of telephone interviews with the chief executives of the firms. Synovate randomly sampled from the Norwegian Register of Business Enterprise, which by law lists all firms in Norway, firms with ten or more employees located in municipalities where 10% or more of the population commute into one of the five major Norwegian city-regions.[3] In total, we approached 5,887 firms and elicited 1,604 responses, a response rate of 27.2%.

As a way to test the hypotheses that different modes of learning and interaction result in different kinds of innovation, we distinguish between product and process innovation and also between radical and incremental innovation. We expect the STI mode to be more conducive to radical innovation and to product innovation, whereas the DUI mode, in particular when it comes to cooperation inside the supply chain, is more likely to be linked to incremental product innovation and to process innovation. For total product innovation, respondents were asked whether their firms had introduced any new and/or significantly improved products during the last three years (53.4% reported product innovation). They were also asked if these product innovations were new to the market, in which case they were classified as radical product innovations (30.6% of all firms), or only new to the firm (incremental product innovations). Similarly, the measure of total process innovation was based on a question about whether the firm had introduced any new and/or significantly improved methods or processes for production or delivery of products during the last three years (47.0%). If these new processes were new to the industry, they were classified as radical process innovations (18.8% of all firms); otherwise, they were classified as incremental ones.

In order to examine firm collaboration patterns, managers were also asked which, if any, of seven different types of partners (other firms within the conglomerate, suppliers, customers, competitors, consultancies, universities, and research institutes) their firm had cooperated with during the past three years. Table 9.1 shows the share of firms that reported cooperating with partners of each type. Suppliers and customers are the most commonly used partners, with three in four firms collaborating with suppliers and almost as many with customers. More than one in three firms also collaborates with competitors, making up a sizable number of firms. In terms of scientific partners, consultancies are the favored type, with nearly half of firms collaborating with consultancies. Almost one in four collaborate with universities and slightly fewer with research institutes.

4. PARTNER TYPES AND INNOVATION OUTCOMES

The first research question we examine is whether collaboration with these partner types improves the likelihood of developing innovations and, furthermore, whether different types of partners are conducive to different types of innovations. In addressing this question, we fit logistic regression models for each of

Table 9.1 Number and Share of Firms Collaborating With Different Types of Partners

Partner type	Number of firms	% of firms	S.E.
Other firms within the conglomerate	830	51.7	1.2
Suppliers	1214	75.7	1.1
Customers	1150	71.7	1.1
Competitors	606	37.8	1.2
Consultancies	774	48.3	1.2
Universities	399	24.9	1.1
Research institutes	346	21.6	1.0

the four types of innovation outcomes presented in the top half of Table 9.2 using dummy variables for each type of partner as independent variables.

The basic regression model takes on the following form:

$$\text{logit}(\pi_i) = \alpha + \beta_1 \text{ Partners}_i + \gamma_2 \text{ Controls}_i + \delta_3 \text{ Region}_i + \varepsilon_i \tag{1}$$

where π refers to the probability of firm i introducing an innovation, with four different regressions being run—one for each of the innovation outcomes (total product innovation, radical product innovation, total process innovation, and radical process innovation). The independent variables of interest are seven dummy variables for the different types of partners (other firms within the conglomerate, suppliers, customers, competitors, consultancies, universities, and research institutes). These variables take the value 1 if the firm has collaborated with this type of partner within the last three years and 0 otherwise.

As usual in firm-level analyses, the model controls for a set of factors that are related both to innovation and to the use of partners. These include the size (log no. of employees), industry (a set of dummy variables referring to one-digit NACE codes), and ownership (share held by foreign owners) of the firm, as well as the less frequently controlled for characteristics of the chief executive: level of education (no. of years beyond compulsory lower-level schooling), age, and directorships held in other companies (log-transformed). We also include controls for the five city-regions in order to examine whether there are any residual differences between the regions after taking into account other factors. ε depicts the error term.

Table 9.2 shows the results of the logistic regression analyses for each of the four innovation outcomes. Different types of partnerships are related to different types of innovation in different ways, but not always necessarily in the direction predicted by prevailing theories. If we take the partnerships that are traditionally linked to the STI mode of innovation, scientific collaboration is, as expected, relatively strongly associated with product innovation. Nevertheless, this association only seems to involve partnerships with universities and not those with research institutes and consultancies. Collaboration with universities is closely related to the likelihood of radical product innovation and, more weakly but still significantly, to total product innovation, whereas it does not seem to affect the likelihood of process innovation. In contrast, collaboration with other types of scientific partners generally has a negligible impact on their likelihood to innovate, with the exception of a large positive association between collaboration with research institutes and radical process innovation.

DUI cooperation with suppliers and customers is closely related to the innovative capacity of firms. Collaboration with suppliers is important for all types of innovation, with the strongest link to process innovation. Collaboration with customers is related to product innovation, but it does not significantly impact process innovation. Contrary to what is frequently stressed in the literature about clusters and industrial districts (Marshall, 1890; dei

Table 9.2   Logit Regression Estimation of the Empirical Model

	Product innovation	Radical product innovation	Process innovation	Radical process innovation
Partner types				
Within the conglomerate	0.39***(0.12)	0.20(0.13)	−0.02(0.12)	0.10(0.15)
Suppliers	0.39**(0.14)	0.33*(0.16)	0.76***(0.14)	0.38*(0.19)
Customers	0.36**(0.13)	0.54***(0.15)	0.03(0.13)	−0.03(0.17)
Competitors	−0.39***(0.12)	−0.55***(0.13)	−0.14(0.12)	−0.09(0.15)
Consultancies	0.15(0.12)	0.18(0.13)	0.16(0.12)	0.03(0.15)
Universities	0.30*(0.16)	0.53***(0.15)	0.21(0.15)	0.13(0.18)
Research institutes	0.26(0.16)	0.20(0.16)	0.26(0.16)	0.79***(0.18)
Control variables				
Manager's education level	−0.01(0.02)	0.01(0.03)	−0.00(0.02)	0.03(0.03)
Manager's age	−0.01(0.01)	−0.00(0.01)	−0.01(0.01)	0.01(0.01)
Manager's log no. company directorships	0.18*(0.08)	0.11(0.08)	0.08(0.08)	0.04(0.10)
Log no. of employees	0.19**(0.06)	0.12*(0.06)	0.24***(0.06)	0.16*(0.07)
% foreign owned	0.48*(0.20)	0.55**(0.19)	0.35(0.19)	0.14(0.22)
Industry	Controlled***	Controlled***	Controlled***	Controlled***
Region	Controlled	Controlled	Controlled	Controlled
Constant	−0.57(0.46)	−2.07***(0.50)	−1.10*(0.45)	−2.75***(0.58)
N	1602	1602	1602	1602
Pseudo R²	0.11	0.11	0.09	0.09

Note: * = P < 0.05 ** = P < 0.01 *** = P < 0.001

The first number in each cell denotes the coefficient, with the standard error listed next to it in parentheses.

Ottati, 1994; Cooke, 1998, 2002; Newlands, 2003), collaboration with customers also does not seem to be restricted to incremental product innovation but is actually even more closely associated with radical product innovation.

In contrast, the other form of DUI-type interactions—outside the supply chain—has a radically different relationship with innovation. Firms that cooperate with competitors in Norway tend to have a significantly lower capacity to introduce product innovation. This association is particularly strong for radical product innovation but still significant for product innovation. Hence while, according to von Hippel (1987), interaction with competitors may yield benefits in terms of a better circulation of information and market knowledge, process know-how, and even training, meaning that free revealing of information to competitors pays (Harhoff et al., 2003), this is clearly not the case for Norwegian firms. Cooperation within the conglomerate mostly does not have a significant effect on the likelihood of innovation, with the exception of total product innovation.

5. WHAT DIFFERENCE DOES GEOGRAPHICAL PROXIMITY MAKE?

The second set of research questions relates to the impact of geographical distance on the propensity to collaborate with industrial and scientific partners, as well as to the effectiveness of such cooperation. In this analysis, we focus on collaboration with partners outside the conglomerate, as the geographical reach of collaboration within conglomerates will fundamentally be shaped by whether the conglomerate itself is a regional, national, or multinational enterprise rather than by the nature of the knowledge flows. As stated in the theoretical section, DUI-type collaborations are expected to involve more transmission of tacit knowledge and practical know-how, which is less easily transferred across geographical distance. Conversely, STI-type collaboration is primarily based on codified and universal knowledge that should, in theory, be less affected by efficiency-loss across geographical distance. Therefore, it could be envisaged that DUI-type partnerships—in particular outside the supply chain—will more often than not take place in close geographical proximity, while extra-regional networks will be more common for STI-mode collaboration. Additionally, geographical proximity will be an asset in DUI-type partnerships, making industrial cooperation within the region more efficient than industrial cooperation with partners outside the region. This relationship is not expected to hold for STI-mode cooperation, which will possibly be even more effective in global networks due to the ability to link up to nodes of excellence.

Starting with the question of firms' propensity to collaborate, we asked for each partner type identified whether the partner was located inside or outside the region. Figure 9.1 shows the share of firms that cooperated with different types of partners inside and outside the region, respectively. Cooperation with partners inside the region is slightly more common than cooperation out of the region, although some categories of partners (other firms in the conglomerate, suppliers, and research institutes) are slightly more frequently located outside the region than inside it. However, there is no clear difference between DUI-mode and STI-mode partners when it comes to the frequency of collaboration inside versus outside the region. The biggest difference in regional versus extra-regional cooperation is for consultancies: 38% of firms collaborate with consultancies in the region and 21% with non-regional consultancies. Even for universities, regional cooperation is most common: 18% of firms cooperate with regional universities and 12% with universities outside the region.

The next question is what difference this makes for firms' ability to innovate. Even if there does not seem to be a systematic pattern of DUI-mode collaboration taking place within clusters or city-regions and STI-mode collaboration in global networks to coincide with the theoretical expectations, it could still be the case that regional DUI-mode networks are more effective than non-regional ones in producing innovation, whereas the opposite is true for collaboration with STI-mode partners. We group the different types of partners into the three categories that we have been using in this chapter: STI mode (cooperation with universities, research institutes, and consultancies), DUI mode within the supply chain (cooperation with suppliers and customers), and DUI mode outside the supply chain (collaboration with competitors). Within each of these categories, we make a distinction between collaboration with partners located inside and outside the region, respectively. Table 9.3 shows, for each category, the share of firms that have collaborated with at least one partner in the category by the partner's location.

The top number in each cell denotes the percentage share, with the standard error listed below in parentheses.

In order to analyse whether these patterns of collaboration affect a firm's ability to deliver innovation, we estimate, once again, logistic regression models for each of the four measures of innovation (total and radical,

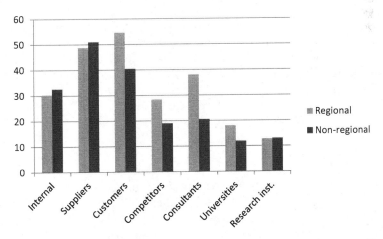

Figure 9.1 Percentage Share of Firms That Have Cooperated With Partner Type

Table 9.3   Share of Firms Collaborating With Partners Within and Outside the Region

Partner type	Regional	Non-regional
DUI non-supply chain	28.4(1.1)	19.0(1.0)
DUI supply chain	67.0(1.2)	61.5(1.2)
STI	48.0(1.2)	29.1(1.1)
N	1604	1604

product and process innovation). The regression model takes on exactly the same form as model (1), but partners are now operationalized differently: Instead of referring to individual partner types, it now refers to the three broad categories of partners and includes separate variables for partners located inside and outside the region, respectively.

Table 9.4 shows the results of the regression analysis. Reproducing the results of the sources of innovation analysis in the previous section, the results show that DUI collaboration outside the supply chain tends to be associated with lower likelihood of innovation. This could be taken as an indication that local tacit knowledge is not conducive to firm innovation in Norway, at least not through the interaction between competing firms. The relationship is statistically significant for product innovation only. Collaboration with competitors outside the region reduces the odds of total product innovation by 26%, while collaboration with competitors within the region reduces the odds of radical product innovation by 40%. However, the coefficients for collaboration with competitors, both within and outside the region, are consistently negative for all four innovation outcomes.

In contrast, DUI collaboration within the supply chain is positively related to innovation, but there is a great difference between collaborating with regional and non-regional partners. This relationship, however, does not go in the direction predicted by the literature. Rather than being more effective in regional networks, interaction with local suppliers and customers does not significantly affect the likelihood of innovation at all. Instead, collaboration with non-regional suppliers and customers is strongly and significantly associated with all innovation outcomes.

STI collaboration with non-regional partners also has, as predicted, significant positive implications for the likelihood of innovation. The association is somewhat weaker than non-regional DUI collaboration within the supply chain, even for the more radical forms of innovation. Furthermore, STI collaboration with regional partners is also significantly positively related to overall and, particularly, to radical product innovation. For process innovation, regional STI partners do not significantly increase the likelihood of innovation, but the effects are consistently positive and larger than for any form of regional industrial collaboration (and, for total process innovation,

Table 9.4 Logit Regression Estimation of the Empirical Model

	Product innovation	Radical product innovation	Process innovation	Radical process innovation
Partner types				
DUI *non-supply chain, regional*	−0.20(0.13)	−0.51***(0.15)	−0.13(0.13)	−0.08(0.17)
DUI *non-supply chain, non-regional*	−0.30*(0.15)	−0.13(0.16)	−0.07(0.15)	−0.01(0.18)
DUI *supply chain, regional*	0.12(0.12)	0.17(0.13)	0.13(0.12)	−0.03(0.15)
DUI *supply chain, non-regional*	0.73***(0.12)	0.72***(0.14)	0.50***(0.12)	0.42**(0.16)
STI, *regional*	0.23*(0.12)	0.40**(0.13)	0.20(0.12)	0.14(0.15)
STI, *non-regional*	0.37**(0.14)	0.33*(0.14)	0.33*(0.13)	0.35*(0.16)
Control variables				
Manager's education level	−0.01(0.02)	0.01(0.03)	−0.00(0.02)	0.04(0.03)
Manager's age	−0.01*(0.01)	−0.01(0.01)	−0.01(0.01)	0.01(0.01)
Manager's log no. company directorships	0.21**(0.08)	0.13(0.08)	0.07(0.08)	0.07(0.09)
Log no. of employees	0.20***(0.06)	0.13*(0.06)	0.24***(0.06)	0.19**(0.07)
% foreign owned	0.59**(0.20)	0.60***(0.18)	0.28(0.19)	0.19(0.21)
Industry	Controlled***	Controlled***	Controlled***	Controlled***
Region	Controlled	Controlled	Controlled	Controlled
Constant	−0.29(0.45)	−1.89***(0.49)	−0.82(0.44)	−2.83***(0.57)
N	1602	1602	1602	1602
Pseudo R²	0.11	0.11	0.08	0.08

Note: * = P < 0.05 ** = P < 0.01 *** = P < 0.001

The first number in each cell denotes the coefficient, with the standard error listed next to it in parentheses statistically significant at the 90% level). One potential explanation of this phenomenon is that collaboration between firms and scientific institutions within the region involves a reasonable amount of cognitive distance (Boschma, 2005) between both partners, whereas the cognitive distance between regional DUI mode partners (suppliers, customers, and competitors) is likely to remain small and not conducive to the generation and circulation of new knowledge. Finally, the effects of the control variables are similar to those observed in the previous analysis, although manager's age now has a significant negative effect on product innovation.

6. CONCLUSION

In this chapter, we have put Jensen et al.'s (2007) idea that both DUI-industrial type and STI-scientific type relationships are basic sources for the innovative capacity of firms to the test. We have examined this theory using a sample of 1,604 Norwegian firms with more than ten employees. We considered four different categories of innovation and distinguished between DUI generally formal types of interaction within the supply chain and those outside the supply chain, usually of a more informal nature. We have also paid special attention to the geographical dimension of the interactions, differentiating between interactions conducted locally and those at a distance.

The results of the analysis confirm that, in the case of Norway, engagement with external agents is closely related to firm innovation. Firms that engage in collaboration with external agents tend to be more innovative than firms that rely on their own resources for innovation. The analysis also validates the hypothesis that both STI and DUI modes of interaction matter for innovation. However, not all DUI modes of interaction matter in the same way. Whereas interaction with suppliers tends to promote greater levels of product and process innovation, both of the incremental and radical type, and interaction with customers is particularly beneficial for product innovation, collaboration with competitors has a detrimental effect on the propensity of firms to innovate and partnerships within the same conglomerate only matter for incremental product innovation.

The introduction of the geographical component also yields interesting results. Interaction with local agents, by and large, tends to have very little impact on raising a firm's innovation potential. The main exception is STI-type interaction with local universities. Interacting at a distance, however, makes a significant difference for the innovation potential of Norwegian firms. Firms that have established links with extra-regional universities, research centers, and consultancies and, in particular, with suppliers and customers outside the region have seen their innovation potential increase radically in virtually all types of innovation.

The results for Norwegian firms challenge some long-held beliefs about where firms get their innovative capacity. Although it is true that both STI and DUI modes of interaction matter, it seems that it is the collaboration of a more formal type that makes all the difference. In our survey we have found significant evidence of interaction of the informal type, such as interaction with competitors and with customers within the region. Interaction which, according to the literature, simply happens because "something is in the air" or as a result of "being there," of sharing the same geographical location (Gertler, 1995). However, there is little indication in the results that this form of interaction and the tacit knowledge it generates leads to substantially higher innovation by Norwegian firms. Excessive cognitive or organized proximity among Norwegian agents in what are relatively small and self-contained city-regions may be detrimental to innovation, with repeated exchanges not leading to the generation of knowledge that can be used and transformed into innovation by local firms (Boschma, 2005; Torre and Rallet, 2005). Too much interaction with local competitors may lead to lock-in and therefore even hamper innovation, in clear contrast with one of the key ideas on which the literature on industrial districts was based. The heterogeneity among agents is what matters for innovation and such heterogeneity is more common at a distance than in close geographical proximity (Srholec and Verspagen, 2008).

Firms are more likely to innovate when they purposely look for partners that may provide knowledge that can then be easily transformed into new ideas. And this is regardless of whether the partners are STI-type partners (mainly universities) or DUI partners within the supply chain. The most important factor is that these partners have to be able to offer the new knowledge that the firms need and this is achieved, in opposition with the theories of agglomeration, regional innovation systems, and local buzz, by searching for specific partners that may not only be at a considerable cognitive distance from the firms involved but also at a considerable geographical distance, as well.

Overall, this research provides a few answers but raises a whole raft of new questions regarding the role of clusters, tacit knowledge, and policy in Norway. It also calls for more in-depth analyses of how collaborations by what are generally relatively small firms emerge with distant partners. Looking into these questions will give us a clearer understanding of what seems a more complex panorama about the sources of firm innovation in Norway than the existing literature would have led us to believe.

ACKNOWLEDGMENTS

This is a shortened version of an article that was originally published in *Research Policy*, vol. 42, no. 1, pp. 128–138. We are grateful to the editor, Ben Martin, and two anonymous referees from *Research Policy* for their useful and relevant suggestions and feedback. This research was funded by the Stavanger Centre for Innovation Research, the Regional Research

Council for Western Norway, and the Research Council of Norway programs DEMOSREG and FORFI. It has also benefited from the support of the European Research Council under the European Union's Seventh Framework Programme (FP7/2007–2013)/ERC grant agreement no. 269868 and of a Leverhulme Trust Major Research Fellowship. The research is also part of the Prociudad-CM program and of the UK Spatial Economics Research Centre. Earlier versions of the chapter were presented at the 2011 Uddevalla Symposium (in Bergamo, Italy) and at the 2012 annual meetings of the Western Regional Science Association (in Poipu, Hawaii) and the American Association of Geographers (in New York). The authors would like to thank participants at these sessions for their valuable input, in particular discussants Olivier Lamotte, Björn Hårsman, and Maryann Feldman. While finalizing the chapter, Rune Dahl Fitjar was a visiting scholar at UCLA where he benefited from discussions with Max Kasy and with the ATS Statistical Consulting Group. Ragnar Tveterås and Björn Asheim have also provided important insights at various stages of the process. As usual, any remaining errors are our own.

NOTES

1 This chapter is a shortened version of an article that was originally published in *Research Policy*, vol. 42, no. 1, pp. 128–138.
2 Although existing theoretical literature has tended to emphasise the importance of geographical proximity in the establishment of firm-university linkages, empirical evidence suggests that this type of proximity in reality plays a limited role in setting them up (Lawton Smith, 2007).
3 Based on 2009 data from Statistics Norway, presented in Leknes (2010). The 10% commuting criterion was based on the Norwegian government's definition of city-regions in its *Greater Cities Report* (Ministry of Local Government and Regional Development, 2003)

REFERENCES

Asheim, B. and Gertler, M. S. (2005). The geography of innovation: Regional innovation systems. In J. Fagerberg, D. Mowery, and R. R. Nelson (eds.), *Oxford handbook of innovation* (291–317). Oxford: Oxford University Press.
Audretsch, D. B. and Feldman, M. P. (1996). R&D spillovers and the geography of innovation and production. *American Economic Review*, 86, 630–640.
Aydalot, P. (1986). *Milieux innovateurs en Europe*. Paris: GREMI.
Barge-Gil, A., Nieto, M. J. and Santamaría, L. (2011). Hidden innovators: The role of non-R&D activities. *Technology Analysis & Strategic Management*, 23, 415–432.
Bathelt, H., Malmberg, A. and Maskell, P. (2004). Clusters and knowledge: Local buzz, global pipelines and the process of knowledge creation. *Progress in Human Geography*, 28, 31–56.
Becattini, G. (1987). *Mercato e forze locali: Il distretto industriale*. Bologna: Il Mulino.

Boschma, R. (2005). Proximity and innovation: A critical assessment. *Regional Studies*, 39, 61–74.

Boschma, R. and Iammarino, S. (2009). Related variety, trade linkages, and regional growth in Italy. *Economic Geography*, 85, 289–311.

Bush, V. (1945). *Science: The endless frontier*. North Stratford: N.H., Ayer.

Cantwell, J. and Iammarino, S. (1998). MNCs, technological innovation and regional systems in the EU: Some evidence in the Italian case. *International Journal of the Economics of Business*, 5, 383–408.

Caraça, J., Lundvall, B.-Å. and Mendonça, S. (2009). The changing role of science in the innovation process: From Queen to Cinderella? *Technological Forecasting and Social Change*, 76, 861–867.

Chesbrough, H. (2003). *Open innovation*. Cambridge, Mass.: Harvard University Press.

Cohen, W. M. and Levinthal, D. A. (1990). Absorptive capacity: A new perspective on learning and innovation. *Administrative Science Quarterly*, 35, 128–152.

Cooke, P. (1998). Introduction: Origins of the concept. In H.-J. Braczyk, P. Cooke, M. Heidenreich (eds.), *Regional innovation systems: The role of governance in a globalised world* (2–27). London: UCL Press.

Cooke, P. (2001). Regional innovation systems, clusters, and the knowledge economy. *Industrial and Corporate Change*, 10, 945–974.

Cooke, P., Gómez Uranga, M. and Etxeberria, G. (1997). Regional innovation systems: Institutional and organizational dimensions. *Research Policy*, 26, 475–491.

Cooke, P. and Morgan, K. (1998). *The associational economy: Firms, regions and innovation*. Oxford: Oxford University Press.

Crescenzi, R., Rodríguez-Pose, A. and Storper, M. (2007). The territorial dynamics of innovation: A Europe-United States comparative analysis. *Journal of Economic Geography*, 7, 673–709.

Feldman, M. P. (1999). The new economics of innovation spillovers and agglomeration: A review of empirical studies. *Economics of Innovation and New Technology*, 8, 5–26.

Frenken, K., van Oort, F. and Verburg, T. (2007). Related variety, unrelated variety and regional economic growth. *Regional Studies*, 41, 685–697.

Gertler, M. S. (1995). 'Being there': Proximity, organization, and culture in the development and adoption of advanced manufacturing technologies. *Economic Geography*, 71, 1–26.

Gertler, M. S. (2003). Tacit knowledge and the economic geography of context, or, the undefinable tacitness of being (there). *Journal of Economic Geography*, 3, 75–99.

Glaeser, E. L. and Gottlieb, J. D. (2009). The wealth of cities: Agglomeration economies and spatial equilibrium in the United States. *Journal of Economic Literature*, 47, 983–1028.

Hansen, T. and Winther, L. (2011). Innovation, regional development and relations between high- and low-tech industries. *European Urban and Regional Studies*, 18, 321–339.

Harhoff, D., Henkel, J. and von Hippel, E. (2003). Profiting from voluntary information spillovers: How users benefit by freely revealing their innovations. *Research Policy*, 32, 1753–1768.

Iammarino, S. (2005). An evolutionary integrated view of regional systems of innovation: Concepts, measures and historical perspectives. *European Planning Studies*, 13, 497–519.

Isaksen, A. and Karlsen, J. (2010). Different modes of innovation and the challenge of connecting universities and industry: Case studies of two regional industries in Norway. *European Planning Studies*, 18, 1993–2008.

Jensen, M. B., Johnson, B., Lorenz, E. and Lundvall, B.-Å. (2007). Forms of knowledge and modes of innovation. *Research Policy*, 36, 680–693.

Kirner, E., Kinkel, S. and Jaeger, A. (2009). Innovation paths and the innovation performance of low-technology firms—an empirical analysis of German industry. *Research Policy*, 38, 447–458.

Laursen, K. and Salter, A. (2006). Open for innovation: The role of openness in explaining innovation performance among UK manufacturing firms. *Strategic Management Journal*, 27, 131–150.

Lawton-Smith, H. (2007). Universities, innovation, and territorial development: A review of the evidence. *Environment and Planning C: Government and Policy*, 25, 98–114.

Leknes, E. (2010). Fremveksten av byregioner i Norge. In A. A. Farsund and E. Leknes (eds.), *Norske byregioner: Utviklingstrekk og styringsutfordringer* (55–93). Kristiansand: Høyskoleforlaget.

Lundvall, B.-Å. (ed.). (1992). *National systems of innovation: Towards a theory of innovation and interactive learning*. London: Pinter Publishers.

Lundvall, B.-Å. and Johnson, B. (1994). The learning economy. *Journal of Industry Studies*, 1, 23–42.

Maclaurin, W. R. (1953). The sequence from invention to innovation and its relation to economic growth. *Quarterly Journal of Economics*, 67, 97–111.

Marshall, A. (1890). *Principles of economics*. London: Macmillan and Co.

Maskell, P., Bathelt, H. and Malmberg, A. (2006). Building global knowledge pipelines: The role of temporary clusters. *European Planning Studies*, 14, 997–1013.

Ministry of Local Government and Regional Development. (2003). *Greater cities report: On the development of greater city policies*. Norwegian Government White Paper no. 31.

Moodysson, J., Coenen, L. and Asheim, B. T. (2008). Explaining spatial patterns of innovation: Analytical and synthetic modes of knowledge creation in the Medicon Valley life-science cluster. *Environment and Planning A*, 40, 1040–1056.

Morgan, K. (1997). The learning region: Institutions, innovation and regional renewal. *Regional Studies*, 31, 491–503.

Newlands, D. (2003). Competition and cooperation in industrial clusters: The implications for public policy. *European Planning Studies*, 11, 521–532.

Ottati, G. dei. (1994). Cooperation and competition in the industrial district as an organisation model. *European Planning Studies*, 2, 463–483.

Porter, M. E. (1986). *Competition in global industries*. Boston, Mass.: Harvard Business School Press.

Rodríguez-Pose, A. and Crescenzi, R. (2008). R&D, spillovers, innovation systems and the genesis of regional growth in Europe. *Regional Studies*, 41, 51–67.

Saxenian, A. L. (1996). *Regional advantage: Culture and competition in Silicon valley and route 128*. Cambridge, Mass.: Harvard University Press.

Sonn, J. W. and Storper, M. (2008). The increasing importance of geographical proximity in technological innovation: An analysis of U.S. patent citations, 1975–1997. *Environment and Planning A*, 40, 1020–1039.

Srholec, M. and Verspagen, B. (2008). *The voyage of the beagle in innovation systems land: Explorations on sectors, innovation, heterogeneity and selection.* UNU-MERIT Working Paper No. 8/2008, UNU-MERIT, Maastricht.

Storper, M. and Venables, A. J. (2004). Buzz: Face-to-face contact and the urban economy. *Journal of Economic Geography*, 4, 351–370.

Torre, A. and Rallet, A. (2005). Proximity and localization. *Regional Studies*, 39, 47–59.

Tracey, P. and Clark, G. L. (2003). Alliances, networks and competitive strategy: Rethinking clusters of innovation. *Growth and Change*, 34, 1–16.

von Hippel, E. (1976). The dominant role of users in the scientific instrument innovation process. *Research Policy*, 5, 212–239.

von Hippel, E. (1987). Cooperation between rivals: Informal know-how trading. *Research Policy*, 16, 291–302.

10 University Collaboration for Sustainable Competitive Advantage

A Resource-Based Perspective

Martin Gjelsvik and Rune Dahl Fitjar

1. INTRODUCTION

This chapter uses the resource-based perspective on strategy to study how firms collaborate with universities and the conditions under which such collaboration can be a strategy for firms to gain sustainable competitive advantage. While universities may offer firms access to new knowledge, gaining competitive advantage from university collaboration is not straightforward. Collaboration with universities is often pursued in an ad hoc manner, led by individual initiative rather than corporate strategy. This study approaches university collaboration from a strategic perspective rooted in the management of the firm.

The open nature of academic science is at times in conflict with companies' need to protect technologies and appropriate value. Furthermore, science starts with known conditions and tries to uncover unknown results, whereas technology and innovation are driven by an idea of the final result, with the researcher trying to solve the necessary conditions to produce the desired outcome (Nightingale, 1998). These dissimilar cognitive foundations raise challenges. The issue is how managers may overcome these obstacles and structure their relationships with universities in ways that provide more value for the firm. In this chapter, we argue that collaboration with universities will only lead to sustainable competitive advantage if the firm can move beyond arm's-length transactions to develop university relations that are rare, inimitable, and nonsubstitutable.

Drawing on semi-structured interviews with managers in firms and at three Norwegian universities, this chapter suggests four mechanisms through which collaboration with universities may help firms obtain idiosyncratic knowledge not easily imitated by competing companies: First, firms need to search for and identify university partners that possess complementary knowledge and capabilities. Second, they must invest in relation-specific assets that make relationships inimitable by competitors. Third, they must possess sufficient absorptive capacity to use the knowledge emanating from the relationship. Finally, they need to govern their relationships with these partners effectively. The firms in our data that are most successful in collaborating with universities use these methods to obtain competitive advantage.

Firms create value from their collaboration with universities when they go beyond formal, arm's-length relationships and purposefully build novel combinations of resources and capabilities through these four mechanisms. This implies that companies actively embrace universities and utilize the differences between industry and academia to their advantage.

This also has implications for how universities should approach firms. Recent attempts to orient universities more toward industry have been based mainly on the linear model of a well-defined, step-by-step innovation process. In this perspective, the third role of universities may be organized in market-like transactions with a focus on arm's-length transactions and contracts. These transactions are "sharp in," indicating a clear-cut, complete, and monetized agreement. They are also "sharp out" in the sense that the provider's obligation of performance and the buyer's expected payment are unambiguous. In this scenario, the university becomes a true market actor on par with private firms. The problem lies in the way the justifiable need to prove the efficient and transparent use of public policy investments can lead to an emphasis on easily measurable outcomes rather than the real drivers of innovation (McKelvey, 2014). From the perspective of the firm and from a broader societal perspective, universities have much more comprehensive roles in the knowledge economy than the linear model assumes (Hughes and Kitson, 2012), and there is much more to it than patents, start-ups, and licensing (Salter and Martin, 2001; Lester and Sotarauta 2007).

The vantage point of this chapter is this broader notion of the universities' roles, and the contention that the organizational dynamics of the broader relationships remain under-researched (Perkmann and Walsh, 2007). However, there is a comprehensive literature on firm-to-firm relationships and alliances (Hamel, 1991; Gulati et al., 2000; Lunnan and Haugland, 2008) and the potential of creating competitive advantage and rents from alliance relationships and the key factors driving them (Dyer and Singh, 1998). We borrow from that literature to study the particular relationship between firms and universities.

2. THEORETICAL PERSPECTIVES: THE RESOURCE-BASED VIEW

We invoke the resource-based theory to study the potential that collaboration with universities may have to enhance firms' competitive advantage. The resource-based view of the firm (RBV) is based on the notion that resources owned by the firm have the potential to provide sustainable competitive advantage when they are valuable, rare, inimitable, and not readily substitutable (Barney, 1991; Peteraf, 1993; Peteraf and Barney, 2003). Resources or capabilities are valuable when they enable the firm to conceive or implement strategies that improve its efficiency and/or effectiveness. If these capabilities are commonplace and easily available, firms may develop similar strategies, products, and services, giving no firm a competitive edge. Valuable and rare organizational resources may thus obviously be a source of competitive advantage. Indeed, firms with such resources will often be innovators, as they are able to conceive of and implement technologies that other firms could neither conceive nor implement due to their lack of capabilities. However, valuable and rare organizational resources can only be sources of *sustained* competitive advantage if other firms cannot obtain them by direct duplication or substitution. In a market, why might a competing firm not be able to obtain the same resources? Resources are costly or hard to imitate when the link between resources or capabilities and a firm's sustained competitive advantage is causally ambiguous, or the development of those resources is dependent on socially complex processes (Dierickx and Cool, 1989). Examples of socially complex resources include interpersonal relations among managers in a firm (Hambrick, 1987), a firm's culture (Barney, 1986), and a firm's reputation among suppliers (Porter, 1980) and customers (Klein and Leffler, 1981). The hard currency often lies in the complex innovation processes and implementation, which evolve in a reciprocal interaction between employees, managers, customers, and suppliers with considerable local learning. The relationship between the firm and a university may be characterized along the same lines, as these relations evolve over time and involve personal relations between firm researchers and university faculty.

To the extent that firm-university collaboration ends up in physical products, it might be argued that they are easily imitated. However, the full exploitation of these products often depends on social relations, in particular between the inventors and the marketers, an entrepreneurial culture, and learning capabilities. Organizations learn from experience, and over time well-established routines cause firms to become myopic (March and Levinthal, 1993), having the tendency to overlook distant times and distant places. They lose their peripheral vision (Day and Schoemaker, 2006), the capability to search for information and opportunities outside their own area. In the words of March (1991), exploitation tends to drive out exploration. For these reasons, firms fail to learn in ways that allow them to innovate and benefit from the changes and disruptions that surround them. Collaboration with a variety of partners from different corners may mitigate these failures.

The notion that firms need to integrate into their innovation processes external knowledge from parties such as suppliers, customers, consultants, and universities or research institutes has become accepted in innovation literature over the past decades. Firms that collaborate with a range of heterogeneous partners are found to be more innovative (Becker and Dietz, 2004; Laursen and Salter, 2006; Nieto and Santamaria, 2007; Fitjar and Rodríguez-Pose, 2013). Furthermore, firms with greater diversity in their partnerships develop skills to improve their ability to absorb valuable external information (Zahra and George, 2002). Diversity is obtained through new combinations of knowledge from complementary sources. Universities may be one such source, as firms and universities are different institutions with dissimilar knowledge bases.

Gulati (1999) models these partnerships from a RBV perspective, arguing that the source of value-creating resources and capabilities should extend beyond the boundaries of the firm by introducing the concept of network resources. These network resources are unique and may enhance the performance and innovative capacity of the firm. This logic is easily transferred from firm-firm relations to firm-university collaborative relationships. However, Fitjar et al. (2013) note that this is dependent on firms making particular investments in a specific partnership rather than simply utilizing resources available to everyone simply by being there.

Standard and tradable links to universities are easy to imitate and can hardly serve as a foundation for sustainable advantage. Building collaborative relations, on the other hand, may help the firm develop inimitable and costly to substitute network resources. Since they often include informal and personal relations, these collaborative efforts may be hard to discover in the first place, especially to outsiders. Second, lasting relations are characterized by high degrees of trust, which facilitates transfer of tacit knowledge. Furthermore, since innovation processes are complex and iterative in nature, collaboration is dependent on relationships, mutual interests, and reputation and less guided by a formal structure of authority, but rather by networks and relational contracts (Macneil, 1980).

The RBV predicts that firms are motivated to collaborate with universities to access complementary resources. This has been confirmed by empirical findings. Hanel and St-Pierre (2006) claim that research activities undertaken in partnership with a university complement rather than replace R&D undertaken by the private sector firms. In order to benefit from external knowledge, however, firms must develop relevant absorption capacity internally that enables them to incorporate that knowledge in their own innovation processes (Cohen and Levinthal, 1990).

On this basis, we expect successful firm collaboration with universities to be driven mainly by four strategic considerations: First, firms must ensure that collaboration with universities is valuable to the firm. This implies searching for and identifying partners that possess knowledge that is complementary to the firm's own knowledge. Second, firms must also ensure that they develop relationships that are inimitable and not readily substitutable by their competitors. This implies investing in relation-specific assets that can only be exploited within the particular relationship between the university and the firm. Third, the firm must develop sufficient internal capacity to exploit fully the outputs from collaboration, which is a requirement for valuable collaboration. Finally, when the right partner has been identified, the establishment of effective mechanisms for governing the relationship helps to reduce transaction costs.

3. RESEARCH METHOD

The chapter is based on semi-structured interviews with firms and universities involved in collaborative relations in three Norwegian regions: Stavanger, Tromsø, and Bodø. These are all relatively small regions that are home to a university with explicit ambitions of contributing to industrial development through collaboration with firms. However, both the industrial structure of the three regions and the research profiles of the universities differ across the cases in order to ensure that the results are not limited to a single industry or type of university. We conducted interviews with firms identified by the universities as collaboration partners, but with varying degrees of relations to these universities.

In each location, we conducted five to seven semi-structured interviews with firms and a similar number of interviews with university representatives. We used similar interview guides for both categories of respondents, as we wanted the opinions and reflections from both sides to the same issues, although with some variation to reflect the specificities of the universities and the firms, respectively.

The members of the project team were mainly recruited from each of the three universities. Their historical and contextual knowledge of key players in the region—both in academia and in business—was particularly helpful for the research. At the same time, we made conscious efforts to ensure the neutrality of our analysis. Two interviewers conducted all interviews jointly, at least one of which was external to the institution in order to ensure reliability. The project manager took part in all interviews in all the regions to ensure consistency in the interpretation of results. To ensure comparability and sharing of data within the project team, all interviews were taped and transcribed. The interviews were then analyzed in a joint workshop with the full project team.

4. RESULTS

While the collaborative relations between firms and universities in our data are organized in a variety of ways, involve different industries and disciplines, and firms and departments of different sizes, they all have one thing in common: the relationship between the firm and the university goes beyond formal, arm's-length relationships to purposefully generate an idiosyncratic combination of resources and capabilities. Firms use a variety of means to achieve this: They identify university researchers who possess complementary knowledge and capabilities to the firm's internal capabilities. They invest in relation-specific assets to develop relations that are inimitable by other firms. Simultaneously, they have various mechanisms to ensure sufficient absorptive capacity to make use of the knowledge developed in the relationship. Finally, they develop effective governance mechanisms that reduce transaction costs between the firm and the university.

4.1 Identifying Partners With Complementary Knowledge

University researchers have access to the brainpower of specialized colleagues and bring a different perspective than that found in corporate environments.

They are usually also less vested in commercial interests compared to other partners such as suppliers, vendors, and consultants who may have their preferred solutions to problems (Perkmann and Salter, 2012). The potential for complementary knowledge is thus substantial. A successful search for a university partner includes two relations: finding the right university and the right person or research group. Firms may improve the chances of finding universities with relevant, complementary knowledge by having ongoing activities of search and screening. Scouts, liaison officers, or gatekeepers are concepts invoked to describe dedicated internal functions in the firm to identify partners and sources of relevant knowledge and technologies. Reputation and prior experience play an important role in this process (Gulati, 1995; Powell et al., 1996). A firm's position in an industrial network and/or the national or global research community can also contribute.

Some search processes are informal and nonsystematic. Having in mind that we focus on relationships, search is often initiated at the individual level. Costs are always involved, motivating limited search. Turning to one's own alma mater typically makes a starting point. Some professors are constantly visible and highly reputed, which also may demarcate search processes. More or less accidental acquaintances at conferences or exhibitions may also initiate lasting relationships. Other firms may conduct broader and more planned searches, often searching at the institutional level: Which university has more to offer? Some firms do indeed read scientific papers in their screening efforts. It also works the other way around when the university on its own initiative markets itself and its core knowledge areas to firms.

Identifying complementarities implies discovering common ground. In today's economy, many firms have become more innovation and knowledge driven, which motivates them to seek university collaboration. In universities, commercialization is no longer confined to the periphery of campus life (Bok, 2003). Moreover, academic administrators increasingly refer to students as customers and education programs and research as products (Washburn, 2005), and branding and marketing are a part of the strategic agenda of universities. In other words, the language and mind-sets have become more similar to that of private business, mitigating the different dominant logics described earlier.

The interests of firms and universities are highly complementary when they strengthen their respective reputations. Through collaboration on cutting-edge research related to the Arctic, firms in Northern Norway market themselves and build their reputations as innovative firms searching new solutions. Simultaneously, the university may build an international reputation by attracting both financial support and partners from renowned global companies. In the competition between universities, high-profile conferences mark their professional territory. Participating firms may provide an economic guarantee, in particular if the conference aims to attract a larger number of academics who cannot afford to pay high fees.

The local university is not always able to offer relevant complementarities to the firm. Some firms approach the university nevertheless, because it may connect them to other universities. This brokerage role may be important, as the use of the university's network reduces the transaction costs of the firm and the time to search for knowledge vital to stay in front of the competition.

Joint firm-university efforts are not limited to bilateral agreements. It sometimes makes sense for firms to fund open, long-term research, although competing firms share the knowledge. Leading industry players, government, and the university may become aware that collective action is needed to address fundamental challenges experienced by the entire industry. The fish farming industry provides an example. The industry has several common challenges related to fish health, nutrition, breeding, product quality, and farming technology.

It also works the other way around, when a large, well-established firm invites the whole research community to explore new frontiers:

> Last year our firm established a comprehensive Arctic program where we invited the research community to come up with the right questions to ask as our business moves north. We will support proposals to how the issues should be tackled. We don't know all the questions, and we don't comprehend all our needs.

Complementarities and synergies are typically invoked to motivate alliances or mergers. They often come with misfits included, however. For firms and universities, the search for complementary capabilities and knowledge includes a careful review of areas in which the relationship actually has a potential for misfits. In the case of firm-university collaboration, there may be complementarity in knowledge content and technological solutions but a lack of fit in terms of organizational processes, incentives, and decision processes. Misfits may occur when both the firm and the university require IP rights. Firms competing on unique technology and solutions are particularly vulnerable if these unique resources are reduced in value through university collaboration. Firms with strategies dependent on IP may avoid universities in their research and innovation processes and use them for recruiting talent only. A large international supplier to the energy industry laments: "We have lost the opportunity to patent because professors had published the results at a conference." It is interesting to note that the extensive group of businesses that develop and supply technology to the oil companies exhibit a different dominant logic (Prahalad and Bettis, 1986) than the oil companies. The former may obtain competitive advantage through ownership of the technology, whereas the oil companies may achieve superior value creation and competitive advantage through smarter *use* of the technology. Hence it is more straightforward to identify and utilize complementarities with the oil companies than their suppliers.

Misfits may arise in established relations based on informal, implicit contracts when the institutional context is altered. Firms used to personal contacts with a selected group of professors may instead experience being referred to a university administration and contract department that insists on ownership of the research results: "The informal communication is crucial. Now, however, the signals have changed: The omnipotent administration obstructs collaboration. The university requires complete contracts and every hour and activity invoiced. They want to publish and own the knowledge." Thus a paradoxical situation has evolved: as the universities are required to commercialize and fill their "third role" as business developer, they become more difficult to collaborate with for parts of the established industry.

Companies may receive public funding in order to undertake research with a university, but contract research is not always straightforward. It does not offer sufficient benefits as two cultures collide: "We want to develop products fast, the university has a slower pace. We expect results; they present concept sketches. They present feasibility studies that they think we can develop and commercialize. The hours are running with no results." In other words, the dominant logics of the firm and the university need to be attuned to each other in order to utilize the potential complementarities. Misfits occur when the university and the firm have conflicting incentives, such as when researchers want to publish the research results, while the firm wants to patent. Competition in the research community motivates especially junior faculty to publish early, which may be prematurely from the firm's perspective. Publishing is associated with concise hypotheses, which may be less relevant for the firm's challenges. Generally, publishing is rewarded internally in the university. The trick for managers is to appreciate the longer-term thinking of academics, as it may overcome their own tendency to look to the next quarter. "Going long" with academics can unlock a range of new possibilities that may offer competitive advantage five or ten years into the future (Perkmann and Salter, 2012).

4.2 Building Relation-Specific Assets

Firms know that universities are different from themselves in many respects. Identifying complementarities and realizing the potential for additional value creation require investments in the specific relation. One firm representative described their relationship with the university as follows:

> It is important to meet face to face and learn each other's different mindsets. In the collaboration with a university, there are things you can and ought to do, and things you definitely should leave alone. There are visible and invisible borders in both camps.

One way for firms to develop lasting relation-specific assets, used by several firms in our data, is by establishing joint research centers with a university. By their contribution to joint centers, firms demonstrate a long-term commitment to the partnerships. An example is COREC (Center for Oil Recovery), which was initiated by an oil company and an oil field license in

2002 to increase knowledge of how to improve oil recovery from existing fields through extensive research, competence building, and education of new students at the University of Stavanger and the research institute IRIS. The research projects within COREC have received both public funding and funding from other oil companies participating in the license. The joint research center has contributed to considerably higher reserve estimates for the offshore oil field and given a boost to the bottom line of the company.

In some centers with public funding, a larger number of companies participate. Government money is more easily accessible when a group of firms or even the entire industry benefit. Under these circumstances, it is harder for the individual firm to turn these benefits into a competitive edge: "We've had enough of centers. We are very selective as the centers are organized with an arm's length distance to us in the projects, offering a lack of individual flexibility." In these arrangements, relation-specific assets from the perspective of the individual firm are minimal, and potential competitive advantage will depend on differentiated absorptive capacities in the respective firms.

Relation-specific assets may also arise in so-called joint industry projects (JIP), often used in the oil and gas industry. This multilateral form of project organization consists of at least one research institution and several firms, along with public financial support. In a JIP, the research institution suggests a work program, including scope and cost, to which the firm responds. A joint industry project typically has both high potential and high risk, but the risks and costs are shared between a larger number of participants, making them easier to handle. Participating students may later become candidates for employment in firms through the latter's sponsoring of masters and project work. These assignments may later evolve to lasting relationships with the university.

In research-intensive industries, the need for knowledge flows between the partners is substantial:

> Our collaboration with the university is long-term, and is based on personal contacts and trust. We have PhD students with supervisors from the university, joint research activities, joint presentations at conferences, and joint activities towards an international professional association. There is more collaboration and less cash. The university takes part in "strategic research" in the company in a truly trustful and open way. They share data and research and produce scientific papers.

The firm recruits from several international and national universities with whom they are engaged in long-term projects. Thus the projects serve as a selection mechanism for new talent. Firms exposed to tough competition and sensitive to other firms being able to imitate their products, seem to prefer bilateral agreements with the university: "We want a close relationship based on trust. We need to trust the university that they don't steal our ideas."

Start-up firms based on commercialization of university ideas represent a special case. These firms tend to cluster around the industries where the local university possesses knowledge and resources at the international research front. Firms located in the university's proximity may develop lasting competitive benefits through their personal relations with the inventor at the university. These benefits turn into sustained competitive advantage when the inventor also acts as an entrepreneur to set up the firm or is hired as a consultant. They may not only provide updated knowledge but also reputation and goodwill, which normally will serve a new and unknown company well. The potential for imitation by competing firms will be limited when the personal relations are exclusive.

Firms sponsoring doctoral degrees invest in potential future relation-specific assets. The student typically works with an issue or problem relevant for the sponsoring firm, and the study is defined in a dialogue with professors at the university. Gaining benefits from these investments requires ongoing contact with the student and the project, which is dependent on the capacity and competence in the firm. In our cases, even in large global companies, lack of capacity rather than financial resources is the main limitation in the relationship. Rich relations develop when the students connect to the R&D department in the firm. Generally: "The deeper knowledge the university has about us, the better. Consequently, we lecture and participate in projects that we use to market our company. We make a footprint when we lecture, worth more than a job advertisement." Another manager claims: "When we sharpen our expectations to academia, they develop products which differentiate us and give us competitive advantage. We market our products at above average prices."

4.3 Developing Dual Absorptive Capacity

Firms are not always able to realize the potential complementarities and benefits in joint research projects with a university. Differences in time horizons and the degree of openness need to be balanced, and both partners need to think through how such rigidities can be turned into mutual benefits. These obstacles exist for all firms; competitive advantages are awarded to those that use their entrepreneurial spirit to overcome them.

In order to utilize the potential of complementarities, knowledge-sharing routines need to be established and developed between the university and the firm that permit the transfer, recombination, or creation of knowledge (Grant, 1996). In the case of university-firm collaboration, these routines are sometimes highly personal, based on trust and tacit knowledge. Personal relations may have a large potential upside and are hard to copy. That is precisely the reason why they may come to an abrupt end if involved individuals leave. This makes the case for more institutionalized and broader communication channels that facilitate knowledge sharing over the long term.

Establishing joint research centers is a way to institutionalize knowledge sharing and create relation-specific assets. COREC, described earlier, may serve as an example. Routinizing knowledge sharing helps firms and universities to improve their absorptive capacity (Cohen and Levinthal, 1990). The concept of absorptive capacity is traditionally conceptualized exclusively as a property of the recipient firm, referring to how its internal innovation processes may also enhance its capacity to absorb external knowledge. However, the way in which knowledge is communicated from the source may also be important for the absorptive capacity of the recipient (Dyer et al., 2007), as exemplified by the following quote: "The better academia knows us, the better they see opportunities for research through our lenses. With very few exceptions, external proposals are highly relevant to us." Accordingly, partner-specific absorptive capacity is important for knowledge sharing in firm-university relationships. Building and extending this capacity is easier for the firm when the university through the relation-specific assets makes its communication and behavior compatible with the innovation processes in the firm.

Another solution is to include significant and research-based customers of the focal firm in the projects. Meeting the end customer face-to-face enables the university-researcher to appreciate how users actually make use of new technologies, ambiguities may be sorted out and utilized constructively (Brun et al., 2008), and the interaction between the developer and the user may increase the benefits of complementary perspectives. Idiosyncratic relations to customers or suppliers are utilized as a supplement to participation in industry-wide projects. SMEs may join industry-wide and government-sponsored projects, as they do not have the capacity in-house: "We don't have a R&D department, and bring the generic knowledge from the joint industry projects to projects with our suppliers. We learn to know what we want and differentiate ourselves."

Firms may further strengthen their absorptive capacity by employing "scouts" or "gatekeepers," specialists who monitor and collaborate with research institutes and universities. They follow up on students, projects, and outsourced contract research. For firms, such a capacity developed over time may constitute a sustainable competitive advantage. Firms also recruit employees with the specific purpose to collaborate with universities and research institutions. These efforts enhance the absorptive capacity of the firms and signal to the research community that the firm is committed to finding novel, science-based solutions. Complementarities may include more than knowledge generation: "The collaboration is based on trust and a solid foundation. It's a win-win situation. The university provides us with a reputation and an image as an innovative firm and a constructive contributor to the industry."

These broad mechanisms of interaction may motivate faculty to approach the firm with relevant proposals. In fact, companies intentionally build these relations to harvest ideas from the university. In large firms, managers usually do not know what their employees know or have the capacity to learn. External researchers with excellent working relations with the firm and familiarity with their goals and strategies may help them out: "We want the institutes and universities to find the best resources we have and collaborate with them."

On the other hand, there is a risk that firms fail to absorb the lessons from collaborative projects. The firm can mitigate this risk by assigning an internal champion to work alongside the academic partner. A large oil company with a substantial number of projects with universities has designated dedicated employees to manage the respective relations:

> I have 50 colleagues with the responsibility to monitor and follow up our research programs. No project is initiated without a dedicated person taking ownership of the project. If that person quits, and we don't find a substitute, we cancel the project. It is crucial that we possess the technical expertise to implement and use the results.

This case underlines that the firm needs to be present at both a strategic level as well as the technical level.

4.4 Effective Governance Mechanisms

Long-term collaborative relationships require effective governance mechanisms. On the one hand, contracts and ownership structures are needed to protect both firms and universities from opportunistic behavior of the other. With considerable and valuable resources involved and at risk, these issues are often settled in a specialized contract department at the university or the university seeks external advice from lawyers. For firms, entering formal contracts represents familiar ground, although the specifics of university contracts may differ. However, effective governance structures go beyond formalities. Growing and high levels of asset specificity in a relationship are best safeguarded through trust and reputation in controlling opportunistic behavior (Gulati, 1995) as high interfirm innovation-related asset specificity create transactional difficulties. Firm performance improves when transaction costs are reduced. However, in firm-university relationships knowledge sharing may have an even greater impact on the bottom line through technology breakthroughs and new products and services. Dyer and Chu (2003) argue that trust in supplier-buyer relations may be a competitive advantage in contexts in which knowledge is a "particularly valuable resource due to product complexity and industry uncertainty."

We find that governance structures include both formal contracts and informal mechanisms based on trust and reputation both in the university and individuals. A so-called framework agreement is built on a formal contract and may include a larger number of projects. These agreements are scalable, in the sense that contracts and routines are developed and then replicated for many underlying projects, including contracts on IP rights and publication of results. Framework contracts may both satisfy the firm's need for time-sensitive projects and results, and the academics' preference for longer-term relationships and the search for entirely new knowledge.

Obviously, transaction costs are reduced once the framework is in place. These agreements are used both for research and for education of PhD students. The students are generally free to publish their results without intervention from the sponsor. There are exceptions, however. There may be limits to what kind of internal data the student can publish. It is crucial that contracts regulate repeated behavior that may have major impacts on the present and future performance of the firm.

In deep and extensive innovation processes, the exact outcome cannot be defined. Consequently, formal contracts are hard to write; and relational contracts (Macneil, 1980) are more convenient and effective, provided that relations are trustful. The driver of the partnership is the motivation to share knowledge (often including confidential knowledge) and the potential upside in the collaboration. The formal contract is there to reduce transaction costs and mitigate against potential breaches of the informal agreements.

The joint industry project (JIP) described earlier is another effective governance structure. In this structure, knowledge is shared across several firms and one or more research institution or university. This is a common governance mechanism in the oil and gas industry where competing firms share and create new technology. Firms taking individual ownership of technology developed in JIPs are the exception, not the rule:

> Our firm and two other oil companies decided not to claim ownership. We would rather see the entrepreneur (an oil service provider) succeed. Then the new solutions will be marketed more broadly. This attitude is a fantastic part of the Norwegian energy industry. The attitude of our firm is to research to use, not to own.

Participating firms in a JIP provide data from their respective oil fields. Interpretation of geological data—that is, transforming data to usable knowledge—constitutes a potential competitive advantage for the oil companies, so the data should not be tied to particular companies or oil fields. The extent to which data may be identified is regulated in the contract. In both JIPs and joint centers, the contract regulates the right to publish. Generally, researchers in the centers are free to publish, albeit with a requirement from sponsoring firms to approve abstracts, sometimes also the papers:

> As a firm, we expect not to be a victim of professorial misconduct. They cannot use our logo in their presentations; we do not want to convey the impression that we accept the results. If a technical solution turns out to be a failure, our company will in that case run a risk of blame. Since an oil company has a strong economy, a plaintiff would prefer to take us to court rather than the university. We should only be mentioned as a financial source.

The collaboration in joint industry projects has become an institution and may be regarded as an integrated part of the innovation system in the energy sector, although it is rarely mentioned in descriptions of the Norwegian innovation system. This could be because the system and its incentives grew organically, outside and beyond targeted policies. Two factors have been decisive. First, oil companies in general pay 77% tax on profits.[1] However, R&D investments are deductible, implying that the company pays only 23% of the costs of research and can deduct the rest from their taxes.[2] Direct financial support to universities is not tax deductible; the support needs to be connected to a project. Second, Norway enjoys a trust-based culture:

> The tax deduction has been decisive. We don't succeed with JIPs in the US. The partners start biting each other, the contracts are incredibly comprehensive, and the only focus is on how to regain the money. In Norway, we sometimes are too relaxed to protect our technology as competitors may patent in order to stop you from developing things. On the other hand, patenting is dangerous, because competitors find out what you intend to market.

Firms need access to new solutions, not necessarily IP rights; they may be indifferent to whether they own a new technology or have an exclusive license agreement. As an exclusive license partner, they want to influence where the IP-owning firm patents.

> We discussed with a university whether to patent. We decided not to, for two reasons: it was hard to define what should be patented, the process became too complicated. We could not stand the fuss. We want freedom to operate and put the solution to work. Secondly, we seek straightforward routines: if the solutions are developed internally, we own the rights; if developed externally, we pay to get access. All hybrids are complicated. Our business is to develop and market good products, not administration.

In most interorganizational collaboration efforts, a joint management function or collaboration hub is established in order to improve knowledge management, monitor the results, and facilitate intervention and accountability, and not least to provide an arena to discuss new opportunities. The "Academia-agreement" between Statoil and a few universities includes an organizational entity aimed to ensure that these functions are carried out. "It is a tool to nurture a long and good relationship with strategically important universities." The long-term collaboration is managed through a committee with three members from Statoil and three members from the respective universities. The collaboration provides seed capital for generating more comprehensive centers and new projects. The oil company is engaged in contract research with a far larger number of universities; hence, the Academia-contract is exclusive and represents a specific investment with a consciously selected few. It serves as an effective governance mechanism through its allocation of resources to prioritized activities and faculties. It also facilitates a flow of both strategic and professional knowledge between the partners. Internal coordination conflicts between a purchasing department and the R&D unit are resolved by lifting decisions into this function. Both education and research activities are included. Since several universities benefit from this type of collaboration, the company has an unparalleled opportunity to draw on complementarities from a differentiated set of universities.

As the borders of the firm are becoming more transparent, the parallels between internal coordination and coordination of external relationships become more salient. In firm-firm collaboration, the relational capabilities can build on the experience of the firm in its internal coordination mechanisms. However, in firm-university relationships, this may not be as straightforward, since the structure and culture of the university are different from those of the firm. Consequently, high-technology firms sometimes recruit employees with university backgrounds as liaison officers or gatekeepers. Companies with a long history of university collaboration are well acquainted with the reputation of the university, so when the university presents proposals for research, the company trusts that sufficient competence is available. However, they may assess whether other universities are more competent.

5. CONCLUSION

Increasingly, firms need to incorporate scientific and technological knowledge into their innovations. To accomplish this objective, business managers need to manage their relations with universities and research institutions. In this chapter, we have used the logic of business strategy to analyze the potential benefits of university collaboration. This perspective departs in many respects from the linear model implicitly guiding much public policy on science and the economic incentives for universities. This model suggests that public investments in basic science lead to applied research and new technology, which in turn leads to economic growth through commercialization of product innovations and new companies.

Based on case studies of university-firm collaboration, this chapter tells a different story. First, universities have much more complex roles in the knowledge economy than assumed by the linear model (Lester, 2005; Deiaco et al., 2012). Our story is more in line with the concept of the engaged university or academic engagement (Perkmann et al., 2013). The latter is defined as "knowledge-related collaboration by academic researchers with non-academic organizations" (p.424). Second, firms need to invest not only in technology but also in their relations to the university in order to identify complementarities and build absorptive capacity both in their firms as well as in the university. These relations are broad and include collaborative research, contract research, consulting, teaching, and informal networking activities, and they are practiced by a far larger proportion of academics than commercialization.

Value creation from university collaboration requires the firm to develop capabilities to search for the right partners (both at the institutional and individual level) and to coordinate activities across the organizational barriers. To exploit fully the potential of complementary resources, assets specific to the linkage, effective knowledge-sharing routines, and governance mechanisms, including both contracts and trust-based relationships, are required. Relational capabilities do come at a cost, but they represent vital resources for firms, often hard or impossible to imitate. In particular, they possess some of the attributes of causal ambiguity and isolating mechanisms that render them sources of sustainable competitive advantage. Market leaders are most vulnerable to imitation or copying and would thus have much to profit by strategically managing their relationships to universities.

Not all firm-university relationships are successful. The firm and the university may be too different to explore and exploit complementarities in knowledge and routines. Furthermore, not all collaboration with academia is motivated by competitive advantages in the individual firm. Some industries may have common challenges in meeting regulatory requirements or environmental issues, so it makes sense to build an industry commons. In addition, joint research projects are generally more attractive for the government to support, as knowledge is shared and not patented by individual firms. In these projects, the university does not only provide knowledge and technology but also acts as a knowledge and financial broker between the government and the industry. Under these circumstances, it is hard for a firm to capture idiosyncratic knowledge.

Collaborating with universities is an activity in which firms learn from experience and develop broader and deeper ways of mutual engagement. We have argued that university relations are too important to be left to chance. Firms that invest early and extensively in university relationships may achieve sustainable competitive advantage. It is a well-established fact that new knowledge builds on prior knowledge. The more knowledge resides within a firm, the better equipped the firm is to acquire and absorb new knowledge. If new knowledge is turned into innovations, a firm may consequently develop a stream of innovations providing both new products and services, as well as novel processes to make productivity gains. These benefits may be gained through a firm's long-term relations with a university, comprising specific relations to that university.

NOTES

1 The normal company tax is 27%. Oil companies pay an additional 50% resource rent.
2 This account is somewhat simplified.

REFERENCES

Barney, J. B. (1986). Organizational culture: Can it be a source of sustained competitive advantage? *Academy of Management Review*, 11, 656–665.

Barney, J. (1991). Firm resources and sustained competitive advantage. *Journal of Management*, 17(1), 99–120.

Becker, W. and Dietz, J. R. (2004). R&D cooperation and innovation activities of firms: Evidence for the German manufacturing industry. *Research Policy*, 33(2), 209.

Bok, D. (2003). *Universities in the marketplace: The commercialization of higher education*. Princeton, N.J.: Princeton University Press.

Brun, E., Sætre, A. S. and Gjelsvik, M. (2008). Benefits of ambiguity in new product development. *International Journal of Innovation and Technology Development*, 5(3) 303–319.

Cohen, M. D. and Levinthal, D. A. (1990). Absorptive capacity: A new perspective on learning and innovation. *Administrative Science Quarterly*, 35, 128–152.

Day, G. S. and Schoemaker, P. J. H. (2006). *Peripheral vision: Detecting the weak signals that will make or break your company*. Boston, Mass.: Harvard Business School Press.

Deiaco, E., Hughes, A. and McKelvey, M. (2012). Universities as strategic actors in the knowledge economy. *Cambridge Journal of Economics*, 36(3), 525–541.

Dierickx, I. and Cool, K. (1989). Asset stock accumulation and sustainability of competitive advantage. *Management Science*, 35, 1504–1511.

Dyer, J. H. and Chu, W. (2003). The role of trustworthiness in reducing transaction costs and improving performance: Empirical evidence from the United States, Japan and Korea. *Organization Science*, 14(1), 57–68.

Dyer, J. and Kale, P. (2007). Relational capabilities: Drivers and implications. In E. Helfat et al. (eds.) Dynamic capabilites: Understanding strategic change in organizations. Oxford, UK: Blackwell Publishing.

Dyer, J. H. and Singh, H. (1998). The relational view: Cooperative strategy and sources of interorganizational competitive advantage. *Academy of Management Review*, 23(4), 660–679.

Fitjar, R. D., Gjelsvik, M., and Rodríguez-Pose, A. (2013). The combined impact of managerial and relational capabilities on innovation in firms. *Entrepreneurship and Regional Development*, 25(5–6), 500–520.

Fitjar, R. D. and Rodríguez-Pose, A. (2013). Firm collaboration and modes of innovation in Norway. *Research Policy*, 42(1), 128–138.

Grant, R. M. (1996). Towards a knowledge-based theory of the firm. *Strategic Management Journal*, 17, 109–122.

Gulati, R. (1995). Does famliarity breed trust? The implications of repeated ties for contractual choice in alliances. *Academy of Management Journal*, 38, 85–112.

Gulati, R. (1999). Network location and learning: The influence of network resources and firm capabilities on alliance formation. *Strategic Management Journal*, 20(5), 397–420.

Gulati, R., Nohria, N. and Zaheer, A. (2000). Strategic networks. *Strategic Management Journal*, 21(Special Issue), 203–215.

Hambrick, D. (1987). Top management teams: Key to strategic success. *California Management Review*, 30, 88–108.

Hamel, G. (1991). Competition for competence and inter-partner learning within international strategic alliances. *Strategic Management Journal*, 12(4), 83–103.

Hanel, P. and St-Pierre, M. (2006). Industry–University collaboration by Canadian manufacturing firms. *Journal of Technology Transfer*, 31(4), 485–499.

Hughes, A. and Kitson, M. (2012). Pathways to impact and the strategic role of universities: New evidence on the breath and depth of university knowledge exchange in the UK and the factors constraining its development. *Cambridge Journal of Economics*, 36(3), 723–750.

Klein, B. and Leffler, K. (1981). The role of price guaranteeing quality. *Journal of Political Economy*, 89, 615–641.

Laursen, K. and Salter, A. (2006). Open for innovation: The role of openness in explaining innovation performance among UK manufacturing firms. *Strategic Management Journal*, 27(2), 131–150.

Lester, R. K. (2005). *Universities, innovation, and the competitiveness of local economies: A summary report from the local innovation systems project-Phase1*. Local innovation systems working paper, 05–005. Cambridge, Mass.: MIT-IPC.

Lester, R. K. and Sotarauta, M. (2007). Universities, innovation and the competitiveness of local economies: An overview. In R. K. Lester and M. Sotarauta (eds.), *Innovation, universities and the competitiveness of regions* (9–30). Helsinki: Tekes.

Lunnan, R. and Haugland, S. A. (2008). Predicting and measuring alliance performance: A multidimensional analysis. *Strategic Management Journal*, 29(5), 545–556.

Macneil, I. R. (1980). *The new social contract: An inquiry into modern contractual relations*. New Haven: Yale University Press.

March, J. G. (1991). Exploration and exploitation in organizational learning. *Organization Science*, 2(1), 71–87.

March, J. G. and Levinthal, D. A. (1993). The myopia of learning. *Strategic Management Journal*, 14, 95–112.

McKelvey, M. (2014). Science, technology and business innovation. In M. Dodgson, D. M. Gann and N. Phillips (eds.), *The oxford handbook of innovation management* (60–85). Oxford: Oxford University Press.

Nieto, M. J. and Santamaría, L. (2007). The importance of diverse collaborative networks for the novelty of product innovation. *Technovation*, 27(6–7), 367–377.

Nightingale, P. (1998). A cognitive model of innovation. *Research Policy*, 27(7), 689–709.

Perkmann, M. and Salter, A. (2012). How to create productive partnerships with universities. *MIT Sloan Management Review*, 53, 79–88.

Perkmann, M., Tartari, V., et al. (2013). Academic engagement and commercialisation: A review of the literature on university-industry relations. *Research Policy*, 42, 423–442.

Perkmann, M. and Walsh, K. (2007). University-industry relationships and open innovation: Towards a research agenda. *International Journal of Management Reviews*, 9(4), 259–280.

Porter, M. E. (1980). *Competitive strategy: Techniques for analyzing industries and competitors*. New York: The Free Press.

Powell, W. W., Koput, K. W. and Smith-Doerr, L. (1996). Interorganizational collaboration and the locus of innovation: Networks of learning in biotechnology. *Administrative Science Quarterly*, 41(1), 116–145.

Prahalad, C. K. and Bettis, R. A. (1986). The dominant logic: A new linkage between diversity and performance. *Strategic Management Journal*, 7, 485–701.

Salter, A. and Martin, B. R. (2001). The economic benefits of publicly funded basic research: A crirical review. *Research Policy*, 30(3), 509–532.

Washburn, J. (2005). *University Inc.: The corporate corruption of higher education*. New York: Basic Books.

Zahra, S. A. and George, G. (2002). Absorptive capacity: A review, reconceptualization and extension. *Academy of Management Review*, 27(2), 185–203.

11 Business Innovation Modes

A Review From a Country Perspective

*Mario Davide Parrilli, Rune Dahl Fitjar,
and Andrés Rodríguez-Pose*

1. INTRODUCTION

The debate on business innovation modes has become particularly important in these days in which firms need to identify the most effective way to innovate and compete in global markets. The heterogeneity of firms questions the possibility of pursuing a standard approach to innovation. The traditional linear mode based on investments in R&D and scientific human capital (the so-called STI innovation mode—science, technology, and innovation) may find alternatives in modes based on practice and interaction across the supply chain (the so-called DUI mode—innovation based on learning-by-doing, by-using, and by-interacting). This latter approach has often been used in more traditional industries, though a strict sectoral correlation has not been proved yet. Country specificities may also matter, but more thorough reviews need to be implemented in order to elaborate more accurate propositions. This is in part what we aim at producing in the current chapter.

In this chapter, we review the empirical studies conducted across different country contexts on the adoption and success of STI and DUI approaches. The debate on the modes of innovation arose partly to generate a response to the puzzle of why some countries have been able to innovate and grow economically, in spite of relatively low investments in specific R&D activities (Asheim and Gertler, 2005; Edquist, 2005, Jensen et al., 2007). This seems to point to the existence of heterodox paths to innovation that are not explained by the direct adoption of higher R&D expenditure rates as recommended by the Lisbon agenda or the Europe 2020 Strategy. Learning-by-doing, using, and interacting (DUI), while less intensive in the use of R&D resources, has proven in certain cases to be as effective as STI type of drivers in the generation of firm-level innovation—if not more (Edquist, 2005; Jensen et al., 2007; Lorenz et al. 2007).

This discussion is at the heart of our research, which takes stock of the studies that have been developed over the past few years (Jensen et al., 2007, in Denmark; Aslesen et al., 2011 and Fitjar and Rodríguez-Pose, 2013, in Norway; Chen et al., 2011, in China; Trippl, 2011, in Austria; Nunes, 2012, in Portugal; Parrilli and Elola, 2012, in Spain; among others) and that aims to shed light on the effectiveness of such innovation modes, as well as on their differentiated use in particular country settings. After a theoretical section in which this debate is proposed and discussed, a review of studies on STI and DUI is carried out on the basis of such empirical works grounded in economies that range from very advanced through medium-advanced economies to emerging countries, including developing and transition economies.

2. THE INNOVATION PARADOX AND THE INNOVATION MODES

The study of innovation can be approached from the micro perspective of the firm or from the macro perspective of the economy. Both approaches have been present in the debate on innovation modes. Most studies have treated the STI and DUI modes as strategies adopted by firms but have typically also underlined that these approaches are embedded in macrolevel characteristics that may make some approaches more effective within particular contexts. Both from a firm perspective and from an economy-wide perspective, innovation has traditionally been regarded as a linear process where investments in scientific research generated new insights that through technological development in firms could be introduced into the market as innovations. This model has served as a basis for the development of R&D departments in firms, as well as for public investments in basic research and in technology transfer. However, recent literature on innovation has increasingly underlined that the transition from research to innovation is anything but linear and automatic and—furthermore—that sources outside scientific research can be equally important drivers of innovation (Rodríguez-Pose and Crescenzi, 2008).

Over the past twenty years, the economics literature on innovation has put forward the constructs of national, regional, and sectoral innovation systems. The comparative approach to innovation systems revealed the existence of different ways of stimulating innovation and growth in various economies (Cooke et al., 2004; Asheim and Gertler, 2005; Edquist, 2005). Particularly, some scholars highlighted that in some countries, firms were capable of generating high rates of innovation in spite of relatively small amounts of investments in R&D activities (e.g., Norway and Denmark). These countries were typically also able to convert these innovation outputs into economic performance very effectively (Edquist, 2005; Lundvall, 2007). By contrast, other countries (e.g., Sweden and Finland)—despite very high levels of investment in R&D—were less successful in transforming R&D into innovation and productivity. This is the "innovation paradox," which is not exclusive to the Nordic countries and which has been identified also in other contexts. For example, for many years Italy (particularly the Third Italy) was able to innovate and grow in spite of relatively limited investments in R&D. Similarly, Barge-Gil et al. (2011) found a number of "hidden innovators" among Spanish manufacturing firms. Kirner et al. (2009) note that low-technology firms perform at least as well as more advanced firms at process innovation and that they lag behind at product innovation partly on definitional grounds.

The systems of innovation approach presented a potential explanation to this paradox by highlighting that innovation is not simply a function of R&D investments. Rather, it stresses the interaction between people, firms, and other actors as the key to developing new knowledge and transforming it into successful innovation. Such interactions take place within a broader institutional or systemic context that implies country specificities. This approach emphasizes the cultural, institutional, and social embeddedness of economic action (Granovetter, 1985; Boschma, 2005) within which firms in various territories make choices about whether and how to pursue innovation. Consequently, co-located firms might exploit common avenues to innovation (i.e., "innovation modes") and thus gain competitive access to global markets. Some countries and regions might rely especially on high intensity of R&D expenditure, whereas others might pursue innovation through a dense set of intra- and interfirm cooperative practices, or even through a combination of both (see Lorenz, 2012). Within this contribution, we focus on the proposition that some economies (mostly developed and transition) may successfully combine the two modes of innovation proposed by Jensen et al. (2007), whereas others are not yet in a condition to harmonically and effectively combine both modes (mostly emerging and catching-up economies).

As stated earlier, the STI innovation mode is based on the adoption of science and technology drivers, such as investment in R&D, scientific human capital, and physical infrastructures (e.g., labs, universities, intellectual property rights). In the STI mode, innovation is heavily based on investments in the production of new codified knowledge (i.e., scientific formulas or compounds), which is subsequently applied and/or transformed into new products, processes, or services. This type of innovation may typically be found in the pharmaceutical and biotech industries, as well as in chemicals, energy, and nano-materials. In these sectors, businesses focus on identifying new principles and properties that are at the basis of new drugs, treatments, materials, and technologies. The DUI innovation mode is based more on practice and cooperation-based drivers, such as learning-by-doing, learning-by-using, and learning-by-interacting, and involves significant experiential and engineering-based capacity. As a consequence, it depends not only (or not mainly) on the generation of (radical) product innovation but more on process, organizational and commercial types of innovation that require more user-producer interactions and adaptations. The DUI innovation mode is centered on problem solving, and it is typically used in traditional manufacturing industries, such as furniture, footwear, but also in automotive, shipbuilding, and machine-tool sectors.

These two modes of innovation are not mutually exclusive. As suggested by Jensen et al. (2007), Aslesen et al. (2011), Chen et al. (2011), and Nunes et al. (2013), STI and DUI can be combined and may in fact mutually reinforce each other. However, other studies question the effective complementarity on the basis of evidence supporting a sort of substitution effect (Parrilli and Elola, 2012; Malaver and Vargas, 2013). This discrepancy might be due in part to different approaches and operationalizations of the concepts used in the analyses of modes of innovation. While Jensen et al. find that firms in Denmark that combine the STI and DUI modes are more innovative, the successful combination of both modes may depend on the availability of crucial drivers of STI and DUI in the firm's surroundings, both in the form of human and financial capital on the one hand, and of social and relational capital on the other. This is not to be taken for granted, as the innovation system needs to count on a number of preconditions to permit their firms to exploit fruitfully the potentials of these different innovation modes. Even across advanced economies, there are significant variations in the availability of finance (e.g., venture capital) and scientific human capital, which represent key assets for the effective application of R&D investments (the STI mode). Similarly, these economies vary significantly also in terms of the density of institutional, social, and relational networks and capital (e.g., accountability and responsiveness of policy-makers; mutual long-term relationships between producers, suppliers and clients), as well as in terms of human capital (e.g., overall educational attainment), which matter for the successful application of the DUI mode.

This chapter raises the possibility that the aforementioned results are all valid and depend not only on the kind of sample and indicators that are being adopted in each case (which differ) but also on country/region specificities that make firms respond more or less effectively to the adoption of a specific innovation mode in different contexts. In the following section, we analyze and compare the different studies in order to address this question.

3. REVIEW OF STUDIES OF BUSINESS INNOVATION MODES: DENMARK, NORWAY, SPAIN, PORTUGAL, CHINA, COLOMBIA, AND BELARUS

3.1 Grounded Meta-Analysis

This research considers and compares different quantitative and qualitative studies realized over the past few years worldwide. This work should help to identify useful behavioral patterns applied by businesses. A holistic methodological instrument is needed to conduct such research. This is the "grounded meta-analysis" (Glaser & Strauss, 1967; Hossler & Scalese-Love, 1989; Stall-Meadows & Hyle, 2010; Apanasovich, 2014b). This type of analysis helps to extract empirical findings from a set of quantitative and qualitative studies together with more qualitative information and evidence supplied by open interviews and observations that represent other rich sources of information. More in general, "this method is chosen because it enables to synthesize the theory, explore methods and findings, and to formulate a complete image of the field of study" (Apanasovich, 2014a: 35–36; 2014b; see also Hossler & Scalese-Love, 1989; Stall-Meadows & Hyle, 2010).

Over the past few years, a growing number of scholars have sought to verify the relevance of the two innovation modes in different country contexts. In this chapter, we examine several recent studies and reflect on potential policy implications of their empirical results. The set of studies that we take into account are based on quite heterogeneous methodological approaches. Some of them follow an exploratory case study approach (Aslesen et al., 2011; Hansen and Winther 2011; Isaksen and Karlsen, 2012), while others estimate correlations between innovation modes and outputs, building on quantitative data (Jensen et al., 2007; Chen et al., 2011; Parrilli and Elola, 2012; Fitjar and Rodríguez-Pose, 2013); some scholars apply factor or cluster analysis to identify different types of innovative business (Jensen et al., 2007; Malaver and Vargas, 2013), or the importance of a range of cooperating agents (Chen et al., 2011), or more simply to verify the consistency of the STI and DUI constructs-based variables (González et al., 2013; Malaver and Vargas, 2013); other researchers pre-assign industries alternatively to the STI mode or the DUI mode (Chen et al., 2011). All these specificities make it hard to compare the different studies directly to draw conclusions about the importance of the various types of innovation modes adopted by small and medium-sized businesses in current globalized markets.

A first relevant comparative methodological issue is the exploitation of quantitative databases. Some studies use data collected through purpose-specific questionnaires. This is the case of the Danish study by Jensen et al., as well as of the Chinese study by Chen et al., the Norwegian cases analyzed by Aslesen et al. and by Fitjar and Rodríguez-Pose, and the Basque case by Parrilli and Elola. Others rely on national adaptations of the Community Innovation Survey, as in the Spanish study by González et al. and the Colombian case by Malaver and Vargas, which are based on broader types of questionnaires that have been set up by statistical agencies in these countries, building on the Community Innovation Survey. This aspect is relevant because it implies important differences across databases in the way the two basic modes are measured.

The variables and indicators used in each study also differ, which might explain some apparently contradictory results. For instance, Jensen et al. (2007) and Fitjar and Rodríguez-Pose (2013) use the variable of "cooperation with customers" as an indicator of the DUI mode, while Parrilli and Elola (2012) excluded this indicator because some industrial interactions along the value chain might still represent STI types of interactions (e.g., pharmaceuticals for biotech or aircrafts for specialized R&D services). This might explain why the latter study shows the DUI mode to have little effect on radical innovation (new-to-market innovations). Some other studies (e.g., Fitjar and Rodríguez-Pose, 2013) were able to separate local versus global STI cooperation and local versus global DUI cooperation on the basis of whether the correspondent relationships connect local agents only or local firms with foreign clients/suppliers and competitors.

In other cases, the methodological gap can be considerable. The work by Chen et al. (2011) distinguishes a priori between STI and DUI industries on the basis of the consideration that traditional industries, such as furniture, footwear, and food, tend to adopt a DUI mode, which generates mainly incremental innovations, whereas high-tech industries, such as pharmaceuticals, ICT, and energy, tend to adopt an STI mode that typically leads to more radical innovations. Chen et al. hypothesize different business behaviors in different types of industries and examine what practices (scope, depth, and orientation of relationships) and agents (technological, research based, or value-chain based) are more likely to benefit these two types of industries (high-tech vs. traditional). This approach differs considerably from the work done by Jensen et al. (2007), which examines innovation modes adopted within firms and across firms, relying on either a set of more experience- and practice-based drivers or a set of more research and technology-based factors.

Table 11.1 compares the methodological approaches used in ten studies of the implications of the STI and DUI modes of innovation. Notably, none of the studies are identical in all dimensions. Indeed, each new paper seeks to add to prior research by approaching the empirical data in a novel way. The last row of Table 11.1 identifies the methodological value added in each study. The original study by Jensen et al. (2007) introduced the concepts and provides the theoretical foundations of this literature. Furthermore, the study emphasizes the originality of trying to verify whether the combination of STI and DUI drivers increases the capacity of firms to generate substantial innovations (new-to-international-markets). This provided a contribution to the literature on innovation systems and business innovation beyond the former idea that countries could promote innovations either by investing more in STI practices or in DUI factors. This seminal contribution has promoted a variety of new works on the topic, each of which provided additional methodological updates.

The work by Aslesen et al. (2011) made two very important methodological contributions. First, it deductively pre-identified two types of DUI approaches: traditional "application development," which refers to an innovation mode that stresses the value-chain connection between manufacturers, suppliers, and clients, and a somewhat less traditional form of DUI called "technological platform," which refers to an innovation mode that entails collaboration and insights absorbed from technology centers. On this basis, the researchers identified a new typology of DUI innovators with different approaches to innovation and competition in the market. Their second contribution is their analysis of the impact of local versus global

Table 11.1 Comparative Methodology Parameters Across STI-DUI Studies

Authors	Jensen-Johnson-Lorenz-Lundvall	Chen-Chen-Vanhaverbeke	Aslesen-Isaksen-Karlsen	Parrilli-Elola	Fitjar-Rodríguez-Pose	González-Parrilli-Peña 1	Nunes-López-Dias	Malaver-Vargas	Apanasovich	González-Parrilli-Peña 2
Database	Disko	Own	CIS based	SPRI	Own	CIS based	Own	Own	CIS based	CIS based
No. Firms	692	209	96	409	1,604	8,300	397	568	525	4,969
Sectors (NACE)*	Any	8(T+H)	4(T+H)	4(T+H)	Any	Any	Any	Any	Any	Any
Inductive-Deductive	I	D	D	I	I	I	I	I	I	I
Factor & Cluster Analysis	Yes	Yes	No	No	No	Yes	Yes	Yes	No	Yes
Regression Analysis	Yes	Yes	No	Yes	Yes	Yes	Yes	Yes	Yes	Yes
Typology of Firms	Yes	No	Yes	No	No	Yes	Yes	No	Yes	No
Method Novelties	Combination of STI-DUI modes	Scope, depth, orient-ation	Split DUI mode, Local, Global	Innov-ation types: prod. proc.org. comm.	Local/Global DUI & STI	Link to short & long-run performance	Only combined modes through cluster an.	Logit anal. associate groups+ innovation	D&U indicators	Agent additionality to firm-university relations

*T= traditional sectors; H= high-technology sectors. Source: Authors' elaboration.

interactions. Chen et al. (2011) also deductively identified DUI and STI approaches. They start from the assumption that industries can be divided between some that are mostly STI oriented and others which are mostly DUI oriented. Their work stresses the importance of studying the scope of openness in knowledge exchanges with other agents, as well as the depth or intensity of such exchanges, and finally their orientation, i.e., the intensity and value of certain exchanges vis-à-vis others in the specific case of DUI or STI industries.

The work of Parrilli and Elola (2012) introduced the novelty of studying not only product or process innovations as the output of the application of STI and DUI drivers but also organizational and commercial innovations. These authors combine the output indicators into a joint "new-to-market innovation" construct, which represents the indicator for radical innovations. Fitjar and Rodríguez-Pose (2013) follow the work of Aslesen et al. (2011) in emphasizing the importance of different types of geographical relations, particularly separating the effect of local relations from national and global relations within the value chain and with competitors and examining the effects of these relations on different types of innovation (i.e., incremental vs. radical). Furthermore, the paper connects specifically the two main innovation modes (STI and DUI) with product and process innovation and seeks to isolate the effects of each mode on separate innovation outcomes. González et al. (2013) connect the innovation modes not only with innovation output but also with economic performance, measured in terms of labor productivity and overall sales value. The paper adopts a two-stage approach that examines not only the effects of STI and DUI strategies on innovation but also whether these innovation outputs actually have an impact on economic performance. In this case, the use of panel data allows for the adoption of temporal lags to check whether the aforementioned impact is stronger in the short run than in the long run or vice versa for both product and process innovation.

Nunes et al. (2013) predefine a set of combinations between STI and DUI modes. Rather than establishing a clear separation between both modes, echoing Aslesen et al. (2011), the authors show their interconnection in different forms. Nunes et al. use a wide set of explicit variables, including some that were used by Jensen et al. (2007), as well as some new variables (e.g., external financing, formal or informal interactions with agents, predominant innovation activities), in order to identify three different types of innovation modes (e.g., low learning DUI innovators, moderate DUI innovators, and stronger STI-DUI innovators). The effects of these combinations are then put to the test in the differentiated context of micro-firms, SMEs, and large companies.

Malaver and Vargas (2013) introduce a hierarchical cluster analysis in order to identify different types of innovation modes (or combinations thereof) in their study of Colombia. The authors subsequently apply a logit model to examine the relationship between the three different innovation modes identified in the former analysis and firms' innovation outputs. The results highlight that some of the identified groups do not produce significant innovations and particularly that the combination STI+DUI is not effective in the specific context of Colombia. In her study of Belarus, Apanasovich (2014a) in turn overcomes the over-reliance of previous studies on indicators of learning-by-interacting as measures of the DUI mode by introducing new indicators of learning-by-doing and using. In addition, this author verifies the effects of DUI and STI practices and their combination not only on product innovation but also on organizational innovation.

At the time of this writing, the most recent contribution was developed by González et al. (2014) in the context of Spain. They study the importance of firm-university relations for innovation output, using the largest database of Spanish businesses (the PITEC survey). Firm-university relations are shown to be most effective when firms not only work with universities alone but also complement this collaboration with other collaborations with STI and/or DUI agents.

3.2 Working Propositions

The original contribution of this chapter lies in the establishment of new working propositions on the role of national or regional (economic and social/cultural) context in shaping the conditions for applying different modes of innovation. These propositions will be assessed in the following section on the basis of the qualitative and quantitative empirical evidence provided by the growing number of country surveys and studies of the modes of innovation. Our general hypothesis is that country specificities matter in the effective adoption of one mode of innovation vis-à-vis other modes (in terms of its impact on innovation outputs). In particular, we hypothesize that the effects of different approaches to innovation are linked to the availability in the country of a number of relevant factors that will be analyzed in the following section. Synthetically, we consider that the effectiveness of the STI+DUI interaction depends on:

1) The degree of development of the country.

Within it, we stress in particular the role of human capital formation in any country context that is considered in the following subproposition:

1.1) The education of the workforce (taken as a proxy for its absorptive capacity).

According to previous studies (Rodríguez-Pose and Crescenzi, 2008; Fitjar and Rodríguez-Pose, 2013), this argument may be explained with the importance of high education as a means to increase the absorptive capacity of employees (good distribution of tertiary and technical education across the population). This puts firms in condition to absorb and exploit knowledge and competencies in the production and commercialization of new goods and services.

In addition, we propose two complementary propositions on the independent effects of STI and DUI drivers and modes in different contexts:

2) In the context of catching-up or emerging economies, the DUI mode is the most commonly used mode across local businesses, but it is likely to be less effective for innovation promotion than the STI mode.

This may be justified on the basis of country/region specificities (e.g., technological development, educational attainment, institutional thickness, among others) (Parrilli and Elola, 2012; Malaver and Vargas, 2013). In catching-up or emerging contexts, firms that apply the DUI mode mostly refer to exchanging old technical knowledge and organizational routines (due to the limited inflow of novel codified knowledge), which tend to have little or no impact on effective innovation processes (i.e., new-to-market innovations). A tiny group of firms are in a condition to invest in STI drivers (e.g., R&D) and, on such bases, are more likely to generate capabilities and capacities to produce effective innovations (Parrilli and Elola, 2012; González et al., 2013; Malaver and Vargas, 2013).

3) In the context of advanced economies (in particular in coordinated market economies in Hall and Soskice's classification), as well as in transition economies, the DUI mode is effective for innovation, particularly where institutional and/or social capital is high. In these contexts, the DUI mode can produce better outcomes when it is combined with the STI mode.

The latter proposition is based on the argument that, in the context of high and distributed absorptive capacities, the DUI mode helps to transfer and incorporate scientific and technological knowledge to a higher extent. In this sense, DUI has a positive effect on innovation output, and this effect is even stronger when it is combined with the application of the STI mode.

On the basis of these propositions, the most advanced countries and regions are more likely to make the combined STI+DUI approach work, as they are endowed with high levels of human capital (not only scientific human capital but also general education across the whole population that represents social and institutional capital more in general), which create conditions in which a large share of the population are in a position to learn-by-doing and by-using. Transition economies with a large share of the population having high levels of education may also be in a position to adopt this combined mode effectively. The DUI innovation mode and its drivers are in general effective in contexts characterized by high levels of institutional and social capital (which might occur in the case of less dynamic yet socially homogeneous economies), where people can be more confident in interacting with outsiders and may place more trust in doers and users to present new solutions.

We will now analyze the evidence from the different country studies in order to examine the validity of the aforementioned propositions.

3.3 Differentiated Evidence on Innovation

In some contexts, notably including some highly developed economies, the combination of STI and DUI drivers helps firms obtain higher levels of innovation outputs. This is true in the case of Denmark (Jensen et al., 2007; Hansen and Winther, 2011[1]) and Norway (Aslesen et al., 2011; Isaksen and Karlsen, 2012), as well as Austria (Trippl, 2011). The most recent study on Norway (Fitjar and Rodríguez-Pose, 2013) does not examine the interaction between the two modes but rather takes into account the effects of different types of DUI collaboration (within or outside the value chain, local or non-local), finding that only one of these types (non-local DUI collaboration) significantly affects innovation. This suggests a need to examine more closely the type of DUI approach taken by firms.

However, a different pattern emerges in studies of another group of countries (e.g., Southern EU economies or Latin America, e.g., Spain and Colombia). The studies of Spain and of its Basque Country region, based on two different databases, do not show the advantage of combining DUI and STI drivers as in the studies from Scandinavia and Austria. In Spain and the Basque Country, the main impetus for innovation arises from a need to close the gap with the more advanced economies and compete successfully in the global market. This leads firms to look for competitive edges in radical innovation rather than in "new-to-firm" incremental innovations (Parrilli and Elola, 2012; González et al., 2013). This is clear in the case of the Basque region, as the effectiveness of research and technology centers in knowledge generation and transformation to valuable industrial applications is being enhanced through political and social pressure for more effective applied research and public/private joint projects. This has led to the structuring of public programs for the intensification of patent registration and new product/process development (Orkestra, 2013). In spite of the current economic difficulties, other Southern European countries (e.g., Italy) are also identifying this new priority of making science more effective for business competitiveness (e.g., Dip. Sviluppo Coesione Economica, 2012 [2]). Thus, in these economies, radically innovative businesses are those that tend to devote resources to STI drivers and scientific personnel (employed in R&D departments), while DUI drivers are currently being neglected. These were more relevant in these economies 10 or 20 years ago in a phase in which incremental differentiations and personalization of product design were sufficient to deliver new entrants a competitive edge (Piore and Sabel, 1984). Groups of firms in Spain still show some sensitivity to DUI drivers, but they do not seem to be in a position to fruitfully combine both STI and DUI drivers (González et al., 2013).

A similar case is Colombia, which has undertaken an important process of economic catching-up and has achieved growth rates at around 5% for many years. Thus the country has been able to develop dynamic industries in agricultural and energy production (e.g., flowers, coffee, cattle growing, oil, gas, hydraulic energy, and mining products), and efforts have been made also in medium-high-technology industries, such as automotive and petrochemicals. This effort and the consequent economic growth are linked, similarly to the Basque Country and Spain, to a high sensitivity of firms to STI rather than to DUI drivers (Malaver and Vargas, 2013, on a sample of more than 5,000 firms in the departments of Bogotá and Cundinamarca). The paper suggests that Colombian SMEs (i.e., particularly a small but relevant group of small firms that are successful and capable of doing so) have realized the need to go beyond their traditional incremental innovation mode and move toward a more science-based innovation (STI) mode in order to produce radical innovation outputs.

This interpretation is supported by findings in China (Chen et al., 2011), which shows quite different effects in medium-low technology industries and in medium-high technology industries. In the context of medium-low tech industries, it is mostly the value-chain relationship with suppliers and clients (DUI drivers) that have a significant impact on innovation output. However, in medium- and high-technology industries, the effect is positive for both types of drivers, although there is a threshold (maximum number) of relationships with innovation agents that firms cannot exceed without suffering a fall in their innovation output. The Chinese case seems quite in line with the Spanish case that also identifies different trajectories for firms, some of which benefit from the exploitation of DUI drivers, whereas others benefit mainly from the exploitation of STI drivers. Furthermore, the mix of the two might prove inefficient in some cases (i.e., traditional medium-low tech industries, see p.371). A dual trajectory may thus emerge also from this case.

At first sight, the case of Portugal seems to differ from this pattern, but a closer look shows a lot of similarities with the former cases. The analyses made by Nunes et al. (2013) indicate that all firms (397 in the survey) apply the DUI approach, although to different extents. The latent cluster analysis shows two broad categories of mainly DUI-oriented firms, classified as "low learning DUI" innovators and "moderate DUI" innovators. The third cluster is the only one that mixes the DUI approach with the STI approach. This category includes several smaller-sized firms (often microenterprises) that work often in medium-high-tech industries and rely on scientific knowledge bases and personnel as well as on dedicated R&D activities. In this case, indeed, the firms seem to stress particularly their scientific and technological profile. The econometric analysis shows that it is this third type of firm, which only represents 13% of the sample (vs. 67% of the first type and 20% of the second), that produces the most significant innovation output. This result justifies the consideration that it is the STI approach that makes a difference, just as in the case of the former four countries. Similarly, Gibson and Naquin (2011: 1304) note that "it seems that there is very little DUI innovation present in Portugal."

All in all, this second group of five country cases seems to indicate that, in emerging and catching-up countries, the class of business that is more likely to produce new-to-market innovations includes firms that mostly adopt the STI mode. However, these represent a minority of firms, whereas a larger group keeps adopting a more traditional DUI mode but with relatively poor outcomes. This preliminary evidence seems to call for a deep and thorough review to verify what kind of policies, programs, and instruments need to be set up to favor the innovation capacity of most businesses in those contexts.

The cases of the Basque Country and Colombia show evidence of this as there seems to be a group of businesses that innovate through the STI mode; in Spain as a whole (and to a certain extent also in China and Portugal), there seem to be firms that are successfully driven by the STI mode and others that are driven successfully by the DUI mode. Therefore, this might also depend on the kind of capabilities that the local production systems (and their SMEs) have developed in these countries, which help them benefit more from the application of either STI drivers or DUI drivers. This may be the case if the development strategy has relied more on the improvement of scientific personnel specialized in R&D activities rather than in the continuous upgrading of general educational levels across the population. The latter type of inputs (DUI) are likely to have contributed strongly in former stages of development of their countries (e.g., 1980s and 1990s) but are no longer enough to help these firms and countries acquire new competitive edges in the current globalized markets in which thousands of companies from several catching-up countries now compete. This in part explains the difficulties that these countries have been facing since the mid-1990s in building up novel innovation capacity across their production systems. Of course, this trend might change again once a new economic situation comes about or, more specifically, when the critical conditions change. This may happen in China, which is experiencing the most significant and abrupt changes in its economic performance, as well as in the conditions that guarantee such results. The Chinese effort to create more solid educational bases (e.g., literacy rate) as well as institutional solidity (e.g., higher environmental standards) might bring about a structural transformation of the innovation modes successfully adopted by its SMEs (Chen et al., 2011). This might also be the case of Italy and Spain (and its Basque region)—which do not face particular problems in terms of human capital (i.e., science-based PhDs and MScs)—as they pass the current constraints linked not only to the EU financial requisites but also in particular to the institutional and social bases (which have been severely transformed by social changes, e.g., as a result of migration) and to the lack of more adequate institutional structures (e.g., the current debate over the excess division in provinces in the Italian case, as well as the inefficiencies that are affecting the autonomous communities in Spain).

In these cases, a renewed innovation capacity may originate in collaborations between the sometimes rather "poorly endowed" local universities and research institutes and innovative firms based abroad (González et al., 2014).

In contrast with this overall pattern, the Belarusian case presents a rather different pattern. In this case, the combination of STI and DUI drivers has a stronger and more benevolent impact on the innovation outputs generated by firms. The results emerging from the Belarusian case stress the importance of combining STI and DUI drivers. The recent analysis by Apanasovich (2014a) indicates that firms that are able to adopt both drivers at a significant level are more likely to generate significant innovation outputs (product innovation) than firms that use DUI or STI drivers independently from one another. The fact that Belarus does not show a similar pattern as the former group of countries might be attributed to the absorptive capacity of the country's workforce. In Belarus, the mean years of schooling are substantially higher than in the former countries, thus raising the internal absorptive capacity (Cohen and Levinthal, 1989), which might favor the simultaneous and positive application of STI and DUI drivers. In this case, one expects that all personnel (e.g., managers and workers) in the firm are able to learn and interact with dedicated STI personnel, thus creating the basis for a positive interaction of STI and DUI factors. While this proposition has not been systematically tested in any of the studies, it might reasonably explain the difference of this country vis-à-vis the former group.[3]

Table 11.2 shows some relevant data for the different countries covered in the case studies discussed earlier. Effectively, the Belarusian case shows a strong similarity to Norway and Denmark with regard to educational rates. China, Colombia, and Portugal are quite different in this respect, whereas Spain looks more similar to the most advanced countries, yet presents quite different results from them.

3.4 The Relationship Between Innovation and Economic Performance

In this subsection, we briefly show the relationships that have been estimated in the aforementioned studies between innovation activities and outputs and economic performance. In a few studies, the combined effect of STI+DUI has also been linked directly to economic performance in the form of productivity or sales. However, as indicated in subsection 3.3, in many cases the effect of DUI drivers is not straightforward and needs to be assessed more carefully, in particular because they can be influenced by a number of factors, including human, social, relational, and institutional capital, which might also split from one another and lead to good combinations of STI and DUI drivers through different avenues (e.g., Belarus more on the basis of a generalized high human capital and Italy more from a restored degree of social and/or institutional capital at the local level in some regions).

Table 11.2 Development Indicators by Country

	GDP per capita (US$ PPP)	Economic Growth (%, 2010)	Development (HDI position)	Education (Mean years of schooling)	Most relevant mode
Norway	55,009	+1.5	1st(0.963)	12.6	STI+DUI
Denmark	37.657	+1.0	13th(0.941)	11.4	STI+DUI
Basque Country*	41,771	+0.5	1st(0.981)	n.d.	STI
Spain	31,000	-0.2	21st(0.928)	10.4	STI or DUI
Portugal	23,700	+1.0	26th(0.904)	7.7	STI
Belarus	15,200	+4.8	67th(0.786)	11.5	STI+DUI
Colombia	10,400	+4.4	69th(0.785)	7.3	STI
China	8,500	+10.3	85th(0.755)	7.5	STI or DUI

Source: Authors' elaboration on the basis of UNDP, HDR, 2013 (webpage) for growth and position, IMF for per capita income. For the Basque Country, estimates of the statistical office www.eustat.es (data 2007 for p.c. income and HDI and 2011 for growth) are used.

Table 11.3 Associations Between Innovation Mode and Output in Different Studies

	Effect of the STI Mode	Effect of the DUI Mode	Best Combination
Jensen et al., 2007	+	+	STI + DUI
Chen et al., 2011	+	+	STI + *dui* or DUI
Aslesen et al., 2011 & Isaksen-Karlsen, 2012	+	+ (if technology DUI)= (if ordinary DUI)	DUI + STI
Nunes et al., 2013	+	+ (if fast DUI)= (if moderate DUI)	STI + *dui*
Fitjar and Rodríguez-Pose, 2013	+	= (if local DUI)+ (if global DUI)	n.d.
Parrilli and Elola, 2012	+	=	STI
González et al., 2013	+	+	STI or DUI
Malaver and Vargas, 2013	+	=	STI
Apanasovich et al. 2014a	+	+	1. STI + DUI,2. only DUI in organizational innovation

Note: with this table the effect on the innovation output is presented (+ positive, = neutral, -negative). Source: Authors' elaboration. Symbols in italics represent a positive effect, but with negligible weight.

3.5 A Synthetic View

From a business/management perspective, these studies indicate the importance of both innovation modes. In general, it seems that the STI mode has a stronger effect as a means to promote a significant/radical innovation output. In addition, it seems that at least in the case of most catching-up and emerging countries and regions, the DUI mode alone does not produce an effective contribution to innovation. A balanced combination of DUI with STI drivers is more likely to be effective in these contexts. It is a prospect that needs to be further developed, as this combination is not yet effective here. This implies that the strengthening of human resources with scientific capabilities and of internal R&D activities to build up a higher absorptive capacity will enhance firms' capacity to interpret and adopt/adapt knowledge produced by the industry leaders. In particular, some studies have shown that traditional DUI represents a limited innovation mode unless it is combined with significant knowledge inputs from leading scientific or international business communities (Aslesen et al., 2011; and Fitjar and Rodríguez-Pose, 2013, on Norway; Parrilli and Elola, 2012, on the Basque Country; Nunes et al., 2013, on Portugal; Malaver and Vargas, 2013, on Colombia).

Simultaneously, some preliminary evidence seems to indicate that the DUI drivers might complement the STI drivers and produce higher innovation outputs than the application of STI drivers alone, mainly in the context of a highly educated workforce and/or a solid social/institutional framework (e.g., most advanced economies and perhaps in transition economies). This might mean that, due to the higher intensity of current global competition—for a majority of firms in several less dynamic countries—the DUI innovation mode that was identified as the critical reason for the competitiveness of SME clusters and districts in the 1980s and 1990s (a time in which SMEs were highly innovative and competitive, Piore and Sabel, 1984; Becattini, 1990) needs to be upgraded. This would permit firms to take on the new challenges that emerging and catching-up countries' businesses face in the current context of globalization.

The DUI approach might still be efficient in some countries and for specific groups of firms, such as when it refers to traditional industries in which only incremental knowledge development and innovations are expected (Chen et al., 2011; González et al., 2013) or for certain types of innovation, e.g., organizational and process innovation (Gonzáles et al., 2013; Apanasovich, 2014a). This is still the exception, as it seems currently necessary to take a step ahead by developing new interactions along the global value chain in order to obtain explicit and tacit knowledge inputs from wherever they are produced. This can be achieved in close connection with the regional and national innovation system that might help firms absorb and transform such knowledge inputs into relevant outputs. Fitjar and Rodríguez-Pose (2013) could also identify the diverse effect of interaction with some agents.

Particularly, international clients help firms develop product innovations, particularly radical types, whereas interaction with international suppliers is more important for process innovations, especially of the incremental type (Fitjar and Rodríguez-Pose, 2013).

From a country perspective (economics), which is a core aspect of this analysis, we note that context seems to matter insofar as similar strategies might have different effects in different countries. Countries at an advanced development level (i.e., Norway and Denmark) can combine fruitfully the STI and DUI innovation modes; this leads to higher rates of radical innovations measured in terms of new-to-market innovations. This success seems to be underpinned by another condition in addition to high economic development, i.e., education. On these bases, a good absorptive capacity is developed across society, promoting effective joint innovation efforts by large segments of the local population and of the personnel in the firms (see in particular Jensen et al., 2007, on Denmark; Aslesen et al., 2011; Isaksen and Karlsen, 2012). Such conditions might be monitored and stimulated through specific policies that strengthen these crucial factors.

A second group of intermediate economies, including Southern European, Latin American countries, and some emerging countries, show the clear predominance of STI drivers over DUI drivers. In many of these cases, DUI drivers do not matter or matter less than STI drivers; and often the combination does not produce additional radical innovation outputs. A more reduced group of firms focus already on science and technology and are able to produce new products, processes, organizational, and commercial combinations that lead to radical innovations. For this group of countries, the DUI innovation mode might have been very useful and effective a few years ago (e.g., in the 1980s and 1990s), but they seem to have advanced to a new stage in which a new type of drivers become strategically important and effective in upgrading the competitive capacity of the country and its firms. However, in these same countries, the aforementioned studies show that the DUI mode might be rather effective for certain groups/segments of firms. It is the case of traditional industries in China (Chen et al., 2011) and a group of traditional firms in Spain (González et al., 2013). In contrast, the DUI mode is clearly less significant and valuable in other contexts and for other groups of firms (e.g., medium-high-tech industries in China, Spain, Colombia, and perhaps also Portugal: Chen et al., 2011; Gibson and Naquin, 2011; Parrilli and Elola, 2012; González et al., 2013; Malaver and Vargas, 2013; Nunes et al., 2013). These findings do not imply that DUI drivers do not matter at all. They only mean that they do not count in the current form. In fact, DUI drivers matter because the large majority of firms tend to work and innovate in an incremental way through some DUI drivers. Specific actions need to be taken in order to make the DUI innovation mode more effective than it currently is (e.g., targeting quality interactions across global supply chains rather than only in locally based communities).

In a third group of countries, which in our meta-study are represented by Belarus only, the effect of combining STI and DUI drivers is positive in spite of the lower development stage. This is hypothetically justified by high levels of human capital (i.e., mean years of schooling, literacy rate) that increase the absorptive capacity of the country/firms to a level that allows firms to involve all their personnel effectively in a joint innovation process (with R&D personnel). This finding has important implications for the previous group of countries. If they want to progress to a combined innovation mode (STI+DUI) in more effective terms, absorptive capacity and human capital need to be stimulated to generate more advanced forms of intra- and inter-firm cooperation.

Table 11.4 Critical Factors and Focus of Innovation Activities

	Key factors	Activities to promote SME innovation
Jensen et al., 2007	Combining STI with DUI	Promoting organizational change toward interactive modes oriented to *problem setting and solving* and supporting R&D and human capital investments (i.e., scientific personnel).
Chen et al., 2011	Scope and depth of opening/interaction	Promoting open learning across firms and clients, suppliers, technology centers, institutions of standards and IPRs.
Aslesen et al., 2011	Diversity of relations of cooperation (STI and DUI)	Intensifying the relations with agents external to the firm to favor learning and technology innovation. Simultaneous support to R&D investment.
Fitjar and Rodríguez-Pose, 2013	Global relations (geographic and cognitive distance)	Spurring formal and informal interactions with international clients and suppliers.
Parrilli and Elola, 2012	STI drivers are much more relevant for innovation	Increasing SME investments in R&D and increasing their scientific and engineering human capital.
González et al., 2013	The firms might follow different innovation modes (STI or DUI)	Identifying the different types of firms and supporting the factors that are related to their main features (STI or DUI).

	Key factors	Activities to promote SME innovation
Nunes et al., 2013	All SMEs adopt a DUI approach, a few also a joint DUI-STI mode	Investment in scientific human capital and support of localized interaction processes.
Malaver and Vargas, 2013	STI drivers are much more relevant for innovation	Increasing SME investments in R&D and increasing their scientific and engineering human capital.
Apanasovich, 2014a	The combination of STI and DUI factors produces higher results	Promoting organizational change toward interactive modes oriented to *problem solving*, and R&D and human capital investments (i.e., scientific personnel).

Source: Authors' elaboration.

5 CONCLUSIONS AND POLICY IMPLICATIONS

This chapter underlines the need to avoid implementing one-size-fits-all policies for promoting innovation (Tödtling and Trippl, 2005) within the modes of innovation approach. While early findings (Jensen et al., 2005; Aslesen et al., 2011) clearly suggested the importance of combining both the STI and DUI approaches to innovation in order to reap the benefits of both, these results may have been conditioned by the specific Scandinavian country contexts of high human, institutional, and social capital in which these studies were conducted. Catching-up economies, such as those in Southern Europe or in Latin America, present a different context in which there seems to be more of a trade-off between the STI and DUI modes, sometimes with limited effects of the latter. In these countries, a few bottlenecks are hindering the adequate operationalization of the DUI mode. These include the low level and the low quality of education, together with serious deficiencies in the labor force that limit the absorptive capacity of businesses.

In these contexts, a reduced number of leading local firms (including SMEs) are capable of investing in R&D and scientific human capital and exploiting the benefits of such investments. This is likely to occur more frequently in specific advanced industries (ICT, biotechnology). The policy of fostering the STI mode would refer to this group of firms (and sectors) that show promise, particularly those firms that have shown potential and capacity to connect and collaborate with universities and research institutes. This should lead to a targeted approach rather than blanket intervention. The innovation brought by these firms can then be diffused locally through the adoption of appropriate DUI types of mechanisms (e.g., promoting interaction along the supply chain).

For a much larger number of firms, an alternative approach would require firms and policy-makers to tackle the bottlenecks that limit the effectiveness of the DUI mode. This implies the need to improve education. In particular, the overall quality of education, on-the-job training, apprenticeship, adult education, and the match between education supply and labor demand should be effectively targeted. Simultaneously, the institutional quality should be upgraded through government effectiveness and corruption control.

Other catching-up economies, including some Eastern European countries, may already have high levels of human capital and perhaps of institutional capital too; these bases create a fertile soil for combining both approaches. In these cases, policy ambitions might include preventing brain drain and retaining human capital in the country. Furthermore, it is important to put this human capital to innovative use through encouraging learning-by-doing and learning-by-using by workers and consumers and feeding new knowledge into the system through STI activities with strong links to industry.

NOTES

1 While Jensen et al. (2007) examine the combination of STI and DUI drivers within firms, Hansen and Winther (2011) consider combinations of STI and DUI stemming from collaboration between high-tech and low-tech firms and find a positive effect for firm cases in Denmark and the UK.
2 http://www.aginnovazione.gov.it/wp-content/uploads/2010/11/Pubblicazione-Napoli.pdf.
3 However, it needs to be said that in the case of organizational innovation, in Belarus, the DUI drivers are the only ones that are associated with innovation across businesses.

BIBLIOGRAPHY

Apanasovich, N. (2014a). *The impact of business innovation on innovation performance: The case of Belarus*. Ph.D. Thesis, Deusto University.
Apanasovich, N. (2014b). Modes of innovation: A grounded meta-analysis. *Journal of Knowledge Economy*, doi: 10.1007/s13132–014–0237–0.
Asheim, B. and Gertler, M. (2005). The geography of innovation: Regional innovation systems. In J. Fagerberg, D. Mowery and R. Nelson (eds.), *The Oxford handbook of innovation* (291–317). Oxford: Oxford University Press.
Aslesen, H., Isaksen, A. and Karlsen, J. (2011). Modes of innovation and differentiated responses to globalisation—A case study of innovation modes in the Agder Region, Norway. *Journal of the Knowledge Economy*, 1–17. doi: 10.1007/s13132–011–0060–9.

Barge-Gil, A., Nieto, M. J. and Santamaría, L. (2011). Hidden innovators: The role of non-R&D activities. *Technology Analysis & Strategic Management*, 23(4), 415–432.

Becattini, G. (1990). The district as a socioeconomic notion. In F. Pyke, G. Becattini and W. Sengenberger (eds.). *Industrial districts and interfirm cooperation*. Geneva: ILO.

Boschma, R. (2005). Proximity and innovation: A critical approach. *Regional Studies*, 39(1), 61–74.

Chen, J., Chen, Y. and Vanhaverbeke, W. (2011). The influence of scope, depth, and orientation of external technology sources on the innovative performance of Chinese firms. *Technovation*, 31(8), 362–373.

Cohen, W. M., and Levinthal, D. A. (1989). Innovation and learning: The two faces of R&D. *The Economic Journal*, 99(397), 569–596.

Cooke, P. (2004). Regional innovation systems: An evolutionary approach. In P. Cooke, M. Heidenreich, and J. Braczick (eds.), *Regional systems of innovation* (3–25. London: Routledge.

Cooke, P., Heidenreich, M. and Braczick, J. (2004). *Regional systems of innovation*. London: Routledge

Edquist, C. (2005). Systems of innovation: Perspectives and challenges. In J. Fagerberg, D. Mowery and R. Nelson (eds.), *The Oxford handbook of innovation* (181–208. Oxford: Oxford University Press.

Fitjar, R. D. and Rodríguez-Pose, A. (2013). Firm collaboration and modes of innovation in Norway. *Research Policy*, 42, 128–138.

Gibson, D. V. and Naquin, H. (2011). Investing in innovation to enable global competitiveness: The case of Portugal. *Technological Forecasting and Social Change*, 78(8), 1299–1309.

Glaser, B. and Strauss, A. (1967). *The discovery of grounded theory: Strategies for qualitative inquiry*. Chicago: Aldine.

González-Pernia, J. L., Parrilli, M. D. and Peña-Legazkue, I. (2013). *The effects of STI and DUI learning modes on innovation output and on economic performance in Spain, Orkestra*. Working paper, no. 1, San Sebastian.

González-Pernia, J. L., Parrilli, M. D. and Peña-Legazkue, I. (2014). STI-DUI learning modes, firm-university collaboration and innovation. *Journal of Technology Transfer*, doi: 10.1007/s10961–014–9352–0.

Granovetter, M. (1985). Economic action and social structure: The problem of social embeddedness. *American Journal of Sociology*, 91(3), 481–510.

Hansen, T. and Winther, L. (2011). Innovation, regional development and relations between high- and low-tech industries. *European Urban and Regional Studies*, 18(3), 321–339.

Hossler, D. and Scalese-Love, P. (1989). Grounded meta-analysis: A guide for research syntheses. *Review of Higher Education*, 13(1), 1–28.

Isaksen, A. and Karlsen, J. (2012). Combined and complex mode of innovation in region cluster development: analysis of the light-weight material cluster in Raufoss, Norway. In B. T. Asheim and M. D. Parrilli (eds.), *Interactive Learning for Innovation: a key drive within clusters and innovation systems* (pp. 115–136). Basingstroke: Palgrave-Macmilan.

Jensen, M. B., Johnson, B., Lorenz, E. and Lundvall, B.-Å. (2007). Forms of knowledge and modes of innovation. *Research Policy*, 36(5), 680–693.

Kirner, E., Kinkel, S. and Jaeger, A. (2009). Innovation paths and the innovation performance of low-technology firms: An empirical analysis of German industry. *Research Policy*, 38(3), 447–458.

Lorenz, E. (2012). Labor market institutions, skills, and innovation style: A critique of the 'Varieties of Capitalism' perspective. In Asheim B. and M. D. Parrilli (eds.). *Interactive learning for innovation* (72–89). Basingstoke: Palgrave-Macmillan.

Lundvall, B. A. (2007). National systems of innovation: Analytical concepts and development tools. *Industry and Innovation*, 14(19), 95–119.

Malaver, F. and Vargas, M. (2013). *Aprendizaje y forma de innovar: una lectura crítica (Colombia)*, Mimeo, Deusto Business School, Deusto University, San Sebastian.

Nunes, S., Lopes, R. and Dias, J. (2013). *Innovation modes and firm performance.* Paper presented at the ERSA conference in Palermo, European Planning Studies, August 30.

Parrilli, M. D. and Elola, A. (2012). The strength of science and technology drivers for SME innovation. *Small Business Economics*, 39(4), 387–397

Piore, M. and Sabel, C. (1984). *The second industrial divide*. New York: Basic Books.

Stall, Meadows and Hyle, A. (2010). Procedural methodology for a grounded meta-analysis of qualitative case studies. *International Journal of Consumer Studies*, 34(4), 412–418. Industrial districts and local economic regeneration, ILO, Geneva.

Rodriguez-Pose, A. and Crescenzi, R. (2008). Research and development, spillovers, innovation systems, and the genesis of regional growth in Europe. *Regional Studies*, 42(1), 51–67.

Tödtling, F. and Trippl, M. (2005). One size fits all? Towards a Differentiated Regional Innovation Policy Approach. *Research Policy*, 34(8), 1203–1219.

Trippl, M. (2011). Regional innovation systems and knowledge-Sourcing activities in traditional industries: Evidence from the Vienna food sector. *Environment and Planning A*, 43(7), 1599–1616.

Index

Note: Italicized page numbers indicate a figure on the corresponding page. Page numbers in bold indicate a table on the corresponding page.

absorptive capacity 3, 4, 9, 15, 50, 78, 80, 123, 152, 154, 161, 179, 183, 188–90, 193, 205, 210, 212, 213, 214, 215; dual absorptive capacity 188–90
academic entrepreneurship 32
action-formation mechanisms 86, 87, 88–90
active inertia 114
Akron tire cluster in Ohio 114
Alpes-Maritimes *département* 126
application development 202
applied typology mechanisms 86–8, 87
ARCSIS (Association for Research on Materials and Integrated Security Systems) 127
Arctic program 185

biorefinery cluster 94–6
bipartite network 130
bonding *vs.* bridging social capital 71, 75
Bouches du Rhône *département* 126
boundary-spanning activity systems 91
business agglomerations 2–3
business development 6–9
business incubators 148
business innovation modes: China 208, 209; Colombia 208–9; conclusions 215–16; differential evidence on 207–10; economic performance and 210, **211**; grounded meta-analysis 200–5, *203*; innovation paradox and 198–200; introduction 9, 197–8; Italy 209–10; Spain 207–9 review of studies 200–15;

synthetic view 212–14, **214–15**; working propositions 205–7
business model change 91, 95

capability failure 25
"catching-up" processes 36
CATI (computer-assisted telephone interviewing) 142, 147
CAWI (computer-assisted web interviewing) 142, 147
centrality measures *133*, 133–6
clusters: analysis and results 93–9; applied typology mechanisms 86–8, 87; conclusions 115–16; defined 85; introduction 3, 7, 14, 85–6, 105–6; methodology 92–3; situational and action-formation mechanisms 88–90; technological gatekeepers 108–15; technology-distant knowledge 106–8; transformational mechanisms 87, **90**, 90–2, **92**; *see also* Örnsköldsvik biorefinery cluster; Oulu ICT cluster
cognitive inertia 112–15
collective learning 70, 123, 130–5, *131*, *133*, **134**
combinatorial knowledge dynamics 32
Community Innovation Surveys (CIS) 161, 166
comparative methodology parameters **203**
competence-enhancing discontinuities 111
competitive advantage *see* sustainable competitive advantage

competitive moves 112–13
competitiveness of firms 16, 124
complementary knowledge 183–6
Constructing Regional Advantage
     (CRA) 23
control variables 153
cooperation-based drivers 199
COREC (Center for Oil Recovery)
     186–7, 188–9
core-periphery networks 132
creative destruction 105, 107–8
CREMSI (Regional Centre of Studies
     for Micro-electronics and
     Interactive Systems) 127
cross-sectoral knowledge 73
customer-producer ties 144

deindustrializing regions 38
demand articulation failure 25
dense networks 110–11
dependent variables 152
diffusion strategy 79
directionality failure 25
disruptive knowledge in clusters 106
distant external collaborations 156
diversity and innovation 73–4
doing, using, and interacting (DUI):
     combination STI+DUI 204–6,
     214; conclusion 174–5;
     constructs-based variables 201;
     defined 161–2, 164; geography
     of 164–6; impact on innovations
     166; innovations as the output
     of 204; introduction 9, 15–16; in
     R&D resources 197; regression
     analysis 171, 172, **173**; SMEs
     in thin regions 77; synthetic and
     symbolic sectors 29, 30; *see also*
     business innovation modes
Domsjö Fabriker (DF) 94
dual absorptive capacity 188–90 *see*
     absorptive capacity

East Asian economies 10
econometric analysis 152, 208
economic performance 210, **211**
effective government mechanisms 190–3
efficiency-driven economies 45
empirical approaches 34–8, *37*
endogenous transformation
     processes 73
entrepreneurial discovery process 4, 5,
     11, 23, 88

European Commission 3, 12, 23
European Patent Office (EPO) 35
evolutionary economic geography 67
experience-based learning 8
exploitation subsystem 50, 111
external knowledge 79, 189
external linkages 110–11

factor-driven economies 45
financial gaps 39, 46, 48
firm collaboration and innovation
     modes: case description and
     data 166–7; conclusion 174–5;
     geographical proximity 170–4,
     171, **172**, **173**; introduction
     6–8, 160–3; partner types **167**,
     167–70, **169**; role of sources of
     knowledge 163–6
firm-firm collaboration 193
firm-university joint efforts 185, 190,
     194, 205
foreign direct investment 77
framework agreement 190
Fruchterman-Reingold visualization
     algorithm 131

geographical proximity 123
globalization 1, 8
green innovations 149
gross domestic product (GDP) 35
grounded meta-analysis 200–5, **203**

higher educational levels 49
high-tech clusters: conclusion 138–9;
     innovation in policy 125–8;
     introduction 123–5; pole
     SCS, defined 128–30; Poles
     of Competitiveness 125–6;
     proximities 135–8, **137**; public
     policy 127–8
high technology clusters 73

identity changes 91–2
idiosyncratic foundations of
     clusters 7
inbound knowledge flows for
     innovation 144
independent variables 152–3
individual spirit 11
industrial diversity 32
industrial path development 72–4
industrial production zones 38
informal communication 186

information and communication technology (ICT) 160, 161, 202, 215
infrastructural failures 25
innovation-driven economies 45
innovation gaps study, Spanish RISs: cluster analysis 56–7, *57*, *58*; concluding remarks 58–9; data 51, **60**; interpretive framework 46–8; introduction 45–6; methodology 51, **52–3**; overview 39–40; representation of *54*, 54–6, *55*; variables 48–51
Innovation Union Scoreboard 34–5
input-output dichotomous perspective 49
institutional failures 25
interdependence between firms *10*, 11
inter-industry learning 69
Inter-Ministerial Committee for Spatial Planning and Development (2004) 125
international collaborations in open innovation strategy 150
interorganizational collaboration efforts 85, 192
intra-path changes 66
intraregional knowledge 8–9
IRIS research institute 187
islands of innovation 73
Italian Chambers of Commerce 146–7

Jabob externalities 73
joint industry projects (JIP) 187, 191–2
Jura cluster 109–10, 114

knowledge-based approach **28**, 28–31, **30**, 124
knowledge exploration subsystem 46
knowledge hubs 38
knowledge-intensive business services (KIBS) 6, 73
knowledge pipelines 135
knowledge relatedness 4–6
knowledge sourcing/sources 7, 8–9, 163–6

learning gaps 39, 46, 47–8
liability of newness 144, 145
liability of smallness 145
local related externalities 79
lock-in situations 2
logistic regression models 167–8, **169**

macro-institutional structures 31–2
macrolevel transformations 87
managerial gaps 39, 46, 47
Markusen taxonomy 127
medium-low technology industries 208
mental models 112
micro-firms 204
multidisciplinary theoretical framework 115
Multiple Factor Analysis (MFA) 51

nanoelectronics clusters 114–15
national collaborations in open innovation strategy 150
National Research Agency (ANR), France 129
national (Spanish) (INE) statistics 49
network openness 106–8
network structures and technological gatekeepers 110–11
new path creation 31, 40
new-to-firm innovations 207
new-to-international-market innovations 202; substantial innovations 202
new-to-market innovations 202, 204, 207, 209, 213; substantial innovations (new-to-international-markets) 202
non-geographical proximity 3
non-local knowledge 32
non-S&T-driven regions 38–9
Northern Italy, industrial districts 109–10
Norway, innovation modes *see* firm collaboration and innovation modes
Norwegian Register of Business Enterprise 166
NSN Nokia-Siemens Networks Unit 99

OECD approach 38–40
open innovation strategies: conclusions 154–7, **155**; introduction 142–3; main features of sampled firms 147–9; mapping collaboration of sampled firms 150, *151*; measures of 152–3; method 146–7; probit regression model 153–4, **154**, 156; start-ups 143–6

openness gaps 39, 46, 47–8
organizational inertia 113
organizational innovation 212
Organization for Economic
    Cooperation and Development
    (OECD) Regional Database
    38–40, 77
Örnsköldsvik biorefinery cluster:
    conclusion 99–100; introduction
    93–4; overview 94–5; time
    period 1 96; time period 2
    96–7; time period 3 97; time
    period 4 97–8; transformational
    mechanisms 96–8
Oulu ICT cluster: conclusion 99–100;
    introduction 93–4; overview
    95–6; time period 1 98; time
    period 2 98–9; time period 3 99;
    time period 2011 onward 99;
    transformational mechanisms
    98–9
outbound knowledge flows for
    innovation 144

partner-specific absorptive capacity 189
    see absorptive capacity
path creation 69–70
path dependency 5–6, 138
path development in RISs: challenges
    and policy approaches
    74–9; conclusions 79–81;
    introduction 66–8; key
    concepts and definitions 68–72;
    organizationally thick RISs 72,
    74, 75–7; organizationally thin
    RISs 72, 77–9; overview 68–70;
    RIS overview 70–2; types of
    72–4
path exhaustion 34, 69
path extension 31, 69, 80–1
path renewal 31, 81
path revitalization 69
physical proximity 3
pole SCS, defined 128–30; Poles of
    Competitiveness 125–6, 129
policy: approaches and challenges in
    path development in RISs 74–9;
    innovation in high-tech clusters
    125–8; public in high-tech
    clusters 127–8; regional
    subsystem 45
practice-based learning 9
primary-sector-intensive regions 38

probit regression model 153–4,
    154, 156
process innovation 212–13
PROMES (Lab for PROcesses,
    Materials and Solar Energy) 127
PROT variable 153
Provence-Alpes-Côte d'Azur
    (PACA) 125
public funding for research 186

radical innovation 202, 204, 207, 209,
    213; *see also* new-to-market
    innovations
regional collaborations in open
    innovation strategy 150
Regional Council (CR) 129
regional evolution 2–4
Regional Innovation Scoreboard
    34–8, *37*
regional innovation system (RIS):
    broadly defined 29; business
    development 6–9; business
    innovation modes 9; conceptual
    approaches 24–34; conclusions
    and outlook 40–1; context
    of 2–6; empirical approaches
    34–8, *37*; evolution 2–4, 6;
    firms, and innovation 6–8;
    fragmented 26; hosting new
    ventures 150; innovation
    gaps 39–40; institutionally
    thick but organizationally
    thin 27, *27*; institutionally
    thin and organizationally
    thin 27, *27*; institutional
    thick 27; introduction 1–2;
    knowledge, as driver 4–6;
    knowledge-based approach **28**,
    28–31, **30**; knowledge sourcing
    7, 8–9; locked-in 26; narrowly
    defined 29; OECD approach
    38–40; originality 9–11, *10*;
    organizationally thick 26–7, 72,
    74, 75–7; organizationally thick
    but institutionally thin 27, *27*;
    organizationally thin 26, 72,
    77–9; smart specialization 23–4,
    31; Spanish (*see* innovation
    gaps); synthetic view of 11–16;
    system-failure approaches 25,
    25–7, *27*, 34; *see also* innovation
    gaps; path development in RISs
regional path development 31, **33**

relation-specific assets 186–8
research and development (R&D):
    driven innovation activities
    37; expenditures 4, 35, 148,
    153; investment in 197–9;
    relationships and development
    188; scientific and technical
    innovation 160–1
research-intensive industries 187
resource-based view (RBV) 180–2
resource dependency theory 112

SAME (Sophia Antipolis
    MicroElectronics forum) 128–9
science, technology, and innovation
    (STI): combination STI+DUI
    204–6, 214; conclusion 174–5;
    constructs-based variables
    201; defined 161–2, 164;
    dominance in analytical studies
    29; impact on innovations 166;
    innovations as the output of
    204; introduction 9, 15–16;
    measurement of 41; partnership
    links to 168; in R&D resources
    199; regression analysis 171,
    172, **173**; *see also* business
    innovation modes
science-based learning 9
Secure Communicating Solutions (SCS)
    125, 128–30
Silicon Valley developments 107
situational mechanisms 87, 88–90
small- and medium-sized enterprises
    (SMEs): in closed innovation
    model 144; competitiveness
    of 212; differentiated context
    of 204; in innovation
    cooperation 35–6; introduction
    3; joint ventures with 189;
    organizationally thin regions 77
smart specialization 23–4, 31, 41, 78
social capital 71–2, 75
social network analysis 59
Sophia-Antipolis 127–8, 132, 138
sparse networks 110–11
spatial concentration processes 124
STMicroelectronics and Gemalto
    132, 134

structure-reinforcing competence 108
supplier-buyer relations 190
sustainability changes 25
sustainable competitive advantage:
    conclusion 193–4; effective
    government mechanisms 190–3;
    introduction 179–80; partners
    with complementary knowledge
    183–6; relation-specific assets
    186–8; research method 182–3;
    research results 183–93;
    resource-based view 180–2
Swedish Governmental Agency for
    Innovation Systems 32
Swiss watch building 113
symbolic knowledge 29
synthetic and symbolic sectors 29
system-failure approaches 25, 25–7,
    27, 34

tacit knowledge 6–8, 66, 110, 161,
    164, 166, 170, 172, 175
technological gaps 39, 46
technological gatekeepers (TGs):
    cognitive inertia 112–15;
    complementary assets 111–12;
    as disruptors and change agents
    108–10; network structures and
    110–11
technological platform 202
technology-distant knowledge 106–8
technology-driven linear model of
    innovation 8
trade regimes 88
transformational mechanisms 87,
    90, 90–2, **92**, 98–9; *see also*
    Örnsköldsvik biorefinery cluster;
    Oulu ICT cluster
transformative change, defined 86
Triple Helix Committee 98
tuning fork technology 110

university-firm collaboration 193
university-industry collaborations 157
urbanization 8
user-supplier relationships 160–1

value-chain relationship 94, 201–2, 208
VINNOVA (Sweden) 94